And others, Robert Watson

Lectures Delivered to the Literary and Philsophical Society,

Newcastle-upon-Tyne, on Northumbrian History, Literature, and Art

Lent Term 1898

And others, Robert Watson

Lectures Delivered to the Literary and Philsophical Society, Newcastle-upon-Tyne, on Northumbrian History, Literature, and Art
Lent Term 1898

ISBN/EAN: 9783337203610

Printed in Europe, USA, Canada, Australia, Japan

Cover: Foto ©Thomas Meinert / pixelio.de

More available books at **www.hansebooks.com**

LECTURES

DELIVERED TO THE

LITERARY AND PHILOSOPHICAL SOCIETY,

NEWCASTLE-UPON-TYNE,

ON

NORTHUMBRIAN HISTORY, LITERATURE, AND ART,

BY

THOMAS HODGKIN, D.C.L., F.S.A.

ROBERT SPENCE WATSON, LL.D.

R. OLIVER HESLOP.

RICHARD WELFORD, M.A.

———

LENT TERM, 1898.

———

Published by the Society.

PRINTED BY ANDDREW REID & COMPANY, LIMITED
NEWCASTLE-UPON-TYNE.
—
1898.

CONTENTS.

		Page.
ROMAN OCCUPATION OF NORTHUMBERLAND	...	1

By Thomas Hodgkin, D.C.L., F.S.A.

NORTHUMBRIAN STORY AND SONG

By Robert Spence Watson, LL.D.

Lecture I.—Northumbrian Folk and Speech	...	25
II.—Northumbrian Faith and Learning ...	...	45
III.—Ballads of Northumberland		69
IV.—Ridley and the Reformation		93
V.—Mark Akenside	... ...	121
VI.—Northumbrian Art and Song		147

DIALECT SPEECH IN NORTHUMBERLAND	... ...	173

By R. Oliver Heslop.

NEWCASTLE A HUNDRED YEARS AGO ...	...	197

By Richard Welford, M.A.

PREFACE.

A few words of explanation respecting the following Lectures would seem appropriate.

For some time it had been felt that a change from the ordinary University Extension Course of Lectures would be beneficial. It was, therefore, decided to introduce a Course on matters especially connected with the County of Northumberland.

Dr. Robert Spence Watson, one of our Vice-Presidents, undertook to deliver the Six Lectures printed in this book; and Dr. Thomas Hodgkin, another Vice-President, Mr. R. Oliver Heslop, Mr. Richard Welford, and Mr. F. W. Dendy most willingly agreed to prepare others. Unfortunately, owing to the illness of Mr. Dendy, his proposed explanation of the Newcastle Guilds was not given.

These Lectures were delivered in the Lent Term of 1898, and were well attended, exciting considerable interest.

The thanks of the Society are due to the gentlemen who have given this further proof, that it retains within its membership, those who are able and willing to strengthen the position it has held from the first, of being one of the leading agencies in the higher education of the district.

ALFRED HOLMES,

FREDERICK EMLEY,

HONORARY SECRETARIES.

October, 1898.

ROMAN OCCUPATION OF NORTHUMBERLAND.

By THOMAS HODGKIN, D.C.L., F.S.A.

The Roman occupation of this part of Britain lasted with some intermission for three centuries,* that of the southern portions of our island for a century longer.†

Even the shorter of these two periods is a long space of time when measured on the scale of human life. It means ten generations of men. How few Englishmen, unless they happen to belong to one of the great historic families, have the least idea what manner of man any one of their ancestors ten generations back was like, or even where he abode! And if we measure this space of time on the life not of the individual but of the nation, we shall find that three centuries may be a long road for a nation to travel. In the year 1598 England and Scotland were still two separate, often hostile, countries. Spain was our most formidable foe, and we had but just recovered from the terror of the Great Armada; the authorised version of the Bible was not in existence; and Hamlet, Macbeth, and Othello had never been seen upon the stage.

In the very field of our present enquiry we have evidence enough how "the slow foot of Time" was working here during those three hundred years. The not infrequent inscriptions which record that some building reared by Roman hands was now *vetustate conlapsum* (tumbled down through age) and required to be restored by a later generation of Romans, bring before us the fact that the Roman occupation of Northumberland was not, as we perhaps used sometimes to think of it, a point, but a line, and a pretty long line in the Past that lies behind us.

---

* From A.D. 80, when Agricola probably crossed the Tees, to A.D. 333, the date of the death of Gratian the last emperor whose coins are found in any considerable number.

† From A.D. 43. the year of Claudius' invasion of Britain, to A.D. 441, the year at which "Tiro Prosper," so-called, places the Saxon conquest of the island.

1

And, yet, it is disappointing and somewhat humiliating to find
that though we, or, at least, our predecessors in this county, were
in contact with the great world-conquering nation for so many
centuries, we and our land spoke but little to the Roman heart, and
produced scarce any effect on Roman literature. When we have
alluded to the account of two British expeditions given by Cæsar
in his Commentaries, when we have read the few chapters in the
Annals of Tacitus which relate to the rebellion under Queen
Boudicca,* and the other more valuable monograph which we owe
to the happy accident that the historian married the daughter of
Agricola, when we have listened to Horace's brave words about
visiting under the protection of the Muses, "even the Britons who
are so fierce toward their guests,"† and when we have gathered from
other poets allusions to British oysters and British wolf-hounds we
have almost exhausted all that the Roman conquerors of Britain
have said to posterity concerning our island. Not a word as to our
beautiful mountains and lakes, not a hint, as far as I remember, of
our treasures of coal, not even a grumble over our changeable climate,
has reached the ears of posterity. When we think of the minute
information which we are bequeathing to future ages as to many a
little native principality in India, and many a Kaffir kraal in South
Africa, how Chitral and Maiwand and Buluwayo will be reproduced a thousand years hence from the letters of English ladies and
the journals of mighty hunters of the lion, it is difficult not to feel
that we have been somewhat unfairly treated in this matter, and
that those masters of many legions who came from afar to conquer
us might at least have taken the trouble to describe us, and to say
what they thought of our country.

But I am sliding into heretical language in talking thus of "us"
and "our conquerors" the Romans. I fancy that I hear the gruff
but kindly voice of my old friend Freeman rebuking me for thus
identifying myself with the men whom Agricola subdued, and see the
thin, eager face of J. H. Green looking reproach at my forgetfulness
that Holstein, not Britain, was *our* home in the first century after
Christ. I accept the rebuke and proceed to repeat the offence. No
doubt the majority of the persons present in this room, if they could
trace back their lineage for eighteen centuries, would find the
majority of their ancestors living in those forest-covered lands between

* The now approved form of Boadicea's name.
† Visam Britannos hospitibus feros.

the German Ocean and the Baltic. Still to us, intruders though we be, this island has grown so dear that we care more about its past than about the past of any other country on this planet. We have given it our own name, Engla-land—a name not unknown in many distant regions of the world—we have identified ourselves with its whole history, and we cannot bear to dissociate ourselves from it even in thought while travelling back through the centuries. No, we will not go back to Holstein. Let the Germans keep what they call the cradle of our race. We will be satisfied if they will leave us England, and we will even, to please our Scottish friends, "glory in the name of Briton," though that name may remind us of the Roman occupation of our country.

Besides, putting these sentimental considerations on one side, it is admitted by the most enthusiastic philo-Teutons among our historians that our Saxon and Anglian forefathers did not utterly destroy the native population which they found in the portion of the country that they overran. The women at least were left, to become the wives and concubines of the conquerors: probably also many of the slaves. Thus there is almost a certainty that even in the present company, could we all, as I before said, trace our ancestry back through the centuries, we should, most of us, find some link, perhaps many links, connecting us with the barbarians who toiled in forced labour at the Wall, or gazed with wonder on the pomp of a Roman *legatus*.

In this lamentable absence, then, of any continuous literary narrative as to the fortunes of our land during three hundred eventful years all that we can do is to attempt to piece together such information as we possess, unsatisfactory as the result arrived at will probably be.

Of this information there are two kinds, and the employment of them will lead us into two methods of enquiry not unlike those which are known in philosophy as *a priori* and *a posteriori*.

Firstly, we have a certain amount of historical information, not very copious it is true, but still fairly continuous, as to the Roman Empire as a whole, the elevation and deposition of emperors, the change of institutions, the success or failure of struggles with the barbarians, and so forth. By applying this information to the case of Britain, which was a province of the empire, we may arrive at some conclusions *a priori* as to what must have been the course of affairs in our island between the years 80 and 380 of our era.

Secondly, the spade and the pick-axe have done something—it is our hope and expectation that they will do much more—towards revealing the traces of the Roman conqueror which have lain buried beneath our soil. "Finds" of coins in various places give us at least a date before which the Roman occupation cannot have ceased, and often, by the greater or less frequency of the coins of a particular emperor, enable us to form a guess as to the time when it was most effective. Statues, inscriptions, tesselated pavements, hypocausts, the bones of men and of animals, all tell us something as to the vicissitudes of the Roman occupation, and enable us in some small degree to reconstruct the social and even the political life of the districts in which they were found.

To this latter portion of our enquiry I hope to revert on some future occasion. At present I propose briefly to indicate what we may learn from the *a priori* method, though it is not necessary or desirable to keep the two lines of investigation absolutely distinct.

From the memoir of Agricola, written by Tacitus, we learn that this able general—the best, probably, of the Roman governors of Britain, notwithstanding his son-in-law's panegyric—brought the Roman standards as far as the estuary of Tanaus (which may be the Tees, either of the two Tynes, or the Tay), and fortified the narrow neck of land between the Firths of Forth and Clyde. It is certain, therefore, that he must have marched through Northumberland ; and as we are told that one especial note of his character as a general was the judgment with which he chose the best sites for the erection of his *castella*, " not one of which was ever stormed by the barbarians or abandoned by the Romans," there is at least room for the conjecture that some of the Roman camps for which our county is famous may have been founded by him. Further than this we cannot go. We cannot at present say with confidence of Cilurnum or any of our other camps that it was built under the orders of Gnaeus Julius Agricola.

The emperor under whom Agricola chiefly served, and who, as Tacitus tells us, was pitiably jealous of his success, was Domitian (81-96), not the weakest, nor perhaps the most cruel, but certainly one of the meanest and most hateful of the long line of emperors. When he was slain by his household servants, the wise and humane Nerva ascended the throne, and with his reign began the Golden Age. of the Roman Empire, which lasted eighty-four years, till the death of Marcus Aurelius. The distinguishing characteristic of this time was that, while it lasted, Rome and the civilised world possessed a form of government which combined almost all the advantages of hereditary and elective monarchy without the faults of either. One emperor after another came to the front, did great deeds for Rome, chose out the fittest man (apparently) in all the empire to succeed him, adopted him as his son, trained him in the art and science of government, and then died, leaving his seat to be occupied, without strife or debate, by the man of his choice, who in every instance signally justified the wisdom of his selection. Thus Nerva chose the Spaniard Ulpius Trajanus, whom the senate, with no false flattery, hailed as *optimus princeps*. Thus Trajan chose Hadrian, a man not of pure moral character, a man with the faults as well as the brilliant gifts of the artistic temperament, but certainly a splendid ruler for Rome. Thus Hadrian chose Antoninus Pius, who can only be described by the one word "noble," a kindred spirit, as it seems to me. to that great English general who desired to have for his only epitaph, "Here lies Henry Lawrence, who tried to do his duty." Thus, lastly, Antoninus adopted Marcus Aurelius, that "philosopher upon the throne," whose hunger and thirst after righteousness makes us marvel how such a man could have lived in the world side by side with Christianity, yet not embracing it; much more .how such a man could by possibility have been found in the ranks of its persecutors.

But there ends the line of the great adopted emperors. Marcus Aurelius, too forgiving to an unfaithful wife, too indulgent to an unworthy son and blinded by parental partiality, left the Empire to Commodus, and leaving it to that bull-necked gladiator left it to ruin.

These eighty-four years were, we may be sure, the best time of the Roman domination in Britain, the time in which the great roads were made, the marshes drained, the forests cleared, the prosperity of the little rising city of Londinium raised to its highest point. Let us look a little more closely into the impress which each emperor may probably have left on our own county.

Trajan's glance was generally directed towards the East, Dacia and Parthia being the scenes of his military triumphs. We have no reason to suppose that he ever visited Britain, and we have some reason to think that North Britain was in a disturbed state during his reign, and even that the Roman arms may have then sustained some signal reverse. The reason for this conjecture is that soon after 108 A.D. the IXth legion, a most unlucky body of troops, which had been almost cut to pieces at the time of Boudicca's rebellion, and had afterwards been stationed at York, vanishes clean out of history.

This is supposed to point to some great onslaught of the Brigantes, the most powerful tribe in the North of England, on the Roman headquarters at Eburacum.

With Hadrian's accession (117 A.D.) a more interesting period of our story commences. This emperor while not anxious to extend the frontiers of the Empire—in fact, he abandoned some provinces beyond the Euphrates which his predecessor had won—was filled with a praiseworthy desire to see with his own eyes the vast realm over which he was called to rule, and to learn its needs for himself. With this object in view he began, probably in the year 119, a tour through his dominions, which lasted eight years. Gaul and Germany were first visited, and in the year 120 (probably) he arrived in Britain. He was, as I have already said, an artist or a poet by nature, a man whose instincts would have led him to spend his days in some beautiful temple-crowned and statue-peopled city on the shores of the Mediterranean. It can have been, therefore, only the stern sense of duty still lingering in his Roman heart which brought him to our fog-wrapt and unattractive island. It is worth while to transcribe a few sentences in which Dion Cassius (no great friend of Hadrian) describes this emperor's manner of performing his self-imposed task.

"Now Hadrian, visiting one province after another, surveying both town and country, and inspecting all the forts and walls, transferred some of these to more suitable places, razed some to the ground and erected others. Thus he personally looked into everything. I do not mean merely what might be called the public property of the army, such as the arms, the engines of war, the fosses the mounds and the palisades, but he examined also the rooms set apart for the rank and file, and was perpetually watching and enquiring into the lives, the homes, the characters of the officers, and often when these had got into an effeminate, artificial way of living, he would change their whole tone and brace them up to the performance of their duty, practising them in every kind of warlike manœuvre, and rewarding some, while he censured others. And in order that they might take benefit from his own example he everywhere used the hardest fare, and either walked or rode on horseback, never on these journeys using a chariot nor setting foot in a carriage. Neither in heat nor cold would he ever cover his head, but alike in Celtic snows and under the scorching sun of Egypt he always went bareheaded. To put it shortly, both by precept and example he so trained and drilled the army throughout the Empire as to bring it into that state of efficiency in which we now behold it, and this was doubtless the chief reason why he remained at peace with all foreign nations. For seeing his admirable state of preparation and sustaining no injury at his hands, but rather after receiving subsidies, they abstained from all disturbance of the peace of the Empire. So well indeed was his army trained that the Batavian cavalry swam across the Danube in their armour, which when the barbarians saw they were seized with terror of the Romans, and turning back to their homes used Hadrian as arbitrator to settle their own differences among themselves."

How these words of the Greek historian help one to understand the well-known passage of arms between the æsthetic emperor and the easy-going, slightly impertinent poet, Florus. The poet addressed his sovereign in three lines, which may be translated as follows :—

> I would rather not be Cæsar,
> Walking through that weary Britain,
> Tortured by the frosts of Scythia.*

To which the emperor made answer :—

> I would rather not be Florus,
> Rambling idly through the taverns,
> Lurking in the dirty cook-shops,
> Tortured by the fierce mosquitoes.†

Such then was the emperor (or, as the Greek historians called him, the "ruler of the Whole"),‡ who about the year 120 visited Britain and stood on the banks of the river Tyne. His presence here was, we may believe, urgently required. The invasion of the northern barbarians, which had wrecked the IXth legion, was probably not yet effectually repelled, if at least we are right in referring to the earliest years of Hadrian's reign the words of the contemporary orator Fronto, "When Hadrian had possession of the

---

* Ego nolo Caesar esse
Ambulare per Britannos
Scythicas pati pruinas.

† Ego nolo Florus esse
Ambulare per tabernas
Latitare per popinas
Culices pati rotundos.

‡ ’ο κεκτήμενος τὴν τῶν ὅλων ἀρχὴν

Empire how many soldiers were slain by the Britons!"* The emperor brought with him a fresh legion, the VIth, from Xanten, on the Lower Rhine to replace the vanished IXth, and this legion stationed at Eburacum retained the same headquarters till the end of the Roman occupation of Britain.

But Hadrian, whose whole policy consisted not in extending but in strengthening the frontiers of the Empire, perceived that it was both possible and advisable to guard the already subjugated portion of Britain by something stronger than a few scattered forts. The narrow neck of land between the estuaries of the Tyne and the Solway offered a comparatively easy line of defence, and across it he determined to erect a continuous series of fortifications—the far-famed Roman Wall. Into the vexed question of how much was Hadrian's and how much was the work of his successors in this most interesting monument of Roman power I am not going now to enter. The question who was *the* Builder of the Wall—the Wall as we now see it—has been debated with some sharpness by two generations of antiquaries, and will perhaps continue to be so debated ; but I do not think any reasonable person doubts that Hadrian was *a* builder of *a* Wall, nor has any sufficient evidence been offered to shake the assertion of Spartianus, the biographer of Hadrian (poor as his authority must be admitted to be, owing to his late date and his lack of critical perception.) "Therefore having in true kingly style changed the habits of his soldiers, Hadrian made for Britain, in which country he set many things right, and was the first to draw a line of wall [across the country] for 80 [Roman] miles, so as to divide the barbarians from the Romans."† We have to notice in passing that the length of the Wall is here very correctly stated. Eighty Roman miles correspond to about 73½ English miles ; and this is the length of the Wall from Wallsend to Bowness. Many other statements by later writers are much less accurate.

I may here so far anticipate what will have to be stated when I come to speak of inscriptions as to say that all the three legions

* Quoted by Mommsen as "Fronto, p. 217, Naber." "Hadriano imperium obtinente quantum militum a Britannis cæsum." If we may translate "obtinente" = "acquiring possession" rather than "holding," the argument for putting these events soon after Hadrian's accession becomes stronger.

† Ergo conversis regio more militibus Britaniam petit in qua multa correxit, murumque per octoginta millia passuum duxit, qui barbaros Romanosque divideret." Spartianus, Vita Hadriani ; in *Historia Augusta*, cap. ii. The earliest date that can be assigned to Spartianus is 288, and some would place him a century later.

stationed in Britain in the year 120 — the IInd (quartered at Gloucester), the VIth (at York), and the XXth (at Chester)—have left memorials of their presence in the Wall, and the reasonable inference is that all took part in its construction.

On Hadrian's death in 138 he was succeeded by Antoninus, who received the surname of Pius (dutiful) from the senate, probably on account of the tenderness which he showed to the memory of his predecessor, veiling with "filial piety" some of the unjust and cruel deeds into which, especially in his later years, and under the influence of torturing disease, Hadrian had been betrayed.

Antoninus did not, like his predecessor, visit Britain himself, but by means of his lieutenants (*legati*) he seems to have ably administered the affairs of this island. Carrying into effect the scheme of Julius Agricola he fortified the other isthmus between Clyde and Forth in a similar way to that in which his adopted father had fortified the isthmus between Tyne and Solway. To quote the words of his biographer, Capitolinus, "By means of his lieutenants he waged many wars, for he both conquered the Britons through his *legatus*, Lollius Urbicus, pushing off the barbarians, and drawing another wall, made of turf, across the island; and he forced the Moors to sue for peace, and subdued the Germans, the Dacians, and many other nations, including the rebellious Jews, by his prefects and *legati*."

The wall between Clyde and Forth lies outside our present province, as the whole district between it and the Cheviots has been unfortunately wrested from us by the Scots. But I note, in passing, that here we have, to our great relief, a Roman work, as to whose author there is no possible doubt, for all the evidence converges upon Antoninus Pius as the emperor under whose auspices it was constructed; and further, that the accuracy of the biographer who informs us that it was *cespiticius* (built of turf) has been in very recent times triumphantly vindicated by the excavations of the Glasgow Archæological Society, who have discovered the lines of black mouldering vegetation in the section of the embankment which enable them to state with accuracy how many layers of grass turf were used in its construction. Hitherto, I believe I may say, we have found nothing in our excavations which entitles us to say that our earthen embankments are cespiticious in their character.

On our own district Antoninus must undoubtedly have left some mark, as his *legati* would certainly not press forward to the Forth and Clyde without making good their advance through Northumberland. And, accordingly, there is good reason to believe that the road which in the Middle Ages received the name of the Watling Street (the word "Street" itself was generally connected with an old Roman road), and which runs from Lanchester to Chew Green, was constructed by the *legati* of Antoninus, who also, probably, placed upon it the still existing camps of Habitancum and Bremenium (Risingham and Rochester).

The reigns of Marcus Aurelius (161-180) and of his unworthy son and successor, Commodus (180-192), were, on the whole, unfortunate for the Roman arms in Britain. This is not altogether surprising when we consider how hardly Marcus was pressed by the invasions of the Marcomanni, who broke through the line of the Danube, and, in fact, began that great series of barbaric invasions of Italy from the north-east which at last achieved the ruin of the Empire. We are told * that the Britannic war pressed heavily on the philosophic emperor, and that Calpurnius Agricola (who must on no account be confounded with the Julius Agricola of the preceding century) was sent to settle it. A " Britannic war " might, of course, be waged on the frontier of Wales, whose mountaineers were probably never perfectly subdued, but it is more likely that the storm burst on the north of the island, and that the Caledonians, breaking through the cespiticious wall of Antoninus Pius, carried their ravages up to, perhaps beyond, the wall of Hadrian. This theory is strikingly confirmed by the fact that coins and inscriptions along the Watling Street and in the camps of Bremenium and Habitancum cease for a time soon after the death of Antoninus Pius, though we meet them again after the great restoration of Roman dominion in the next century. Under such a profligate and cruel emperor as Commodus nothing was likely to go well, and we learn with little surprise † that "the tribes in that island overpassed the wall which separated them from the Roman camps, made widespread ravages, and cut to pieces a Roman general with the soldiers under his command, whereupon Commodus, alarmed, sent Ulpius Marcellus against them."

The historian then proceeds to give us a curious account of the personal habits of this ascetic general. Frugal and modest in all his

* By Capitolinus (Vita Aurelii in *Historia Augusta*, iv. 8).

† From Dion Cassius, xviii. 8. It is noteworthy that the name of the general, Ulpius Marcellus, is not mentioned by the *Historia Augusta*, one of the many proofs of the fragmentary character of that history.

ways in time of peace, when he started upon a campaign he at once assumed the proud bearing of a commander. Determined, however, to avoid to the uttermost the luxury which demoralises an army, he set himself to war against it both in his officers and in his own person. To prevent any of his subordinates sleeping too long he was accustomed in the evening to cover twelve tablets made of lime-tree bark with as many memoranda addressed to one or other of his officers and entrust them to an orderly with instructions to distribute them at odd hours all through the night, that the centurions and tribunes might feel that their general was awake, and it behoved them also to watch. He was in truth himself a very scanty sleeper, but in order that he might be yet more wakeful he restricted himself to the utmost in the matter of food. An old man, apparently, he suffered from sore gums, and any hard food made them bleed and caused him great pain. In order, therefore, to destroy his pleasure in eating he would always send for his bread all the way from Rome in order that when it arrived in the camp it might be so hard and stale that he with his sore gums might have no temptation to excess. We ask ourselves whether we are reading the story of a proud Roman general or of an emaciated hermit of the Thebaid. However this Spartan treatment of himself probably obtained for him the respect of his soldiers. His campaign in Britain was successful, the barbarians who had broken through the wall were thoroughly chastised, and Marcellus returned to Rome, where it was a cause of wonder to many that he was not put to death by the jealous emperor as a punishment for his too great success.

This campaign of Marcellus probably took place in the year 182. It will be observed that we have now completed one century of Roman domination in Northumberland, a century marked on the whole by success and triumph. The two centuries that we have yet to traverse will exhibit a very different landscape. But first of all we meet with the figure, not attractive but sturdy, and full of rough energy, of a great restorer of the Roman power here and elsewhere, a native of Africa, the Emperor Septimius Severus (193-211). From the wild welter of confusion into which the world was plunged after the murder of Commodus, one emperor being proclaimed in Rome, another on the Danube, another in Britain, and another in Syria, Severus emerged sole conqueror. He was the emperor who had been acclaimed by the legions in Pannonia, and he had the great advantage of being nearer to Italy than either Pescennius Niger, who commanded in Syria, or

Clodius Albinus, who commanded in Britain, while Didius Julianus, who ruled in Rome, having literally bought the imperial title of the Prætorian guards, had only the swords of those Prætorians, a degraded and demoralised palace-soldiery, to rely on. Thus, as I have said, all these rivals fell before Severus, the African. There is nothing in his fight with Albinus for us to notice, though Albinus commanded the legions of Britain, since that quarrel was fought out not in Britain but in Gaul ; but, incidentally, this struggle for empire re-echoed even in the wilds of Northumberland. For we are told* that the Maeatae, a race of men who lived close to the wall—perhaps the wall of Antoninus—had invaded the Roman province and carried off many captives, when on account of the strain put upon the Empire by the struggle between Severus and Albinus, possibly owing to the departure of the legions for Gaul, Lupus was unable to resist the barbarians by force, and was obliged to buy peace with gold and to ransom the captives—not many in number—whom the Maeatae had carried off. This Lupus was no doubt the same as Virius Lupus, who was after-wards proprætor under Severus, and of whom we find inscriptions at Bowes and Ilkley, in Yorkshire.

The expedient of buying off barbarian invaders answered no better with the Maeatae in the second century than with the Danes in the tenth century. Possibly, too, the defeated legions of Albinus returned to their quarters in Britain in no good humour with the new master whom the fortune of war had given them. By the year 208 the affairs of the province had become so disordered that the emperor thought it necessary to come himself in person to set them straight. He came with a heavy heart, for he knew that he should never return to Rome and to the gigantic palace, the Septizonium, which he had reared at the southern end of the Palatine. He was now in the sixty-third year of his age, tortured by gout, tortured still more in spirit by the deadly feud which he knew to be raging between his two sons, Bassianus (or Caracalla) and Geta. Moreover, many undoubted signs pointed to his approaching end. The stars foretold it as seen from the astrological observatory which he had constructed on the roof of his palace ; the seers confirmed the verdict of the stars ; and three letters of his name had been accidentally brushed off from the great statue of the emperor which stood at the portals of his palace, and past which he rode forth to battle. Manifestly this omen foreboded that in the third year of his expedition the emperor would die.

* Dion, lxxv. 5.

However, the stern old Roman, all omens notwithstanding, crossed the mountains and seas to come to the scene of his duty. Though not a man of high culture, he was a student of Homer, and perhaps repeated the line :—

εἷς οἰωνός ἄριστος ἀμύνεσθαι περὶ πάτρης.

"The best of omens, is our country's need."

He probably spent some little time in the south of Britain attending to the administration of the province, and, among other changes, removing the IInd legion from their old quarters at Gloucester and stationing them at Caerleon-upon-Usk, so as to be nearer to the Welsh highlands. Then he came northwards, doubtless reviewed the VIth legion at York and the cohorts and *alae* of the allies along the line of the Wall, and pushed on to fight the Maeatae. It is clear that he regained his hold upon our county, for Habitancum and Bremenium, now again by their inscriptions attest the presence of Roman soldiers, and no doubt the whole of the Watling Street as far as Carter Fell became once more a safe Roman highway. After that his dealings with the wild Maeatae and Caledonians do not specially concern us, but we hear of long and toilsome marches over desolate moors and treacherous morasses, of gigantic labours in hewing down forests and cutting away hills, of marshes filled up and rivers bridged. In these labours, and by the harassing guerilla warfare of the Caledonians, we are told that 50,000 Roman soldiers perished, but still the indefatigable old man pressed on, borne in a litter on account of the gout which racked his limbs, and reached at last, we are told, the northernmost recesses of Caledonia. Bent on exploring the secrets of Nature, he marked the rising and setting of the sun both at mid-summer and mid-winter, and must therefore have spent full six months in this Caledonian campaign, which was ended by the submission of the barbarians, who consented to the loss—probably the very temporary loss—of a considerable part of their poverty-stricken country.

The campaign thus described is generally referred to the year 209. In the following year, 210, as no great expedition is recorded, room is found for the one exploit which most deeply concerns us, and which is related only by one somewhat late authority.* "The greatest glory of his reign was that he fortified Britain by a wall drawn right across the island, reaching at both ends to the ocean." The historian who writes

* Spartianus in *Historia Augusta*.

this sentence seems to forget that he has already recorded the same fact concerning Hadrian nearly a hundred years before. He does not say "another wall," or "repaired the wall," but simply "he fortified Britain with a wall." Hence much difficulty and many heart-burnings among antiquaries, tempers lost, and friendships severed by the fierce debates between the defenders of the Hadrianic and Severian origin of the wall from Tyne to Solway. "Not mine to settle so vast a quarrel." I but record my sincere conviction that both Hadrian and Severus may truly be called builders of the wall ; that the irruption of the barbarians in the reign of Commodus and the subsequent disorders had so broken down the great barrier that a real rebuilding was necessary, which in some places may have been as laborious as if it had been an original work ; and that with such knowledge as we possess it is, and perhaps always will be, impossible to decide what stones were laid by order of the artistic Hadrian and what by order of the rough and brusque Severus.

It was perhaps towards the end of this year 210 that Severus rode forth with his son Caracalla and a long train of generals, to receive the submission of the Caledonians and the surrender of their arms. The place of meeting must surely have been somewhere on the moors of Northumberland. For a state occasion like this the old emperor abandoned the litter, and subduing his agony, mounted on horseback. His son, who rode behind him, came silently close up to him, and making his horse rear in order to give to what was about to follow the appearance of an accident, was on the point of transfixing his father with his sword. The cries of the other generals arrested the murderer's arm, and caused Severus to look round and behold his son's sword flashing in the air. He said nothing at the time, but ascended the judgment-seat and proceeded with the ceremony of the day, receiving the claymores of the Caledonian Highlanders. Then he quietly sent for Caracalla, and along with him his two ministers Castor and the great jurisconsult Papinian. Castor was well-known to be the confidant of the father and hostile to the son ; perhaps Papinian was looked upon as belonging to the opposite party. To them, from his judgment-seat, Severus spoke, sternly rebuking his son for having attempted such an impious deed, and that too in the presence of Romans and barbarians, " But if you desire to slay me, end my life here. You are young and strong ; I am an old man and racked with disease. But if on reflection you shrink from doing the deed with your own hand, here is Papinian the prefect, who is bound to obey your orders as emperor. Give him the word, and let him slay me." Of course the command was not obeyed ; but this was the only rebuke given to the parricide. Often had Severus blamed Marcus for not putting his son Commodus to death, and now his own similar or even greater leniency was to leave the Roman world a prey to a monster as cruel and even more despicable than the brutal son of the gentle philosopher.

Next year (211) came tidings of another revolt of the Maeatae who were joined by the Caledonians. Filled with fury, Severus ordered his legions to march into their land, repeating to the officers the terrible words of Homer :—

> Let not one of the race escape the steepness of ruin,
> And your avenging hands ; not even the babe at the bosom.*

He was intending himself once more to go forth in his litter to traverse the morasses of Caledonia, but the passion of revenge was too much for that old frame, weakened by disease and worn by that madness in the brain which comes from " being wroth with one we love." He sickened and died at Eburacum on the 4th of February, 211. Some men said that Caracalla assisted Nature and hastened the old man's departure, but this may be a calumny. He was sixty-five years old, and had reigned seventeen years. Evidently a forceful, though not a lovable man, his death-bed sayings were long remembered by those who stood round his couch in the *prætorium* at York. To his sons he said, " Be of one mind " (a vain counsel), " enrich the soldiers, and never mind about any other class of your subjects." He sent for the porphyry urn in which his ashes were to be conveyed to Rome, remarked how small it was, and said, stroking it, " Thou wilt be large enough for the man for whom the world sufficed not." His energetic temperament showed itself on the point of death, for his last words were " Come now, give me something to do."

If I should seem to have described at disproportionate length the life and character of this emperor, I may plead in my excuse that no other emperors have left a greater mark on history as connected with North Britain, or on Northumbrian history as inscribed in stones, than Septimius Severus and his family. Especially is this the case with his worthless son, whom the inscriptions speak of

---

* Τῶν μή τις ὑπεκφύγοι αἰπὺν ὄλεθρον
Χεῖρας 9' ὑμετέρας· μηδ' ὅντινα γαστέρι μητήρ
Κοῦρον ἐόντα φέροι. μηδ' ὃς· φύγοι αἰπὺν ὄλεθρον.

by the honoured names of Marcus Aurelius Antoninus, but whom
the mob of Rome, and history following in their wake, refuse to know
by any other name than Caracalla,* from the fact of his having
presented every Roman citizen with a long Gallic mantle reaching
to the knees—as we should say, a long Ulster coat—which was
generally known by that name.

On the death of Severus the campaign of vengeance against the
Caledonians seems to have been abandoned. Both the young emperors
—for Caracalla and Geta had together assumed the imperial title—
were doutless anxious to exchange the hardships of British warfare
for the delights and the pomps of Rome. In the year 211—the year
of their father's death—they left Britain, and as they sailed forth
from the Tyne an altar was raised to Jupiter on South Shields Lawe
expressing the prayer of the offerer for their safe return home.†

They did indeed both return in safety, through no merit of Caracalla's, but because his brother Geta was too constantly guarded by
stalwart centurions for Caracalla's bravoes to reach him. But when
they had reached Rome, the deadly feud between the two brothers was
notorious to all the city. They took up their quarters at different
ends of the Palatine hill. Their palaces were guarded as if each were
face to face with a deadly enemy. There was a talk of dividing the
Empire between them; that one brother living at Rome and the other
at Antioch might be safe from the dreaded fratricide. At length, on
pretence of a meeting for the purpose of reconciliation, Geta was lured
into his mother's apartment. Caracalla was not there, but a multitude
of his centurions appeared on the scene. Geta knew their errand, and
ran to his mother and clung round her neck, wailing out—"Mother,
mother, help! they are killing me." He was dragged from her embrace and slain. His blood was sprinkled upon her robe, and she even
received a wound in the hand in trying to defend him. Yet she dared
not shed a tear or utter a groan, for she knew that the diabolic rage
of her son would be turned upon her if she dared to lament his
victim.

All over the empire the names and titles of the murdered Geta
were studiously erased from the public monuments. They were effaced
from the triumphal arch of Severus at Rome, from military inscriptions at the Welsh Caerleon-upon-Usk, at Greta Bridge in Yorkshire,
at our own Risingham, and Hexham. I well remember the delight
with which the late Dean Stanley gazed upon the obliterated letters in

---

* More accurately Caracallus.   † 537 *Lapidarium Septentrionale.*

the crypt of Hexham abbey, recollecting that he had seen exactly the same obliteration on a monument in Egypt, far up, I believe, towards the Second Cataract. So world-wide while the Roman Empire lasted could be the workings of a fiendish man's revenge upon his brother.

Utterly detestable as was the character of Caracalla, and short as was his reign (for after six years of empire he was assassinated by a groom when he was on his march through Syria), he accomplished two things which will ever keep his name in the foremost rank of famous emperors. The first was the erection of those stupendous baths, the Thermæ Antoninianæ at Rome, which, even in their ruin, almost appal the gazer by their vastness, and which are certainly at least as wonderful as the more often pictured Colosseum.*

The other great achievement of Caracalla was his extension of the rights of Roman citizenship to all free inhabitants of the Empire. It is true that we are told† that this was done solely in order to subject the provincials to some taxes from which they had till then been exempt, and that Caracalla might thus refill the treasury exhausted by his boundless prodigality to his soldiers. Still the measure was surely in itself a wise one ; the crowning of an edifice of which the lower stages had been reared by the great Julius and some of his wisest successors ; and had the times been less hopelessly out of joint, and could some scheme of representation for the provinces have been devised, it might have made a mighty addition to the world's happiness. What the effect of this edict of Caracalla may have been on our district of the British province can be only a matter of conjecture ; but my guess would be that it made here but little difference, the majority of the inhabitants being either soldiers, who had acquired or could acquire the citizenship by length of service, or else mere barbarians, who neither desired the *civitas* nor could have exercised any of its rights if they had possessed it.

On the death of Caracalla, followed soon after by the deposition and murder of Macrinus, who had prompted his assassination, the Roman

---

* Spartianus (*Historia Augusta*) says of these baths that the great hall, which he calls *Cella Solearis*, was a building which, as all architects agreed, defied imitation, for brackets (or girders : *cancelli*) of copper or brass were placed under the ceiling, whereby the whole ceiling was tied together, and thus a width of span was obtained of which learned mechanicians had denied the possibility.

† Dion, lxxvii. 9. οὗ ἕνεκα καὶ Ῥωμαίους πάντας τοὺς ἐν τῇ ἀρχῇ αὐτοῦ, λόγῳ μὲν τιμῶν, ἔργῳ δὲ ὅπως πλείω αὐτῷ καὶ ἐκ τοῦ τοιούτου προσῇ, διὰ τὸ τοὺς ξένους τὰ πολλὰ αὐτῶν μὴ συντελεῖν, ἀπέδειξεν.

army in Syria raised to the imperial throne a handsome youth named Varius or Elagabalus, whose mother and grandmother gave out that he was not merely a kinsman, but an illegitimate son of the murdered Caracalla. So strong was still the stolid loyalty of the soldiers to the memory of the man who had squandered the treasures of the state in extravagant donatives among them, that they wrapped in the purple and bore in triumph to Rome this effeminate Syrian lad, whose only distinction hitherto had been his handsome face and the devotion with which he had served as priest in the temple of the Sun-god, otherwise named Elagabalus, at Emessa, in Syria. For the worship of this divinity he was a zealot, and it is the only sign of anything like earnestness in his shallow nature that he was so devoted to his celestial patron whose name, of Semitic origin, he himself assumed.

Once installed in the great mansion on the Palatine the silly lad gave himself up to every sort of degrading and vicious indulgence. He of course called himself Antoninus : that profession of respect for two noble predecessors was now the usual prelude to a reign as different from theirs as darkness from light. But his four years of reign seem to have been a perfect orgy of lust and gluttony and every kind of shameful vice as well as folly, a sort of scientific demonstration of the outrages on common sense and common decency which might be committed by a weak brain intoxicated by the possession of absolute power. I will not defile my lips by speaking of his wicked deeds : I will only mention one or two of his extremely foolish ones. He promised his servants rewards if they would collect for him spiders' webs. They are said—let who will, believe it ?—to have collected 10,000 lbs. weight of the gossamer threads, at which he hugely rejoiced, saying that he now understood how large Rome was. On New Year's Day he used to send to his parasites with great pomp vessels which when opened disclosed only frogs, serpents, scorpions, and other loathly creatures of the reptile race. In vessels of this kind he used to enclose an infinite quantity of flies, calling them mild bees. He would exhibit chariot races, at which he himself would be present, eating dinner or supper, and would force elderly men, his guests, sometimes of high rank in the state, to drive the *quadriga* before him, while he himself reclined at his insolent banquet. He sometimes gave a party, to which he invited eight bald men, eight one-eyed, eight gouty, eight deaf, eight black guests, and also especially eight very tall and eight very fat men, so that there might be a shout of laughter over their inability to find room on the same couch. And so on, through page after page, the historian tells the story, at first amusing, but at last wearisome, of the wild pranks of the imperial buffoon.

The one sensible act which the effeminate Syrian priest, who posed as master of the world, performed was his association in the Empire of his cousin, Severus Alexander, a lad of fourteen, of extraordinary promise, both of mind and character—promise which was abundantly fulfilled, for in truth the young emperor who came from this strange Syrian stock is, though not one of the strongest, one of the loveliest and purest rulers that ever adorned a throne. You may still see in the museum at Chesters a stone with this inscription :—

SALVIS IMPERATORIBVS

FELIX ALA II ASTVRVM

" When the emperors are safe the second squadron of the Asturians is happy." From certain signs, which will be mentioned shortly, it is inferred that the two emperors whose health brought such joy to the hearts of the garrison at Cilurnum were Elagabalus and Severus Alexander. The inscription expressed hollow flattery for the one, but genuine loyalty for the other. The Roman soldiers were not yet so demoralised as not to regard with unutterable disgust the folly and debauchery of the effeminate young man whom they had enthroned at the Palatine, but all that was manly and soldierlike among them was ready to rally enthusiastically round his young colleague. Elagabalus perceived the change in the flow of the current of loyalty, and sought to deprive Alexander of the dignity which he had conferred upon him. The Prætorian guards heard of the design, and compelled him by their menaces to relinquish it. There was a forced and feigned reconciliation ; a rumour, false as it proved, of the death of Alexander ; a mutiny of the soldiers which Elagabalus tried to repress by high-handed measures. The cup of military discontent ran over. Elagabalus was murdered by the Prætorians, and thrown into the Tiber, and Alexander succeeded to his uneasy throne.

This revolution, like that by which Caracalla rid himself of his partner in the Empire, has left numerous marks on the Roman monuments in Northumberland. Without exception, I believe, in the many inscriptions in which the name of Antoninus Elagabalus once occurred, it has been erased from the stone, and looking on these tablets one can almost hear the chip, chip of the mallet with which some stout soldier has vented his indignation at having been even for four years compelled to crouch and grovel before a thing like Elagabalus. In the inscription which once recorded the happiness of the soldiers at the safety of their emperors, the epithet Antoniniana, which connected them with the Syrian priest who assumed that profaned name, has been erased by the hammer, and in another inscription of the year 221 recording the restoration of a building *vetustate conlapsum* all that records the name and titles of the loathed Elagabalus has been with equal passion obliterated from the stone.

After a prosperous reign of fourteen years, Alexander, whose only considerable fault seems to have been that he was too obviously governed by the advice of his mother, Mammaea, was slain by his mutinous soldiers, and the brutal Thracian Maximin, the only full-blooded barbarian who ever received the imperial diadem, reigned in his stead.

The advice given by Severus to his sons, which was virtually "Pamper the soldiers; never mind about the rest of your subjects," had been too faithfully followed. As soon as a conscientious ruler like the young Alexander (or in later days Aurelian or Probus) tried to enforce a stricter discipline, and to bring back the soldiers to the type of the brave and patient legionary which had been the ideal of earlier days, he was sure to fall a victim to a barrack-room conspiracy, and some military demagogue who had exasperated the resentments and flattered the vanity of the soldiers reigned in his stead. In this way, after the murder of Alexander, in a period of fifty years, fourteen emperors ascended the throne, besides numerous aspirants to the diadem who strutted for their little day in the distant provinces of the Empire. This period, from 235 to 284, might almost be called the real time of the downfall of the Roman Empire, for though under the strong and wise rule of men like Diocletian, Constantine, and Theodosius, the process of disintegration was arrested, and some appearance of strength and cohesion was given to the decaying Empire, it was after all but a temporary reprieve. The barbarians, in those fatal fifty years, had learned that the legions were not invincible. the cancer of corruption had eaten deep into the civil service, even the process of reorganisation could only be accomplished by sacrificing the last semblance of liberty and turning the Imperator who had once been but the foremost citizen of the republic into the counterpart of an oriental despot, approached with idolatrous prostration and surrounded by eunuchs and cowering slaves.

I am not going to weary you with the names of the ephemeral emperors of the middle of the third century ; nor, indeed, do I propose to follow the course of imperial history any further in detail, for soon after the death of Severus Alexander the connection of our county as a whole with Roman affairs almost ceases. An inscription at Bremenium does indeed record the name of Gordian III., the excellent young prince who succeeded the murderer of Alexander (237-243), but soon after that, inscriptions north of the Wall fade away entirely. The line of the Watling Street, with its supporting stations of Habitancum and Bremenium was apparently lost ; and for effective purposes the grasp of Rome on Northumberland was limited to the little strip of land between the Wall and the Tyne—if indeed the *cohortes* and *alae* always held that strip.

Our historians tell us practically nothing about the affairs of Northern Britain during this period ; but, arguing from the analogy of other parts of the Empire, and knowing the utterly demoralised . state of the Roman army, we may well believe that some of the incursions of the barbarians, which broke through the line of the Wall, wrapped the camps in fire, and strewed their floors with the ashes and rubbish, on which later builders came to raise their poorer imitations of the work of Hadrian and Severus, happened during this miserable time—especially during that most wretched part of it, the reign of Gallienus (261-268), which from the number of pretenders to the purple who appeared in different parts of the Empire, is known as the time of the Thirty Tyrants.

The events of Romano-British history after this time left but little mark on this part of Britain. We know from other sources that the Hollander, Carausius, a man of mean extraction, who was charged to suppress piracy in the German Ocean, made the imperial fleet the instrument of his own ambition, had himself proclaimed emperor in Britain, and forced even the proud Diocletian to acknowledge him as his colleague, and that thus for at least six years (287-293) Britain was virtually the seat of an independent Roman Empire, until Carausius was slain and Constantius Chlorus restored the lost province to Rome.

We may be certain that during these six years the cohorts along the line of the Wall obeyed the rule of this upstart usurper, but we have no proof of it, for his name is not recorded in any of our museums.

So, too, that great event, the elevation of Constantine to the imperial dignity at York (A.D. 306), with all its world-changing results, is one as to which the camps on the Northumbrian moors are entirely silent. We have in all only two or three inscriptions of Constantine and his family to produce—nothing like the wealth of monumental evidence for the reigns of Severus and his descendants.

We hear towards the latter half of the fourth century (360-362) of ravages of Britain (extending even to the "city which was anciently called Londinium, but is now called Augusta") committed by the Picts and Scots, with whom are now joined the terrible nation of the Attacotti, who, according to Jerome, were accustomed to feed on human flesh. Undoubtedly these men, before they reached so far south as Londinium, must have thoroughly broken down the defence of the troops stationed along the line of the Wall—probably also that of the legion quartered at York. Theodosius, father of the famous emperor (368-369) certainly cleared the southern part of the province of these savage invaders. Perhaps, also, as Ammianus Marcellinus tells us, he re-established all the frontier stations which had been demolished. That he re-annexed to the Empire the lost region between the wall of Hadrian and that of Antoninus, and called it by the name Valentia, after the then reigning emperor, Valentinian, appears to be asserted by the same historian ; but his language is vague ; he evidently speaks with no precise knowledge of the country : and the fact alleged is most improbable.

What is undoubted is that fourteen years after the British victories of Theodosius (383), a Spaniard, Maximus, who had obtained high command in the Roman army in Britain, raised the standard of revolt against the young Emperor Gratian, crossed over into Gaul, probably taking the bulk of the Roman forces with him, was acclaimed as Augustus by the soldiers of his rival, and reigned as emperor at Trier for five years, till he was overthrown by Theodosius the Great. To this date I am disposed to assign the practical disappearance of the Roman standards from the valley of the Tyne, though I must admit that some of our best authorities hold that the actual line of the Wall was still occupied till the middle of the following century. It seems to me, however, probable that the withdrawal of so large a part of the imperial army to the other side of the Channel so weakened the Roman line of defence that the fierce Pictish invaders effectually undid the restoring work of Theodosius and broke down the hated barrier, not to be again restored. It is true that in the *Notitia Dignitatum Utriusque Imperii*, the civil and military directory of the Empire, which was probably edited for the last time about the year

402, the list of troops "*per lineam Valli*" still appears in all its strength and as holding all the forts along the Wall. But would not a dying state like the Roman Empire under Honorius be just the organisation to keep up its paper defences and its spectral cohorts after they had ceased to have any real existence, and does that chapter of the *Notitia* outweigh the admitted fact of the almost entire disappearance of Roman coins after the reign of Gratian? I know not. This is a question which we may hope that further excavations will solve, and in the earnest desire that this may prove to be the case, I will for the present conclude my story of the Roman occupation of Britain.

NORTHUMBRIAN STORY AND SONG.

LECTURE I.

NORTHUMBRIAN FOLK AND SPEECH.

Let me begin my course of lectures by explaining what I mean them to be, for I have found no title which will quite express this.

Nor do I find it easy of explanation. I make no profession of antiquarian, archæological, historical, or philological learning. I cannot expect to be able to tell many of my audience that which is new or startling; cannot expect to teach them. Thirty years ago I had the honour of lecturing to this society for several successive winters on our language and literature. They were not then much thought of or lectured about, but had been my constant study since my early youth. Although a better state of things has begun, and some of our most excellent workers and distinguished scholars are and have been in residence in one or other of them, still, speaking generally, our old university men even yet seem to cherish the belief that, whilst all other languages and literatures require scientific exposition, and may be regarded as more or less educational, a knowledge of our own comes by nature, and can not, need not, or should not, be taught. In spite of delusions in them as elsewhere there is much systematic instruction in this most important subject. Learned bodies, such as the Early English Text Society, the Chaucer Society, the Ballad Society, the new Shakespere Society, the Dialect Society, and so forth, have carefully edited manuscripts and texts, and issued admirable dissertations upon them, and upon the points of interest which they illustrate. German scholars have been working in these rich mines with the patience, thoroughness, and exactitude which pre-eminently distinguish their methods of study, and German universities have learned professors with learned assistants who devote their lives to the scientific educational exposition of the language and literature which are still grudged a full entrance to the old universities of their native land.

And one result of this great increase of material upon which to found and form judgments has been that we have learned once more that there is no finality in learning. We have had to give up many a cherished belief. The dear old Heptarchy has gone the way of the toad in the rock, and all the interesting bad characters of our childhood's history books have been satisfactorily converted, or, at all events, white-washed. It is really refreshing and encouraging to reflect how very much more the people who live a thousand years hence will know about us than we do about ourselves. Then may Thomas Bewick be known as the inventor of the locomotive, and George Stephenson as the author of *Italy and her Invaders*.

So having, in every decade of an average long life, had to begin all over again, I cannot hope to be a teacher of those to whom the new learning is the only true learning.

But I have one qualification for my task : I am a devoted Northumbrian, with an intense love for and belief in the Northumbria of old and the Northumberland of to-day. I have wandered through every nook and into every cranny of the grand old county since I was a little child, and still visit with ever-renewed delight the hills and vales, the peles and castles, which are so abundant, so varied, and so full of interest for us all. I have lived with the shepherds in Cheviot and the fisher folk by the sea. The legends, the ballads, the histories of the Border side, were our delight in extreme youth ; and they are so still. Who amongst us does not love this wild, free northern land of ours ? Rude though our climate be, it is bracing, and genial in the warmth of its embrace. Where can you find such heather as that which makes our fells one unutterable glory of colour in the summer's prime ? The "wild, wandering waste of sea," which brings the biting, bitter "wind of God," as Kingsley calls it, to our shores, can be "even the gentlest of all gentle things," can assume a sheen and radiance of many colours which neither Adriatic nor Mediterranean could outvie.

And our story, and that which our great men have done for us, are worthy of this Northern land. I hope in my lectures to show what this has been and how it has been, or rather to hint at or sketch this. I shall, for the most part, confine myself to Northumberland as we now know it : but, in the early days, that is not possible for it did not exist ; and the old Northumberland from the Humber to the Forth, whether one kingdom or divided into Bernicia and Deira, must be brought to some extent under our consideration. For geographical distinctions are, in such cases, mere names, and of little consequence.

The people who lived in the land, and what the thinkers amongst them thought, and what the doers did, these alone are vital.

For convenience sake, and whilst fully admitting the impropriety, I shall call the old Northumberland by its Latin name of Northumbria, and shall use the Latin names Bernicia and Deira as denoting respectively the land between the Tees or the Tyne and the Frith of Forth and the land between the Humber and the Tees or the Tyne. These names were unknown to the English unlearned folk, and the divisions themselves were arbitrary and varying.

Northumbria was, in many a great emergency, the saviour of England. Northumbria was the cradle of its religion, and decided the form of its religious faith. Northumbria struck the key-note of the poetic song which is one of England's greatest glories. Northumbria led the van of Christendom in learning as in art. And what Northumbria did Northumberland has continued to do in some measure, and will continue to do in full measure when we all fully recognise and live up to the privilege and responsibility which are implied in the proud boast, " I am a Northumbrian."

We will now come to particulars.

Northumberland is an epitome of the world. All of the general features of the habitable globe may be found within its borders, except volcanoes and glaciers which, indeed, it did possess in its more youthful days, but which it no longer requires. But it has never been a show county, and few even of its inhabitants who are not bicyclists have any idea of the variety and beauty of the scenery which it contains, none who are not anglers really know the wealth and multitude of its charms. Even when the poet comes to speak of "mountainous Northumberland," he does not dwell upon the features of natural scenery which it boasts. He turns at once to that which man has added to nature, and, in his charming sketch of the coast so familiar to us, it is with this that he chiefly occupies himself. You will remember that the good Abbess Hilda is voyaging, with some of her nuns, to Lindisfarne from the famous monastery of Whitby :—

> And now the vessel skirts the strand
> Of mountainous Northumberland :
> Towns, towers, and halls, successive rise,
> And catch the nuns' delighted eyes.
> Monk-Wearmouth soon behind them lay,
> And Tynemouth's priory and bay ;
> They mark'd, amid her trees, the hall
> Of lofty Seaton Delaval ;

They saw the Blythe and Wansbeck floods
Rush to the sea through sounding woods;
They passed the tower of Widderington,
Mother of many a valiant son;
At Coquet-isle their beads they tell
To the good Saint who owned the cell;
Then did the Alne attention claim,
And Warkworth, proud of Percy's name;
And next, they cross'd themselves, to hear
The whitening breakers sound so near,
Where, boiling through the rocks, they roar,
On Dunstanborough's caverned shore;
Thy tower, proud Bamborough, mark'd they there,
King Ida's castle, huge and square,
From its tall rock look grimly down,
And on the swelling ocean frown;
Then from the coast they bore away,
And reach'd the Holy Island's bay.

The man who wrote that knew what he was writing about, and selected, as Sir Walter Scott nearly always does, those features of the landscape which chiefly impress the mind, and characterised each by the appropriate adjective. He had spent considerable time at Langley Ford, in Cheviot, in 1791, when twenty years of age, and had been specially attracted by Flodden Field, which in his verse he was to make live once more, but he made many a peaceful raid on other occasions into our beautiful county which he knew well and appreciated thoroughly. "I have had an expedition through Hexham and the higher parts of Northumberland, which would have delighted the very cockles of your heart, not so much on account of the beautiful romantic appearance of the country, though that would have charmed you also, as because you could have seen more Roman inscriptions built into gate-posts, barns, etc., than perhaps are to be found in any other part of Britain. These have been all dug up from the neighbouring Roman wall, which is still in many places very entire, and gives a stupendous idea of the perseverance of its founders, who carried such an erection from sea to sea, over rocks, mountains, rivers, and morasses. There are several lakes among the mountains above Hexham, well worth going many miles to see, though their fame is eclipsed by their neighbourhood to those of Cumberland. They are surrounded by old towers and castles, in situations the most savagely romantic; what would I have given to have been able to take effect-pieces from some of them. Upon the Tyne, about Hexham, the country has a different aspect, presenting much of the beautiful though less of the sublime."

We have gained much from the intimate knowledge which the great Border poet thus obtained, for the scenes of the first and second and most of the sixth cantoes of " Marmion " are laid in Northumberland, and we thus obtain a share in one of the few works of this Borderland which will not willingly be let die.

In these lectures I have already said that I must perforce distinguish between Northumberland and the old Northumbria of which it was but a part, and which, in its greatest days, stretched from the Humber to the Frith of Forth. In this larger sense, Sir Walter Scott was as much a Northumbrian as Cædmon, if, indeed, it be any longer permissible to speak of Cædmon at all. When I had the privilege of conducting the class in this society upon the English language and literature which I have already mentioned, I lectured in all good faith upon this Cædmon, the first English poet, and published what I said. In those days my words met with some acceptance, but, since then, there has been much minute and learned research into the whole subject of our early literature, and good, solid work has undoubtedly been done. This branch of learning, however, has not escaped from the fever of unsettlement, of change for change's sake. In these latter days the not inherently probable theory that the nearer you are to any one or thing, the less you know about him or it, has had extensive vogue : Cædmon has not escaped the fate which has overtaken even Shakespere, and the uninteresting parts of his poems are said to have been borrowed from the Heliand, an old Saxon or Low German poem of the ninth century, and the more interesting and poetical parts to have been written by Cynewulf, an English and Northumbrian poet of great merit, and whose date is at the least a century and a half after Cædmon's. But I venture to think that the last word has not yet been said upon this matter, and that it may prove that the Venerable Bede, writing as he did twelve centuries nearer to Cædmon's time than we are, and who was born in Cædmon's life-time, and in his own Northumbria, knew perhaps rather more certainly than we do what the facts about this poetry really were.

But this raises another, and an interesting and important question. When the English first came to England, and for four centuries afterwards, nearly all their singing was done by Northumbrians ; the old Northumbria was the home of the best and greatest poets. It has never been so since. The northern part which passed to Scotland has kept up the old traditions, or, rather, from time to time there has been an outburst worthy of the older times, but the part south of the Tweed has remained comparatively barren. No poet, scarcely any writer, of the first rank can North-umberland, Durham, or Yorkshire boast. True that Elizabeth Barrett Browning was born in Durham, but she left it when a little child.

We shall see when we come to consider the ballads of our county that we find in them a very similar state of affairs. There was some-thing in the Borders north of the Cheviots and the Tweed which favoured the poetic element, and which was not found in the Borders south of the Tweed. But what this something was I cannot tell you with certainty. It was not the climate, for in that respect the dis-tricts are alike bad : it was not the natural features, for in this respect the districts are alike good, the southern portion having perhaps a slight advantage in the special beauty of its rivers. It was not the speech, for the changes which this underwent in the two parts were not dissimilar. It was not the natural man, for he also had a close resemblance in each case, both in origin and in the many intermixing processes which he had undergone. As to the early singing, some-thing may be due to the fact that the English who conquered Northumbria came from the same district of the main-land, Angeln, the real old England, and brought with them the traditions and possibly examples, of great poetic song, for we cannot say certainly whether so grand an epic outburst as Beowulf, for example, belongs to England or to Angeln. We may one day be able to trace exactly the intellectual influences which swayed the Lowlands of Scotland but from which our side of the Borders was cut off, but, speaking of the later days, at the moment I can only ask you to bear in mind that the Scotch borders were comparatively near to Edinburgh, the capital of their kingdom and the centre of Scottish light and learning, whilst the English borders were far removed from all courtly and learned influences. I cannot go further than the simple suggestion that these facts may, in some measure, tend to explain the difficulty which I have mentioned.

But let me be careful when I speak of intermixing processes, for I have no wish to lead you into the ethnographical and etymological quagmires which lie around the previous question of the natural man. If we get into these, six lectures will not suffice to deliver us from them. It is sufficient for us to know that when the Romans con-quered Britain, when the Teutons made Britain England, when the Vikings themselves or their descendants took possession of England, in each case they found two peoples here who, to the conquerors, were native to these islands. There were the Britons, at first everywhere in Britain south of the Tweed, and in the kingdom of Strath-clyde which lay to the west of a line drawn from Dumbarton to Chester ; and there were the Picts, or the Picts and Scots, to the north. As Britain became England, the Britons in England proper were to some extent absorbed, to a greater extent, probably, exterminated ; but the west part of the island, consisting of Strath-clyde, Wales, and the peninsula of Cornwall, Devonshire, and part of Somerset, remained in the hands of the free Britons. Strath-clyde ceased to be a kingdom early in the eleventh century, but the native tongue only ceased to be spoken in Cornwall in our own day, and even yet the Cornishman speaks of "going into England." It is still the speech of the Highlands of Scotland, and of a great part of Ireland, and, having spent several weeks in the country districts of Wales, I do not think it too much to say that their native tongue is everywhere still in Wales the speech of the Welsh people. And this in spite of great efforts having been made to kill them, English being taught in schools throughout the kingdom, and children being punished for speaking their mother tongue. A good Highlander, now a valuable member of Parliament, told me that the soundest thrashing he ever got was for answering in Gaelic a question' asked in English.

But what about the Picts and Scots? Here lie the quagmires close ahead. "Scotia's Isle" is Ireland, of course, not Scotland ; what we now call Scotland being merely a geographical expression to denote that land, the lower half of which was England and the upper half Caledon ; and the Scots were destitute aliens who landed in Albin or Caledon (which we now strangely call Scotland) from Ireland—a Gaelic colony from Ireland. Of this there is no manner of doubt, but who were the Picts? Were they Gaels, or were they Goths who had, before the Roman invasion, conquered the Gael or Celts ; or were they Britons whom the Romans never conquered ; or were they Hyperboreans, or Scandinavians, or Pruth-neach from the Lower Vistula ; or does the expression simply mean, what it seems to mean, that they were painted men—men who continued to come out in the full war paint which Cæsar expressly says their brethren, the Southern Britons of his day, indulged in, long after those Britons had, in conformity with the usages of their Roman masters, taken to clothes ?

It is of little consequence, and we will leave it. Much melancholy learning has been expended upon it, and those whose tastes lie in the direction of useless knowledge can find enough of it accumulated around this controversy. The world has grown rather too old for the arguments which were once the staple of intellectual existence, those about questions which are quite insoluble by man.

> Myself, when young, did eagerly frequent
> Doctor and Saint, and heard much argument
> About it and about, but evermore
> Came out by the same door where in I went.

I was saying, when I turned aside to give warning of surrounding dangers, that the natural man, north and south of the Tweed, had a close resemblance, both in his origin and the intermixing processes he went through. Speaking generally, it was in each case the Celt conquered by the Roman, next conquered by the Englishman—call him Angle or Saxon if you like it better—then the result directly conquered by the Viking or Scandinavian from Scandinavia, and afterwards indirectly from Normandy.

But now let us look for the traces of the intermixing processes of which I have spoken. Where shall we look for them? There is only one place where we can certainly find them, and that is in our language. Now, from the grammatical point of view you cannot mix a language. You may simplify it, but what remains will be of the original source. From the etymological point of view you may mix any language to any extent. Again, a language does not die when it ceases to be spoken, it dies when it begins to be regularly and systematically written. Before that, growth is possible, is perhaps certain: after that, decay is sure. And thus a highly developed grammar, a complex grammar, does not necessarily imply a highly developed civilisation. The Bask, the language (according to those who use it) which was spoken by Adam and Eve, and which was introduced into Spain before the confusion of tongues consequent upon the too successful building operations in connection with the Tower of Babel, has the most intricate and complicated of grammars. It is supposed also to be highly philosophical, but it is too difficult for the use of mankind generally. It is said that even the devil himself, who is generally credited with special ability, gave up the attempt to learn Bask in despair, after three years of unsuccessful endeavour.

Let me, before I proceed to examine our Northumbrian tongue, just briefly recapitulate the salient points of the language-principles which I have been laying down.

Grammar, the mode of expressing the relationships of words, is the frame, the bony skeleton, nay, rather the very life of a language. It does not grow or change after the language becomes a written one, excepting in the direction of simplification, which is a long word simply, in this case, meaning loss. It cannot be blended with the grammar of another language. Vocabularies may be mingled to any extent. The words of one people may become those of another ; this process is constantly going forward in all civilised countries : languages have adopted foreign words even to the exclusion of their own, but they preserve their grammars. We have, in our dictionary, some 45,000 words, not a third of which are truly English or even Teutonic. We can write sentences which (excepting particles and auxiliaries) have not a native word in them. But our grammar, the way in which our words alter to denote altered relations or different circumstances, is purely English.

I shall have, before long, to call your special attention to one or two facts in connection with our own grammar, which seem, in some measure, to contradict the position which I have just taken up. I shall go carefully into these when the time comes, and you shall judge for yourselves how far they contradict or confirm that position. I only mention this now to put you on your guard.

Since Britain became England, one language and one only has been spoken in it by the English. Two processes have been going forward in that language all the time, those of grammatical simplifi- cation and verbal amplification. But we speak to-day the same tongue which Cædmon sang in and which Alfred wrote. The changes which it has passed through are the fruits of the two processes I have men- tioned, and of those only. No tongue, once spoken here and called Anglo-Saxon, perished with the Norman Conquest. The tongues spoken in these islands when Alfred ruled or William the Norman conquered them are spoken in them still. I doubt whether any dialect, at all events of the English tongue, any of those family differ- ences which marked the differing parts of the main-land from which the English settlers came, has died out. By the differing parts of the main-land, I mean, in the case of Northumbria, the different districts of Angeln, the true old England. Neither the Norman Conquest nor any subsequent event has disturbed the supremacy of the English tongue. When the English folk first took possession of Britain and made it England, the land of the English, and gave it their tongue in the place of Cymric and Gaelic, the Celtic dialects which then obtained, the English language was highly inflected. The invasions of the Northmen and the Norman Conquest did much to simplify this, and the latter added vastly to the English vocabulary, and the two processes of simplification and amplification have since gone on until now we have scarcely anything left which can be called grammar, and we have twice as many foreign as English words. But, all that is left of grammar is native; the words in most usual demand are native; we can write sentences, chapters, even books, without foreign assistance, whilst no book or chapter can be composed without English aid.

English, then, may be called the staple of the tongue we use in Northumberland, but we wish to see whether there are any linguistic traces left of the tongues which were used here before the English came, and what effect has been produced by the subsequent political convulsions to which our county has been subjected.

We find but few and faint traces of the centuries of Roman rule, and those of which we can speak with any certainty are perhaps only to be discovered in proper names. Chester-le-Street, the camp on the road, is a bright example of a tiny group, and we have Chesters in different parts of Northumberland. But although Italy has greatly influenced our vocabulary, both in the ancient and the modern form of its spoken tongue, that influence came later and in other ways. There is something startling in the few traces anywhere left of the Roman conquest and occupation of Britain. They held these islands for nearly three times the duration of our rule in India. They have left evidences in every part of England that their occupation was intended to have a permanent character. We have in Northumberland the most important of these evidences, not only in our great Roman Wall, and the many stations which form appendages to it, but also in the camps and entrenched towns which have been dug out from the dust of ages to tell us of the pride, power, and pomp with which Imperial Rome ruled her most distant possessions. The sculptured stones, often of much artistic merit; the mosaic pavements; the ingenious methods of banishing the northern cold and damp from their luxurious villas; their admirable bathing arrangements; the gateway entrances worn into deep ruts by the passage of chariot wheels; the stepping-stone contrivance in the streets, designed to keep the patrician feet free from the frequent floods; the domestic appliances and costly urns and splendidly embossed silver dishes; these recall to us the days spent in wandering through the more famous and extensive remains of Pompeii and Herculaneum. Deeply interesting and frequently pathetic are the inscriptions on the common monumental tablets and votive altars : the loving brother to his good comrade; the bereaved husband to his most sacred wife, who had reached the age of thirty-three *sine ulla macula*. These, and many more similar remains, are found from time to time, but when the Romans departed they left behind not a trace in the practice or lives of the conquered of their arts or their religion, and scarcely a vestige of their language. The walls they had built, the roads they had made, indeed remained, but the walls to serve as quarries for centuries for those who put up what Romans would have scorned to dignify with the name of building; and though the roads, being made by the finest road-makers the world has seen, continued and even still, in scattered instances, continue to do their work, the art of making them vanished when the Romans went. The Britons could not even defend the walls which the Romans had built.

But in our English tongue, and in the varieties of it specially spoken in Northumberland, there are more remains of the languages spoken by the Britons than there are of the great Roman tongue. Putting on one side, for a moment, the names of places, and speaking only of the names of things, we are at once struck by the fact that the words which remain are of the commonest kind. They refer chiefly to articles in daily use, and are entirely without reference to objects of mastership or superiority. We have, for instance, cabin, button, bran, quay, garter, flannel, hem, pail, pan, pitcher, lum, trace, coat, coble, clout, girdle, basket, darn, kiln, gruel, gown, mop, size (paste), and the like. Now what is suggested by this fact ?

Considerable ingenuity has been expended upon the question whether the English exterminated or absorbed the Britons. The fact of the complete disappearance of all traces of the laws, arts, religion, and language of Rome, which the Britons must, to some extent, have acquired, at least temporarily, undoubtedly points to extermination ; the number of common words in everyday use points in the opposite direction. Is not the truth probably to be found between these extremes ? The Britons fought, though vainly, and, at times under valiant men or women, fought well. There was no voting, apparently, in those days as to whether women who did the same work as men should have similar recognition. The fighting was hand-to-hand work, and multitudes of men would no doubt perish in it. But those who remained and the non-fighting women and children would be kept and applied to uses similar to those to which Englishmen fourteen centuries later apply such Matabele and Mashona as they do not put violently to death.

This is what we seem to learn from the faint linguistic traces which remain to us, but, speaking of these very things, Dr. Hodgkin in his great history of *Italy and her Invaders*, beautifully and wisely says, " to the questions, so intensely interesting to us, how all these things happened, how the struggle was regarded by those engaged in it, what manner of man the Roman provincial seemed to the Saxon, and the Heathen to the Christian, what were the incidents and what the nature of the strife—to all of these questions we can scarce obtain more answer than comes back to us from the spirits of those with whom we once shared every thought, but who, summoned by the touch of an unseen hand, have left us for the Land of Silence."

I need not say that we find traces of the Britons in many of the names of places. Our river Tyne, for example, may be the British Tuinn, waves, or Tuinna, water's edge, or it may simply mean double, referring to the two rivers which join to form it ; our Derwent, dur, water, and gwent, an open bit of country. But the most interesting to me are our Esk, or Ouse, as in Ouseburn. Both come from the same word, the British uisge, meaning water, and so does whiskey. Thus it is superfluous to speak of whiskey and water, you only say, in so doing, whiskey and whiskey. The greater part of our rivers retain their British names, and this is sometimes the case where you would scarcely suspect it. Thus we call the head waters of the Till the Breamish. The Till is the Breamish until it passes under the county bridges at Powburn. It was a rapid, impetuous stream in its youth, and so you get this fact recorded in its name, breme, rough or rapid, uisge, water : Esk, Ouse, Usk, Ish, are all varieties of the fine old word which has been perverted to the service of Bacchus. When indeed the beck becomes a river, and the impetuous restlessness of youth is exchanged for the dignified placidity of age, then the name is also changed, but it is still British, and describes the altered character. Slow, quiet, but deep and dangerous is the Till as it flows down through the fertile vale of Wooler to join the broad, bright streams of the Tweed, and the old rhyme which pleased us in our childhood's days has a grim truth about it :

> Tweed says to Till,
> " What gars ye rin sae still ? "
> Till says to Tweed,
> " Though ye rin with speed
> And I rin slaw,
> Where ye droon ane man
> I droon twa."

It seems almost superfluous to say again that the staple of this intermixing process is English. It is English, the vocabulary of which is being mixed. It has inherited a few Latin words, it has retained and appropriated useful and convenient British words. But the next step in the mixing process was quite of a different character. It was carried forward by a people who came at first as bold and lawless sea pirates, seeking for wild adventure and plunder only, but who soon determined upon conquering the goodly land of the English, and carried out their determination to a successful issue.

We have no good account in our English histories of this marvellous people; no account which lets us see the Vikings at home, and traces closely and clearly the intimate connection between their land and ours during, at least, two hundred years. Thomas Carlyle has sketched this powerfully and well in his *Early Kings of Norway*, and I strongly advise those who have that love for the land—now one of our chief holiday resorts—which all who know it feel, to make a careful study of his little book. There is something strangely akin in the early history of the two rival countries. England was peopled by men from different parts of the northern shores of the main-land of Europe. The early history of these successful invaders was one of constant strife between the kings of small and varying portions of the conquered territory, until at length under Egbert in the year 860 the whole of the English race submitted to one common rule. The last to submit itself to him was Northumbria.

So in Norway the early tale is that of many small and varying territories under different lords, or jarls, as they were called, and the early predatory incursions into our islands were conducted by bands of Northmen who acknowledged no common leader. But the work of uniting the land under one common head, and making it a kingdom, which it has practically continued to be ever since, was carried to a successful issue by the powerful influence of Harald Haarfagr, and under circumstances which are so romantic, that you will pardon me for briefly stating them. His father, Halfdan, known as Halfdan the Black, had begun the work which his great son completed.

Harald Haarfagr, the fair-haired Harald, loved a beautiful and proud lady, Gyda by name. But, when he made advances to her in due form, she replied that (to quote Carlyle's words) : " Her it would not beseem to wed any jarl or poor creature of that kind : let him do as Gorm of Denmark, Eric of Sweden, Egbert of England, and others had done ; subdue into peace and regulation the confused, contentious bits of jarls round him, and become a king ; then, perhaps, she might think of his proposal ; till then, not."

This answer, lofty and contemptuous though it were, was quite to Harald's mind, and he resolved to win the proud and peerless beauty in the way which she had dictated. He vowed that he would let his fair hair grow, and would neither cut nor even comb it, until he could rightly claim the haughty Gyda as his bride. It was a long and tough job. Twelve weary years of constant fighting ensued. Every year fresh jarls were subdued. Not only the Vikings of the mainland, but those who had settled in the Orkneys, Shetlands, Hebrides, and the Isle of Man, at length acknowledged Harald's sovereignty, and, when twelve years had passed, his right-hand man, Ragnwald Jarl, was commissioned to undertake the due barbering of the now royal head, and the long-coveted prize was won. Gyda was brought home in triumph, the greatest queen of the North.

These were the great days of Norwegian colonisation. The Vikings who would not submit had to flee, and they conquered and settled down in the lands which they had formerly harried : Iceland, the Faroe Islands, parts of Scotland and Ireland, France, and England, all felt and still feel the effects of Gyda's pride.

As you sail up the stern western coast of the noble peninsula, how strange this story seems. At quiet, pretty little Aalesund, lying peacefully, upon its two islands, under the shadow of the great hills, on the outer edge of that wondrous Skjaergaard which makes the voyage up the Norwegian coast so agreeable (for the most part) to squeamish travellers, how hard it is to realise that it was from this spot that Ganger Rolf went forth to conquer that important bit of France which bears the Northman's name to this day. That giant Rolf, whom no horse could carry and who had therefore to gang on foot and so was called Rolf the Ganger, was foremost amongst the Vikings who gave to Europe the little leaven of determined power which may truly be said to have leavened the whole lump. It was towards the beginning of the tenth century that Rolf got final possession of Rouen.

I should add that Harald Haarfagr is said to have continued to reign for sixty years after his winning of Gyda. He did not make, perhaps, the most faithful of husbands, but he proved himself as good and powerful an administrator as he had been a triumphant fighter.

I have said that the Norsemen came over at first upon mere predatory expeditions, but that the time came when they were bent upon conquering the land and succeeded in doing so. Before the year 870 the whole of Northumbria had passed into their hands. But their conquest was quite another thing than that of the English had been. The English had, as we have seen, come over to the land of their adoption in great numbers, and had dispossessed the people who dwelt there, exterminating or absorbing them, or driving them back into remote parts of the country. The Norsemen who wished to settle here were comparatively few in number, and drew their reinforcements from a land which can never have contained a great population. We are apt to forget what a vast amount of territory the kingdom of Norway covers. In breadth it varies between about 250 miles in its northern half, and 450 miles (between the mouth of the Hardanger fjord on the west and Björkö on the east) at its broadest part towards the south. But from the North Cape to Lindesnaes, its most southerly point, it is 1,160 miles long, the entire coast line of the Scandinavian peninsula, measuring upwards of 2,000 miles in length, the part between Cape Lindesnaes and Vadsö alone accounting for 1,250 of these miles. A circle drawn from Lindesnaes as the centre, and with the North Cape as the radius, will pass through Italy very little north of Rome, whilst the trend of the land is so greatly from east to west that, although its most western longitude is that of Amsterdam and a little more westerly than Marseilles, I have frequently heard it debated whether you are more of an Eastern traveller when you are at Constantinople or the North Cape. Constantinople is, indeed, a little more to the east, but it is only a question of a few miles.

But although Norway occupies so much ground, there is but little of it that is really habitable. There is only some 3 per cent. of it which is built over or cultivated. Forests, some of which are all but impenetrable, and the lower fjelde where the saeters are, and where cattle can graze and perhaps a little hay can be made, form 22 per cent. Lakes, fjords, and glaciers occupy $7\frac{1}{2}$ per cent., and the remaining $67\frac{1}{2}$ per cent. is without cultivation of any kind, being the abode of the bear, the wolf, the elk, the red and reindeer, the eagle and the greater owls, and the favourite haunt of the true sportsman. And you will thus see that the population of the land can never have been a great one. Those who know Norway understand well why the Norseman loves the sea ; why the boys who are born in inland places still long to be sailors ; how vast a part the sea has always played, and must always play, in Norwegian life. Not only does it thrust its way lovingly into the land, often for more than a hundred miles, but, in a great part of Nordland, the vast region which lies within the

Arctic Circle, you find no roads, often not even foot-paths, and you must pass from one place to another, make calls, send for your doctor, go to church, in an open boat. The men who were born in that land in early days were sea-kings as a matter of course, and Frithjof Nansen, he who, in the words of our pitman-poet, Joseph Skipsey, at one time assistant-librarian in this institution, "dared to do what no Viking had done," has shown us in these later days that the endurance, the courage, the indomitable energy, and the spirit of adventure, which carried the Vikings triumphantly over the known world and beyond its confines, are still the proud possession of their undegenerate sons.

The Norsemen conquered Northumbria and settled in it, but they were absorbed by the English people. They became Englishmen; they did not make Englishmen Northmen. But where did they settle in Northumbria? The question is a difficult one to answer. We must again apply the test of language, and here we are met by a serious initial difficulty. When we come to consider the names of places, we find comparatively few of such which are Norse in the Northumberland of to-day. Further north we have the familiar "fjord" in the Frith of Forth, and again, on the west, in the Solway Frith; but it is not until we reach the south of Durham and Yorkshire that we find in abundance the familiar ending "by," a town or village, "dal," a valley, or "foss," a waterfall. On the other hand, we have everywhere in Northumberland the well-known "fjeld," a hill or, perhaps I might say, an elevated table-land from which mountains spring, in our "fell," and it has been claimed that the "wick" of Berwick and Alnwick is the common Norse ending for a dwelling-place. But this is highly problematical.

There is a good Celtic word, "gwic," a village, bay, or creek of the sea. We have the old English "wick" (vic) and the Norse "vik," which are the same word, but with different meaning; the old English "vic" signifying "dwelling," and the Norse "creek." Berwick is surely Celtic, Abergwic; Aber being the place where waters meet, or where a small river falls into a large one, or where a river falls into the sea. Thus we get the village of the creek where the river falls into the sea.

Again, with Alnwick, we have the Gaelic word, Alain, which means handsome, bright, clear, and thus we get the village on the clear water, for we find the word "Alain," or some word closely similar, constantly applied to rivers.

JOSEPH SKIPSEY.

We should gather, I suggest, from these facts, that the greater part of the Northmen found our Northumberland too rough a country for habitation when they had more fertile and gentler lands ready to their hand in the broad plains of Yorkshire.

Yet I am not prepared to give up the view that there is a very real and close connection between our county and Norway. Of course to those of us who are fortunate enough to possess a true patronymic in our surnames, Norway is, in a direct sense, the real old fatherland. Still, in many parts, there as in Iceland, the son is incontestably his father's child. Eric Magnus-son is Eric the son of Magnus, who was, in his turn, Magnus Sigurdson, and Eric's son will be Olaf Ericson. But this is not enough. To those of us who have lived many months in Norway, our county's speech is pregnant of that beautiful land. We never walk through our Bigg Market without thinking of the dancing bears of sheaves of byg, barley, which form so important and charming a part of the autumnal land-scape in Norwegian valleys. We speak of our little streams as becks, until they become big enough to be called burns. We ask a Cheviot shepherd or a Nordfjord farmer who has had an accident how he fares, and he tells us in either case that he is "braw nu." The Low-lander sings "hame fain wad I be," but the Northumbrian says hjem with the Northman. Both speak of the pluff or plov instead of the plough. In our Groat Market, we have the place where gröd was sold, the groats, out of which gröd, the Norwegian porridge, is made. When we return from fishing or climbing in either land, we groan over the painful impressions which the same "cleg" has made through our knickerbocker stockings, and we have used alike, in either case, a "stang" to fish or or climb with. We take a "keek" at Trond-hjem Cathedral, "and then, hev a keek at the moniment, tee," when we get to London. Honey "clags" to our fingers in both lands, a "darg" in both is a day's work, we "teem" out of one vessel into another, and the "dag" which soaks us through, whether in Norway or Northumberland, is in each alike the prelude to a "mirk" (mörk) night.

And so I might go on piling up examples to show how full our local speech in Northumberland is of pure Norsk words. In many cases, no doubt, there is very small difference between the Norsk and the Old English, as in the case of "kirke," "circ," a church. This is to be expected, for the Angles came from that part of the main-land which closely adjoined Denmark, and the boundary between the

English of the continent and the Scandinavians of the Danish peninsula was but an imaginary one, whilst the languages of the three
peoples amongst whom Scandinavia was divided, were almost identical.
But quite irrespective of words which may belong to English or
Norsk indifferently, and quite irrespective of words which are
acknowledgedly Norsk, but which may be met with in literary
English, our local speech is literally full of good, strong, picturesque
words which are Norsk and nothing else.

I may, perhaps, mention that there are not so many Norsk words
in literary English as we should naturally have expected to find.
They are, however, all good, everyday, working words, many of them
relating to the sea and sea-faring life—bilge, crew, screw, windlass,
yacht, and so on. But starboard and larboard are the most interesting of these, for they speak to us directly of the early Viking days.
When you are at Christiania, on no account omit to visit the sheds in
the court behind the university where the Vikings' ships, found at
Thune and at Sandefjord, are preserved. You will find the rudder on
the right-hand at the stern of the boat (for the Vikings steered on
one side only), and, inside, you will find a table on which the steers-
man stood. On the other, the left side of the boat, there is no table
for there is no rudder. Now "styrre," is the Norsk for "to steer,"
and "bord" means a "table :" so "styr-bord" is the steering table,
and the "styr-bord" being always on the right-hand side, "styr-bord"
or, with us, "starboard," corresponds with right. So "larboard"
means the side without a table, and probably comes from "lav," low,
shallow, flat, and "bord" a table. The left side being the flat side,
that without a table, "lav-bord," or, with us, "larboard," corresponds
with left.

But I have said enough about the effect which the conquest of
the Vikings had upon the English vocabulary ; had it any upon the
English grammar? I think that it had an effect in one or two ways
which is, at the first blush, somewhat startling. The English verb
"to be" is rather remarkably irregular. How the present tense should
run "I am," "thou art," "he is," "we, you, they, are," is surely
puzzling. It would appear as though our verb "to be" held really
the fragmentary remains of, at least, three verbs which all meant
nearly the same thing. I must not, in a course of lectures such as
I have undertaken to deliver, stop to elaborate a point like this, but
I must content myself with stating that the southern form of the
present plural in Old English was "sind" or "sindon"—far enough

away from "are." We find a northern form of the present plural—"aron," but not until we get to the time of the Durham Ritual, probably the tenth century. But the old Norsk form was "Erum, Erut, Eru," and it is highly probable that we took our northern form of this present plural from our Northmen conquerors, and that it, being the more convenient form, triumphed over the southern form, and thus permitted our northern speech to have some share in literary English.

It is not without interest to note that our auxiliary verb to-day bears traces of the three originally distinct and independent verbs which have been broken up, and the fragments welded together to form the present verb "to be." We have three plurals in the present indicative, sind, beoð, aron. The last was the northern form, and is of Scandinavian origin ; the first died out before the middle of the thirteenth century, and its place was taken by the second. We find this second in many writers of the sixteenth and the beginning of the seventeenth centuries :—"The powers that be ;" "They be the fairest flowers." It is still used in some parts of the south :—"I be a-going," "We be ready." Tindale uses the northern "are" in his translation of the Bible in 1530, and, in this century, it won the victory over the southern forms and became of general use in literature.

But you will ask me, if part of our most useful verb is Norsk, how can you justify the assertion made at an earlier part of the lecture that the grammar of a language cannot be mixed ? Here surely is a blending of the Norsk and the English grammars.

Yes, but you must bear in mind that it is the systematic reduction of a language to writing which fixes it so that afterwards its only alterations are those of loss. It is when a language really becomes a written language, and there is a fixed standard to appeal to, that changes cease. Now, we have no writings which tell us anything of the English language whilst it was in a state of flux, that is during the wars of the different English families with one another, or during those with the Northmen. The different families of English may well have used different grammatical forms, and those forms would, in the nature of things, alter from time to time, and be amenable to outside influences. But when the West Saxons carried the day, and, through Alfred the Great's literary skill, made their form the literary language of the land which was to bear their northern brethren's name, then the northern brethren's form of speech became only a dialect of that which was thenceforward to be called the English tongue, and when once manuscripts of recognised authority accumulated, possibility of grammatical growth ceased.

Let us now see how far we have got on our way. We began, after a brief introduction, by noting how, upon the whole, that part of the old Northumbria which is north of the Tweed has been richer in purely intellectual accomplishments than the part which is south, and this led us to see how far this difference can be accounted for. We inquired into the effect which the repeated processes of blending with other peoples had produced upon the dwellers in the land, and examined the speech of those dwellers to ascertain this effect. We found that the language which has been spoken in Northumberland for fourteen centuries is English; that so much grammar as has survived the inevitable process of constant simplification is still English; that our vocabulary is more foreign than English. We found in our language scarcely a trace of the tongue of Rome spoken here for more than three centuries of sway. Both in very common words and in proper names of places we discovered much which recalled the Britons whom the English displaced, and we learned how, when our Viking ancestors came to stay, and were absorbed by the people, the English folk, whom they conquered, they brought of their own words, and even, before English was to any extent a written tongue, made an important change in our most important auxiliary verb, and possibly affected the structure of our language in other ways. We must not carry the question of verbal amplification or structural simplification further.

LECTURE II.

NORTHUMBRIAN FAITH AND LEARNING.

In my first lecture I dwelt more upon the language of our county, and the grammatical and etymological changes which it had gone through than upon what I may call its intellectual history. We saw that from the time when the English took possession of it to the present day English had been spoken in it, and that the dialects which we find in it to-day are variations upon the literary language which the West Saxons, and not the English folk of Northumbria, gave to England, but the grammar of which had been modified in certain important details by Northumbria. We saw also that our dialects, as well as those of other parts of England, are the slowly decaying relics of the different manners of speech of the different districts of the mainland from which the English people came. And, finally, we noted how great a local influence the conquest of Northumbria by the Northmen had, and how this is still shown in our popular speech.

But there is one source of change which I only hinted at ; and it is one which, though of comparatively little consequence from the political point of view, is of such paramount importance in the intellectual history of our county, that I shall devote this evening to speaking to you of it and its consequences. I allude to the peaceful Roman conquest carried out to its ultimate conclusion by the monks commissioned for that purpose by successive popes of Rome. Many words especially of an ecclesiastical character, such as cloister, minster, monk, and the like, were added by this bloodless victory to the English language, but this addition was in no sense peculiar to Northumbria. It is the influence which the men who brought these words had upon our social and intellectual life which will concern us to-night. This it was which brought back our island into the circle of civilised peoples. In this story Northumbria, and especially that portion which we are specially dealing with, our own Northumberland, played the most distinguished part.

But Christianity did not, in the first instance, come to us immediately from Rome ; it came to us more directly from Ireland. There are few more fascinating subjects in history than that presented by the tale of the early development of that island. When this

country was being conquered by our heathen forefathers and reduced for the time into a state of barbarism, Ireland was sending
out her missionaries to convert other lands to the Christian faith,
and had already attained a high position in all which makes what we
call civilisation of true value. It had fair and certain laws ; it had a
wide and general system of education ; it had great libraries of richly
illustrated manuscripts ; and it had attained to a high point of
perfection in the art of decorative metal working. But it would
indeed be difficult to say when the Irish were not an artistic people.
In the pre-historic days of which we can only speak with a
stammering tongue, yet of which a multitude of traces are to be
found at every turn in Ireland, the men, who burned their dead,
showed by their skill·in providing wonderful homes for the ashes,
by lavishing ingenious ornamentation on the interiors of such homes,
and by providing urns of rare beauty of decorative design to hold
the remains of their beloved and honoured, that they were gentle
and cunning workmen. It is sufficient praise to say that, when
Christianity replaced the earlier unknown form of religious belief
which caused its devotees to carry out so many and such wonderful
works, the hand of the Irish workman only retained its cunning.
The elaborately carved crosses of the tenth and eleventh centuries ;
the richly sculptured churches of perhaps as early a period ; and the
varied contents of the cromlechs, cairns, and barrows of unwritten
days, all speak the same art tongue which he who understands can
read in the exquisitely executed brooches, chalices, and illuminated
manuscripts which have been preserved to us from the early Christian
days, and which, it has been truly said, "exhibit a perfection of
handiwork unrivalled for its ingenuity, delicacy, and richness of
design."

To us the most important and interesting of the early Irish saints
is St. Columba. His very birth-place is significant of the retirement
and obscurity which seem to form the favourite soil for the production
of great religious reformers. It is not without a wide and full meaning that we are enjoined, when we seek to hold communion with the
Father of Spirits, to enter into our closet and shut the door. The
greatest of religious reformers, those who have changed the face and
form of the intellectual world, have all fled from their kind to the
voiceful solitude which nature affords. Moses, Christ, Mohammed,
have each in turn received the mystic education of the desert. There
the voice of man is not ; in the vastness, the loneliness, the sublimity

of apparent space, the only sound the weary and waiting one may hear is "the voice of the Lord God walking in the garden in the cool of the day."

St. Columba was born far from the desert of which I have spoken, but close to that watery waste which has ever inspired the deepest of human poetic susceptibilities, the ocean itself. And poetic susceptibilities and religious enthusiasms are closely akin. The poet and the prophet may be, should be, one. Alas, I know many poets who have none of the prophetic insight, but I know no great prophet who is not a poet, and no great poet who has not the prophet's spirit. The Psalm writer's "great and wide sea wherein go things creeping innumerable ;" Cædmon's "whale-road ;" Dante's "deep, illimitable main ;" Shelley's "mountainous waste ;" Byron's "throne of the invisible ;" Blake's "fathomless and boundless deep ;" William Morris's "hungry sea" or "tumultuous sea ;" Swinburne's "slow, passionate pulse of the sea ;" Poe's "sounding sea ;" Tennyson's "sounding furrows ;" these, and a thousand more epithets, show how many aspects the same ocean presents to the mind of man. Who amongst us who has spent solitary hours by the great Atlantic sea but understands how you may be solitary yet not alone. The ocean and the desert are as one in their magic power. Habitual stillness reigns everywhere over each, stillness which speaks. Each, too, from time to time, gives forth a dreadful and destructive voice. But, in the quiet of calm, the soul which has learned to see recognises the Spirit of God moving on the face of the waters.

Nowhere is the Atlantic Ocean more impressive than on the west coast of Ireland, and it was in a little lonely glen running down to the noblest part of that coast, in south-west Donegal, that St. Columba was born. It is now as remote a spot as you could find in the British Isles, but the whole of Donegal is filled with deeply interesting evidences of a much greater population in pre-historic and legendary days than in these. Glencolumbkille lies between the measureless sea and the lonely moors, and it is probable that if we could know with certainty the early influences which had been most instrumental in moulding the life of the great missionary we should find that each of these mighty factors had borne its part. Columba was descended from royalty, and, for a time, he certainly belonged to the church militant, taking part in several of the great battles which were of constant occurrence, and in which the uniform of the Prince of Peace might frequently be seen. Whether it was a result of these, or that he began to feel the need of rest and peace, or warfare of a spiritual kind, he settled in the lonely island of Iona in 563, and that island became a centre of religious light. It was also ere long a place of much political importance, and kings and bishops resorted to it for shelter, countenance, and advice. It sent out its missionaries amongst the inhabitants of the eastern mainland, and the English of the north were indebted to it for their first instruction in Christianity.

The Irish Church was, at this time, quite distinct from the Romish Church. It had been founded when the earliest Christian missionaries visited these islands, and had not been exposed to the perils under which the early British Church in England had succumbed. It differed from the Romish Church in the method which it adopted for calculating the period for the observance of Easter, and in the practice of the tonsure, but there was no really vital point of difference between them. Irish bishops were greatly more numerous than were the bishops whom the Church of Rome afterwards introduced into England, and the system of dioceses did not obtain. They were tribal and local, with comparatively restricted powers. Irish bishops had been present in the Catholic synods held in southern France and Italy, but, although bishops were received in Iona as honoured guests, the head of the ecclesiastical community was the abbot and not a bishop.

But let me briefly explain what I mean when I say that we were indebted to Iona for our first instruction in Christianity.

I need not repeat the well-known tale of how, in 596 A.D., Gregory I. sent missionaries to England under the guidance of St. Augustine, and how our Northumbrian king, Edwin, became a Christian by marriage, his wife bringing with her to the North Paulinus, who was consecrated bishop of the Northumbrians in 627. He baptised the people of Bernicia and Deira in crowds. His is the holy well at Holystone, near Harbottle, and from him does Palinsburn obtain its name. But when Edwin was killed in the battle of Hatfield in 633, Queen Ethelburga and Paulinus fled, for the bishop, having imprudently declared that the king's successes arose from his acceptance of the true faith, was not unnaturally held responsible for the terrible reverse which that fine old pagan Penda brought about.

Oswald, the next king of Northumbria, had taken refuge at Iona in his youth, and, on his accession to the throne, he sent to the island for a missionary to take up the work of religious preaching and teaching. Aidan, who came (after one priest had given up the task in despair) was a man of remarkable zeal and untiring patience and gentleness. He settled in Lindisfarne in 635, and soon won his way to the hearts of the rude Northumbrians, by his simplicity, devoutness, and constant self-denying labours amongst them. I must note that the good King Oswald frequently accompanied Aidan on his missionary enterprises, and acted as his interpreter.

Well did Lindisfarne deserve the name, which it soon obtained, of the Holy Isle. It is one of the spots in our land which we visit with peculiar feelings of love and reverence, for there did the Christian faith take deep root, and become abiding and active. We can there, thanks to the loving labours of recent years, bring before the mind's eye the early life of the missionary isle as it really was when, lying under the shadow of the royal abode at Bamborough, the religious influence and political importance of Lindisfarne surpassed even those of Iona, the mother isle.

Thus, then, we Northumbrians received our earliest abiding light from the lone sea coast of south-west Donegal through Iona's little isle, and, with that light, came learning, came leadership, came high political importance. But that political importance would never have attained its height if Northumbria had continued to draw its spiritual leaders from the isolated Irish Church. I have mentioned the differences between the Irish Church and the Church of Rome. In those days these differences appeared to be much graver in kind than they probably seem to any one nowadays. In its early stages religion clings to outward and symbolic forms,

Since ever by symbols and bright degrees
Art, childlike, climbs to the dear Lord's knees.

And we can see, as we read the Venerable Bede's loving but sad words about the holy Aidan, how mighty a thing this difference about the right time of holding Easter was to him. Such views are not to be laughed at: they need not, and, in such a case, they do not imply pure formalism. We are, perhaps, too ready, in these days of supposed spiritual enlightenment, to condemn those who, now or in bygone days, have required something more than a spiritual conception to lean upon. As I grow older the necessity of cultivating sympathy even with what we hold to be error seems ever more important. It will not weaken your earnest striving for the truth: it will but help you to combat the error in the wisest and best way, which is ever the kindest. It was at length agreed that the proper

4

time of keeping Easter, and the proper method of the tonsure, should be settled by formal debate. · The spot hit upon for this great function was one of surpassing interest. It was the Abbess Hilda's monastery at Streoneshalch, the port of the beacon, the Whitby of to-day.

There is no more inspiring character amongst English women than that of the Abbess Hilda. Of royal descent, a convert to the ministry of St. Paulinus, she came at an early age under the influence of Aidan, and was taught by him. She soon showed that she was a born ruler of men : she became head of a small conventual establishment, possibly at South Shields, then of a larger one at Heruteu, our Hartlepool, and finally built and tended the great monastery at Whitby, which, under her fostering care, rapidly became the chief seat of learning and religious training in the North of England. Now it is memorable to us chiefly because one of the poor brethren, because he was unable to sing, became the first of the great English singers of whom we know anything. But, in Cædmon's time, kings and princes sought there the guidance and counsel of the noble and beloved abbess, who ruled her devoted subjects with the gentle firmness which only a woman owns.

And it was hither that King Oswy came in 664 to preside at the great discussion which was to decide whether we should hold Easter on the fourteenth day of the first lunar month of the Jewish year or on the Sunday next after the fourteenth day of the month nearest to the vernal equinox, and the latter or Roman view carried the day. But much more than this was decided at that conference ; England's place in the world of thought and action was fixed. Our country became one of the European confederation ; it entered into close and constant communication with the other peoples of the Continent; it began to develop an intellectual life, and at once to play a part amongst civilised nations. It had many a difficulty to overcome, many a trial to pass through, before its place was fully won, but the step which must lead to it was irrevocably taken at that conference at the Abbess Hilda's monastery of Streoneshalch.

This was in 664, and the decision come to appears to have been immediately and peaceably acquiesced in, and now for a time there was a quiet existence in the great monasteries, and libraries were formed, and learning was cultivated, and there was a beginning of vernacular literature, not entirely confined to religious themes. But the English spirit was a serious one. There was a certain heaviness and gloom which characterised all the religious and literary effort of the period.

Our English forefathers had but small sense of humour and were quite without wit. They were more closely allied with the Frisians than with those whom we should now call North Germans. Energetic, resolute, solid if somewhat stolid, gloomy in thought but bright in action, it is with the Dutchmen that we compare them until they have been leavened by the dash of the Scandinavian fresh from his sea-roving or polished by his settlement amongst·the light-spirited Kelts of north-eastern France.

Whatever the subject may be or whatever the medium chosen, the treatment is alike grave and serious. The splendid epic romance of "Beowulf," Cædmon's Paraphrase, Bede's History, the Runic inscription on the Ruthwell cross, even Cynewulf's riddles are alike in their solidity of purpose. They are downright, each with an object in view for which it goes with determined vigour, and imbued with an intense and lofty teaching spirit. And this special characteristic of all our oldest poetry has been characteristic of all our noblest verse throughout the many centuries which separate Robert Browning and Cædmon. From time to time we have had a true poet who, in the wild exuberance of unbridled youth, has hotly preached and ardently practised the unmeaning or untrue doctrine, "Art for art's sake." But for him, too, years have brought the philosophic mind, and he has learned that the art which does not help as well as delight is a poor and stunted thing.

Our forefathers began very slowly to show signs of brightness as well as power, and, if our island had settled down after the southern part of it became England, we should never have occupied a leading position amongst the nations of the earth. I do not think that it is quite reasonable to attribute the somewhat uniform and uninspiring character of our early literature simply to the influence which the good monks wielded over the early English intellectual world. We must also remember the pit from which our fathers were digged. Their work has its own merits, but brilliance is not one of these ; and we may truly say that brilliance has never been a true characteristic of English literature in the same way as it has ever been characteristic of French thought. But we cannot be too thankful that we are a twice-conquered people, and that our conquerors in both cases came from the race which, always doing much physically and politically, but only turning to intellectual labours when absorbed by some other race, have been for Europe the little leaven which has leavened the whole lump.

But here I must go back a little that we may see in more detail the precise part which our own portion of Northumbria played in the work which I have mentioned. I have already spoken of Lindisfarne and the monastery which was founded there by the monks from Iona. This was the source and centre of religious life in the north, from the Humber to the Forth. It was emphatically a missionary station, and from it went forth the devoted men who carried the good news of great joy to the northern folk. The first sixteen bishops of Northumbria had their residence there. It would be hard to say which of the truly great men connected with it was of the holiest life, but Aidan and Cuthbert, of whom I have already spoken, are the names which rise at once in our minds when holiness of life is mentioned.

I find it somewhat remarkable that Aidan should have been a man of so much resource and so free from conventional ideas that he should at once have ventured to engage women in his great work. It is not less remarkable that the women whom he selected should have proved so worthy of his choice. He had a strong belief in education. He himself instructed twelve English youths, one of whom, Eata, became a bishop and played an important part in the subsequent religious movements of this district. Every church and monastery which he founded became a school where his monks gave the English children as complete an education as even the great Irish monasteries afforded. Melrose, Tynemouth, South Shields, Hartlepool, Coldingham, and Whitby were amongst the places where Aidan built a church or established a monastery. There would seem to have been quite a craving for knowledge amongst the English youth, and they are said to have gone from monastery to monastery to find the teacher who was most able to help their special need in study.

But there is another side to this picture. True conversion, that is the turning away from an old and congenial course of life to a new and straiter one, is always a rare thing. The English had rushed to baptism like flocks of sheep when the king and his thanes adopted it as they still rush where fashion and society lead, but they had only changed nominally. The missionaries had constant trials, difficulties, and dangers to encounter; they had to meet the fickleness of kings as well as that of the multitude. There were many lookings back to the old times and old gods on the part of the half-baked converts. There is a tale said to be told by Bede, although I do not find it in my edition of his history, of how when certain monks, who had been driven out to sea near the mouth of the Tyne, were in danger of being swamped, those who would have helped them were stayed by exulting beholders who cried, "Let them alone : this will teach them how to live differently from others. Let the fools, who would take our old gods away from us, perish."

Within forty years from the commencement of the great Celtic mission from Iona to Northumbria at least twelve important monasteries had been founded. To those I have already mentioned must be added Hexham, Carlisle, Lastingham, Ripon, Wearmouth, and Jarrow. The last two were not founded under Columban or Irish rule, as I shall show shortly ; the others were. The Irish monasteries were under the rule of abbots, not of bishops. St. Patrick had established in Ireland a kind of tribal episcopacy. The bishops were great in number, as every important family claimed to have at least one episcopal office, but they had no regular dioceses and had small authority. The Irish Church was essentially monastic. We have no trace of any definite and general rules finding universal acceptance. The discipline of each monastery rested with the abbot who presided over it, and there was thus a wide variety of practice. It was this type of monastery which was introduced by Columba into Iona, and this type which was introduced by Aidan into Lindisfarne. Several of the monasteries were double, that is, they contained nuns as well as monks, but to their credit be it told that, excepting in the case of Coldingham, no hint of any impropriety, at all events in the earlier years of their existence, has been thrown out against them. A double monastery was frequently presided over by an abbess; this was, indeed, the case at the famous Whitby monastery under Hilda's rule.

Aidan then introduced into England, or, rather, into Northumbria, Irish monastic institutions and the peculiar Irish beliefs of which I have already spoken, and which had to give way before the Italian beliefs which the Romish missionaries advocated. But, although there was strong feeling and plain speaking upon these matters, the savage feuds and bitter rancour of most petty disputes about religious details were avoided, and, upon the whole, there was a general and highly creditable exhibition upon all sides of the true spirit of Christian love. Let me read you the words which I have already alluded to, and in which the Venerable Bede concludes his account of this holy man :

"I have written thus much concerning the person and works of the aforesaid Aidan, in no way commending or approving what he imperfectly understood in relation to the observance of Easter; nay, very much detesting the same, as I have most manifestly proved in the book I have written, *De Temporibus*, but, like an impartial historian, relating what was done by or with him, and commending such things as are praiseworthy in his actions, and preserving the memory thereof for the benefit of the readers, namely, his love of peace and charity; his continence and humility; his mind superior to anger and avarice, and despising pride and vainglory; his industry in keeping and teaching the heavenly commandments; his diligence in reading and watching; his authority, becoming a priest, in reproving the haughty and powerful, and at the same time his tenderness in comforting the afflicted, and relieving or defending the poor. To say all in a few words, as near as I could be informed by those that knew him, he took care to omit none of those things which he found in the apostolical or prophetical writings, but to the utmost of his power endeavoured to perform them all."

Aidan came to us in 635, and died in 651. Two years after he founded his monastery at Lindisfarne there was born upon what we now call the Borders, in Northumbria certainly and possibly in Northumberland, one who was also to be a bishop of Lindisfarne in due time, and whom I have already named as worthy to be ranked with Aidan himself. St. Cuthbert has the advantage over him of being truly native to the soil, and, of all our early heroes, he has taken the strongest possession of the popular mind. We still visit the mouth of the Till where the remains of a chapel mark the spot where his coffin rested when his uneasy corpse refused to remain at Melrose Abbey :—

> Not there his relics might repose;
> For, wondrous tale to tell!
> In his stone coffin forth he rides,
> (A ponderous bark by river tides);
> Yet light as gossamer it glides
> Downward to Tillmouth cell.

And which of us has not seen the sculptured stone in the glorious cathedral which rose over St. Cuthbert's remains on the banks of the Wear, and upon which is preserved the legend of the strange way in which it was at length discovered where his bones could find rest from their weary wanderings.

Well may we northerners be proud of Durham Cathedral, for there is none other in majesty of situation, in splendid simplicity of architecture, I might almost add in historic interest, which can compare with the glorious pile which rejoices the eyes of every traveller who passes along our famous east coast route between the North and the South of England. It is unique amongst the cathedrals of the world : " none but itself can be its parallel."

In early youth St. Cuthbert was a shepherd lad; active, bold, and strong, and unequalled, Bede tells us, amongst his youthful comrades in all the sports in which they delighted. But he was also one of those to whom, in the solitary tending of his sheep, the voices of the natural world spake of its Creator. To him, in the words of the Shepherd King of Israel, "the heavens declared the glory of God, and the firmament shewed His handiwork." When he learned that the good Aidan was dead, he resolved upon a religious life, and, at the age of fifteen, he entered the monastery of Melrose, which was then presided over by the Abbot Eata, one of the youths who had been trained and educated by Aidan himself. Time will not permit me to dwell upon the events of his laborious and devoted life. He is said to have possessed a rare gift of persuasive eloquence, which made him a welcome visitor in the wild districts which he traversed in his constant missionary work. But the grand secret of his success was that without which all preaching is vain, he was consistent in word and deed ; his example preached even more eloquently than his precept ; in Geoffrey Chaucer's pregnant words :—

> Cristes lore, and his apostles twelve,
> He taught, but first he folwed it himselve.

It was Abbot Eata who took Cuthbert with him to Lindisfarne, when, after the decision had been given at Whitby in favour of the Romish doctrines, Bishop Colman, instead of contesting the verdict, withdrew, with those monks who could not abandon the belief in which they had been reared, and returned to Iona. After twelve years of patient labour there, Cuthbert betook himself that he might be undisturbed to one of the lonely Farne Islands, whither, as Bede tells us, Bishop Aidan had been wont often to retire to pray in private. Here he lived by the labour of his hands, and here, or more probably on the little island near Lindisfarne, which still bears his name, as legend will have it he laboured nightly, using a rock as his anvil, to produce what modern science says are certain little shells of the genus *entrochus*, but which popular legend speaks of in quite another way :—

> Fain Saint Hilda's nuns would learn
> If, on a rock by Lindisfarne,
> Saint Cuthbert sits, and toils to frame
> The sea-born beads that bear his name.

Here too, on the Farnes, we still find St. Cuthbert's birds, the eider ducks, which he tamed and which will even now allow the gentle visitor to caress them on their nests.

But so eminent a man could not withdraw himself entirely from the outside world. He had many visitors. Great events, of which I shall have to speak, were convulsing the outside political world, and eight years had not passed when the king Egfrid, with his chief thanes and most of the monks of Lindisfarne, came to beg him to return to active life. At a great synod, held in 684, at Twyford, on the Aln (possibly Alnmouth, although Whittingham also claims the distinction), and presided over by Archbishop Theodore of Tarsus, who is so strangely introduced into our early ecclesiastical history in which he played so great a part, Cuthbert had been unanimously chosen bishop of Hexham. After a prolonged struggle, and with many tears, he at length gave way, persuading, however, his friend Eata to accept Hexham, whilst he himself became bishop of Lindisfarne.

In the great hall at Wallington where there resides a Northumbrian who has played many parts in the literary and political worlds, and who has played them nobly and well, there are eight frescoes by William Bell Scott (for many years the master of the School of Design in this city) representing events in Northumbrian history. Amongst these are three which illustrate the period to which I refer in this lecture, the death of the Venerable Bede, the descent of the Northmen upon Tynemouth, and the visit of King Egfrid to St. Cuthbert to induce him to leave the Farne and accept high office in the Church. It is well that such events should be thus recorded, and it is interesting to find that, to the artist and those who commissioned the work, it seemed that the period and the men about whom we speak were the most important in our county's history.

The office of bishop over a big diocese like that of Lindisfarne, which stretched even to Melrose, was no sinecure. Cuthbert worked as hard when he was the great and powerful bishop as he had done when an unknown missionary. He taught, he exhorted, he visited and examined the neighbouring monasteries, and he became to his people the object of love and reverence. Legends cluster thickly around him. Many miracles which he is said to have worked are recorded by Bede. Amongst other things for which we are supposed to be indebted to him is the loving cup which is still passed round at great banquets. Visiting a certain important man, he noticed that he was in misery, and found that his wife was at the point of death. He at once sprinkled her with water which he had blessed, and she was able to rise, and, acting as cupbearer, to present to him, in the name of her children, a cup of wine; and, since then, this cup, which was called from the cause which moved her to offer it "the loving cup," has been offered by the host to the most distinguished guest who, in turn, hands it to his neighbour.

The last place which Cuthbert visited was the priory of Tynemouth where the abbess, Verea, received him with much state. But he was worn out by the severe exertions of his two years' episcopacy, and he retired once more to his lonely isle to wait for his release. In two months it came. He was but fifty years of age when he died.

I have only time to mention one other of the early bishops of Lindisfarne, and his is a very different character to that of the gentle monk of whom I have been speaking. Wilfrid was a Northumbrian, and, like so many others of the leading churchmen in those early days, he was of noble family. He was born in 635, two years before St. Cuthbert, and two years after King Edwin, the great and good king of Northumbria, was killed in battle by Penda who, with Cadwalla the British king, made a terrible slaughter in the Church forces of the Northumbrians. It was then that Paulinus, who had baptised Edwin, fled for safety into Kent, and the mission of the church of Rome to the North of England seemed to have failed for ever.

But there is no finality in religious or secular politics. This Wilfrid was to be the principal factor in the firm re-establishment of Christianity in Northumbria, and in the triumph of Rome over Ireland. He was an ecclesiastic of the type of Thomas A'Becket or Wolsey rather than that of Aidan or Cuthbert. He loved to live in the world and to take part in its rough and tumble life, and even he got enough of it before he got through with it.

When he resolved at fourteen years of age to adopt a religious life, he obtained King Oswy's consent through the intercession of Queen Eanfled, King Edwin's daughter, who was the first person baptised by Paulinus in Northumbria. He distinguished himself as an earnest student at Lindisfarne, where he was educated during the time when it was under the rule of Columban monks. He seems to have formed some misgivings as to the teaching of these monks, or, as Bede puts it, being a clear-sighted youth he observed that the way to virtue taught by the Scots was not perfect, and he resolved to visit Rome, a journey which no English Christian had yet made. But he spent a year at Canterbury first where, of course, he learned the other side of the Easter question. Another youth of whom we shall hear more anon, "called Biscop, or otherwise Benedict, of the English nobility," and now known in history as Benedict Biscop, was also at Canterbury, and he joined Wilfrid in his journey.

That journey is easy enough now when made in a luxurious *coupé* with beds and tables and every possible convenience, but it must have been a very different thing when Wilfrid and Benedict made it. They had, of course, the excellent roads made by the Romans to help them, and excepting in the unsettled character of the country, they were probably little worse off than John Milton or even Joseph Addison when they visited Italy many centuries afterwards. But I never rush through the Mont Cenis or over the St. Gothard without an ever-increasing admiration for those who ventured so far when travelling was a toil, accommodation uncertain, and perils by the way of hourly occurrence.

The companions separated at Lyons, where the graceful and sprightly Wilfrid was detained by the bishop of that city, who straight-way fell in love with him, as every one, in his early days, seems to have done. He wished, indeed, to keep him altogether, and offered (Bede says) "to commit to him the government of a considerable part of France" (by what authority does not appear), "to give him a maiden daughter of his own brother to wife, and to receive him as his adopted son." But Wilfrid, in spite of these inducements, went to Rome, studied there diligently for some months, and returned to Lyons, where he stayed three years and received the Roman tonsure. His friendly bishop was put to death by the French queen, Baldhilda, once an English slave, and Wilfrid wished to die with him but that boon was refused him, for it was one thing to kill a subject and quite another to kill an Englishman, and he returned to England. When he was twenty-six years of age, in 661, he was made abbot of Ripon, and, in 665, he was chosen to be bishop of York.

The rest of his life was a strange one. Wilfrid it was upon whom, at the great discussion in 664, at the monastery of Streoneshalch, the port of the beacon, the burden of advocating the Romish practices fell, and ably and triumphantly did he perform his task. This meant much for the English Church, and perhaps even more for England. It left the way open for Theodore of Tarsus (who entered into Wilfrid's labours, and has frequently received credit for that which was not all his) to organise the episcopacy in a systematic way upon geographical lines, and, as we have seen, it brought England at once into touch with the great nations of the European continent.

But Wilfrid had developed certain hard and precise lines of character which made him inclined to press a victory too far. His refusal to have the rites of consecration as a bishop performed by any bishop of his own land was equivalent to declaring that he questioned their orthodoxy. The fact that he was to be the head of the Church in Northumbria, but that he was to rule from York instead of Lindisfarne, was another blow at an already defeated foe. True that the parties most closely interested, Bishop Colman and the Columban monks, behaved loyally throughout, and, when they could not give way, quietly withdrew. But there were heart burnings in many breasts at the Romish victory at Whitby, and Wilfrid did not attempt to lessen the soreness which he had been the chief agent in producing. No one felt this more than our noble Abbess Hilda, who, as a faithful disciple of the good Aidan, had earnestly longed for the defeat of the Romish monks. She had great influence with King Oswy, who had entrusted the bringing up of his daughter Elfleda to her. When Wilfrid went to Compiègne to be consecrated with much pomp by Agilbert, the bishop of Paris, who had been bishop of the West Saxons, he stayed away for three years, which certainly looked as if his home work was not uppermost in his mind. On his return, he found that the king had appointed Ceadda bishop of York in his stead, and he withdrew patiently to his old monastery of Ripon, but was soon invited to Mercia by the king Wulfhere. Here he did a great work in organising the Christian forces, and he was able, through the bounty of the king, to found several monasteries in other parts, amongst the most famous being that of Hexham. Egbert, the king of Kent, next required his services at Canterbury, where he acted for three years as the chief bishop of the English Church. During this time he showed a new side to his character, introducing into Ripon builders, who in those days were also architects, and monks who were able to teach the Gregorian chant which was then in use in Canterbury. He was a born organiser, and loved the strict rule and order of St. Benedict, and this he made the system of the monasteries over which he had rule.

I must not stay to tell how, by a series of fortuitous circumstances, Theodore, an Asiatic monk born at Tarsus, became archbishop of Canterbury in 669, and took up Wilfrid's work, at once restoring to him the bishopric of York, nor how the great task of thoroughly organising the episcopacy, I might almost say of creating the organisation of the English Church, was carried out by this brave old

Eastern ecclesiastic, who was sixty-seven years of age when he under-took the duty. The appointment of this man from the remote and alien East, a foreigner of foreigners, proved a successful experiment, but one which, happily, has never been repeated.

For nine years Wilfrid devoted himself to the work which always lay near to his heart. He organised his great diocese with remark-able skill and care; at York, at Ripon, and at Hexham, he carried out noble architectural works, the like of which had, until then, been undreamed of in Northumbria; he made his schools both good and popular; and the North, through his exertions, became famous for the widespread knowledge of music and for its splendid perform-ance.

But the day came when he quarrelled with the then king, Egfrid, who persuaded Archbishop Theodore to depose Wilfrid, and to divide his diocese into three, York and Hexham being two of these, and Lindisfarne being subsequently added. The king and the archbishop had, perhaps, scarcely realised the kind of man they had to deal with. He appealed to them to alter their decision, which he told them plainly was bare robbery. When they refused, he went off to Rome to appeal to the head of the Church. Driven by a storm into Fries-land, he there became the first English missionary to Germany, and devoted himself during the whole winter to preaching and working amongst the Frisians. How did he make himself understood by them? Were his native tongue and theirs so nearly alike that they could make out his meaning? We should learn much if these questions could be certainly answered. When he at length reached Rome, his case was heard and he was successful; but, returning home with the pope's decree for his restoration to his see, King Egfrid threw him into prison, where he remained in solitary con-finement for nine months. As he refused to acknowledge that the decree he had gained was false, he was sent to a worse prison at Dunbar, there to be kept in irons. Released at length, he took refuge in Mercia, and then in Wessex, but he was hunted out of each in turn. There was no refuge for him amongst Christians, but the king of Sussex, who still held the old faith, received him kindly, and there he succeeded in bringing the last of the English who worshipped other gods to call themselves Christians. It is a strange and sad history, showing once more as has been so often shown before and since, that to change the label on the bottle does not alter the liquor inside.

He founded a monastery at Selsey which, long centuries afterwards, became a famous place when Sussex was the centre of iron manufacture in England, and here he laboured for five years, going through many strange and terrible experiences of which I have not time to tell you. But, at long last, Theodore saw and confessed the great error into which he had fallen, and, in 686, Wilfrid was restored to the bishopric of York, and his monasteries of Ripon and Hexham were again given him. He had not even yet learned fully the lessons of adversity. He began, at once, to quarrel with the monks of Lindisfarne, and had to give it up within a year to a new bishop. He next had difficulties with Aldfrid, now the king of Northumbria; and was once more deposed from the see of York and exiled; but was made bishop of Lichfield by Ethelred, the king of Mercia, and lived there, so far as appears, quietly and usefully for eleven years. He was then persuaded to attend a gathering near Ripon which had been arranged by King Aldfrid, and which was presided over by Theodore's successor as archbishop of Canterbury, Berchtwald. Here he went through a kind of trial, and was condemned to retire from all his offices and to live entirely at Ripon. This he refused to submit to, and with danger and difficulty got back to Mercia. He was an old man now, seventy-one years of age, but again he appealed to Rome, and set out for the third time for the Imperial City. Here he went through a hard ordeal. Berchtwald sent men to accuse him, and the pope himself (John VI.) presided over the council of bishops which tried the cause. It lasted for four months and occupied seventy sittings, but Wilfrid was triumphant once again. Yet, once more, upon his return, the king refused to recognise the judgment, and brave old Wilfrid was yet again expelled. This was for the last time, for, before his death, justice was done to him, and he retired to the management of his favourite monasteries of Ripon and Hexham. The last four years of his life were spent quietly, chiefly at Hexham. He was seventy-six years of age when he found certain rest in 709.

This man was, indeed, of a different order to the other Northumbrians of whom I have spoken. He was one who lived for the nation more than for any part of it. "Ever a fighter," he learned but slowly to be gentle and moderate in the hour of victory. His life was, for the most part, a hard struggle for the right. He conquered at last: he did much for England, and great things for Northumbria; and both may well be proud of him.

You may perhaps remember that, when he first set out for Rome,

Wilfrid travelled as far as Lyons with Benedict Biscop, who seems really to have fallen in love with Rome, for he visited it six times in all, and he employed there both thought and money in the most charming of all pursuits. Benedict was a collector of books, or, it would be more correct to say, of manuscripts: a scholar himself, he gathered together not merely such works as might be expected to grace the shelves of an early monastic library, but Greek and Latin classics, books of such science as was then available, and the like, and he was also a virtuoso, and collected great stores of pictures, embroidered robes, silver vessels, and other objects of art. These were all intended for the famous monastery of Wearmouth, which he built and adorned, and the still more famous monastery of Jarrow, which was also his work.

But before he could settle in the North and build great monasteries, he did an interesting service in the South of England. When Rome was resolved to make Theodore of Tarsus archbishop of Canterbury, the pope associated with him Abbot Adrian, who was by birth an African, and Benedict Biscop, who seems to have acted as interpreter. When England was at length reached, he was appointed by the archbishop to be head over the chief monastery in Canterbury, and there he stayed for two years, but then he came to the North, which he seems only to have left afterwards when he repaired to France or Italy for workmen to build and bedeck his monasteries, or for objects to adorn them, and to make them of wide use. The Wearmouth church was of stone, and was ornamented with pictures and probably with mosaics, for the beautiful art of mosaic work had been restored and applied to architectural purposes in Italy nearly two centuries before the time of which I am speaking (676). He brought back with him glass-makers from France, for glass-craft was unknown in England, and they not only glazed the windows of the monasteries but they also taught the English the way to make the glass themselves.

When we began (here in Newcastle) to manufacture the Swan incandescent electric lamps in quantity in 1881, there were no men in England who could make the right kind of glass, so Mr. James C. Stevenson and Dr. Merz became our Benedict Biscops, and travelled over to Ilmenau in Germany, whence they induced skilled men to come over and teach us Northumbrians the way to make this special glass. History repeats itself.

Wearmouth was founded in 674: Jarrow in 682. When they were ready for use, each was supplied with a splendid library, and each became a nursery of scholars. The works which these libraries contained, and the scholarship which they encouraged, were no doubt opposed to the extension of a literature in the people's tongue. That flourished in Northumbria at this time, as we shall shortly see, and the more learned literature flourished by its side. We Northumbrians were clearly gainers, and great gainers, by the enlightened labours and liberality of Benedict Biscop. I had almost omitted to mention that music in our part of the district owed as much to him as it owed to Wilfrid in the more western part, for, when he was at Rome for the fifth time, Benedict Biscop persuaded John, abbot of St. Martin's and precentor at St. Peter's, to accompany him on his return, and John set to work at once in a systematic way to improve the musical education of our monasteries. Thus we received from Benedict Biscop large intellectual benefits, given lavishly in many directions and with both hands.

The immense boon which he had conferred upon the intellectual life of England was destined to be speedily shown. A little boy of seven was sent to his care at Wearmouth in the year 680, a little boy called "prayer," Bede, as Nansen called his little girl "life," Liv. I fear that, but for this boy, few of us would have given much thought to the worthy collector of books and builder of monasteries. He became a marvel in his own day, and is still a marvel in ours. He is one of the noblest and most beautiful characters amongst our English men of thought and letters, and the foremost literary man of the Christendom of his time. Removing to Jarrow so soon as it was opened, and when still a child, he grew up to make it the literary centre of western Christendom. None other school could compete with that in which the gentle and humble Bede was the foremost teacher. Here the classics, forgotten or denounced in Italy, found a congenial home. Here theology, medicine, such natural science as the world possessed, music and philosophy, were taught, studied, and written about. Here was the fountain-head of our historical writing, and a knowledge of the men of whom I have spoken was preserved for our instruction and admiration. And, with all this, it is the Venerable Bede's name which is connected. Scholar, teacher, writer, historian, biographer, the pages of history record the name of no literary man more diligent or more earnest. Nor did he neglect to punctually perform the services of the church. Alcuin, the friend of Charlemagne, and himself an educational missionary of vast merit, and a Northumbrian, writing to the monks of his monastery, told them how Bede was wont to say "I know that angels visit the brethren at the canonical hours, and what if they should not find me among the brethren? Would they not say 'Where is Baeda? Why comes he not with his brethren to the prayers appointed?'"

You know the beautiful story of his death told in a letter written by one of his students, Cuthberht to Cuthwine, a fellow-student. It is worthy to be placed high amongst the many triumphant life endings with which history abounds. Hard is he working at his translation of the Gospel of St. John into English, dictating to his loving scribe when he can no longer himself hold the pen. The sands of life are running fast. The evening of the day, and of the precious master's day, has come. "There is yet one more sentence, dear master, to write." He answered "Write quickly." After which, the boy said "Now it is finished." "Well," he said, "thou hast spoken truly, 'It is finished.'" Then he bade his friends place him where he could look on the spot where he was wont to kneel in prayer. And, lying there upon the pavement of his cell, he chanted the *Gloria Patri*, and, as he uttered the words "the Holy Ghost," he breathed his last, and "so he passed to the kingdom in heaven."

He left behind him some forty works, the principal of which was his *Ecclesiastical History of our Island and People*. It is, to my thinking, as interesting and refreshing a book as a Northumbrian can read. Most of his writings are of a religious character, but amongst them you will find works on *The Nature of Things, Orthography*, and *The Art of Music*. He wrote the life of St. Cuthbert both in prose and verse.

It is scarcely to the credit of us dwellers on the Tyne that there should be no monument amongst us to this man who was the leader of our Western army of great literary men. Can we do nothing in this good old society of ours to see that this fault is remedied?

And now our question is, What was the position of literature amongst the Northumbrians during the time of which I have been speaking? We had amongst us many men who wrote in Latin; the knowledge of Greek which had practically died out in Italy was never wholly lost in Northumbria. But what of our own English speech, that tongue which, as we have seen, passed through so many intermixing processes? Here we have a record of which we may indeed be truly proud, for we have the earliest literature in the people's tongue which is certainly known to Western Christendom. True, we have but little left to us, although the remains are much more extensive than is popularly recognised. All the most important part of it is poetical. We have, no doubt, some poems which were brought over by the English from their Continental homes, such as the "Wanderer's Song," but we have also many which belong to us, and the earliest English poet who is known to us by name is Cædmon who sang in Hilda's monastery of Whitby. There is a strong probability that a yet greater poet, Cynewulf, whose date is uncertain, but who is placed by one of the latest writers on this subject, Professor Ten Brinck, followed by Mr. Stopford Brooke, as not later than the middle of the eighth century, was also a Northumbrian. The grand tale of "Beowulf," the only traces of which are English, is probably a century at least older than Cædmon's Paraphrase. And, finally, Bede tells us that Cædmon's example was followed by others, and we may say that for two centuries, from 600 to 800, our Northumbria was the home of poetic song.

I do not wish to exaggerate the absolute poetic merit of what remains to us of this early English verse. It is direct, simple, genuine, often with much poetic force. From time to time we come to a phrase which is full of the deepest and truest poetic spirit. I would instance Cædmon's description of hell. As you read it you feel that he speaks of what he has seen ; that, like Dante, he had passed through the hope-deserted portal, and gazed upon the dread torments of the damned ones, face to face. He tells of the grim, bottomless abyss, filled with intensely burning heat, bitter reeks of smoke, swart mists, night immeasurably long, and, ere dawn, cometh the east wind and frost bitter cold. When, unable to bear the blending of fiercest fire and most freezing frost, the lost ones seek another land, they come to one that is "lightless and liges full," void of light and full of flame. I know none other words which call up such a dread picture as these.

But the deepest interest which attaches to this early poetry is that, in it, we are at the source of that magnificent volume of noble song which is one of the chief glories of our land and its wondrous story. The voice may be often uncertain ; there is gloom and sadness often in the strain ; the poetry is even then, what it has so often been since, prosaic enough ; it lacks brilliance ; it is devoid of wit, and even its humour is heavy enough ; but it has great conceptions, is true and earnest, is always lofty in aim and helpful, and our old English bards struck the key-note of the song which Shakespere and Milton sang, and which we still hear in the glorious verse of Tennyson and Robert Browning.

For two hundred years the good work which I have faintly sketched went quietly and successfully forward. Then darkness and destruction came suddenly upon it. The Northmen fell upon the coast of Northumbria, harrying and ravaging wherever they went, but their especial objects of prey were the great monasteries. In 793, the English Chronicle says, "dire fore-warnings came over the land of the Northumbrians, and miserably terrified the people; there were excessive whirlwinds and lightnings, and fiery dragons were seen flying in the air. A great famine soon followed these tokens, and, a little after that, in the same year, on the 6th before the ides of January, heathen men lamentably destroyed God's church at Lindisfarne, through rapine and slaughter." The year following, Wearmouth and Jarrow fell a prey to these fierce sea-robbers. There is no record of any further attack until seventy-three years later, when the full conquest of Northumbria was carried out, but I see no reason to doubt that the piratical incursions continued at intervals. From the end of the eighth century, the period of peaceful culture, of song and study, of thought and learning, ceased for Northumbria, and, although in time, anarchy gave way to order, and religion again asserted its benign influence, the supremacy in light and leading had finally departed.

I opened my first lecture with the words of Sir Walter Scott; I shall close this with those of one who is himself of Northumbrian extraction, Algernon C. Swinburne, and who ends his *Winter in Northumberland* with the following verses, the first lines being a stirring sketch of the dire descents of the Northmen of which I have just spoken, and those which follow a noble psalm of praise.

As men's cheeks faded
On shores invaded,
When shorewards waded
The lords of fight;
When churl and craven
Saw hard on haven
The wide-winged raven
At mainmast height;
When monks affrighted
To windward sighted
The birds full-flighted
Of swift sea-kings;
So earth turns paler
When Storm the sailor
Steers in with a roar in the race of his wings.

O strong sea-sailor,
Whose cheek turns paler
For wind or hail or
   For fear of thee?
O far sea-farer,
O thunder-bearer,
Thy songs are rarer
   Than soft songs be.
O fleet-foot stranger,
O north-sea ranger
Through days of danger
   And ways of fear,
Blow thy horn here for us,
Blow the sky clear for us,
Send us the song of the sea to hear.

Roll the strong stream of it
Up, till the scream of it
Wake from a dream of it
   Children that sleep,
Seamen that fare for them
Forth, with a prayer for them;
Shall not God care for them,
   Angels not keep?
Spare not the surges
Thy stormy scourges;
Spare us the dirges
   Of wives that weep.
Turn back the waves for us:
Dig no fresh graves for us,
Wind, in the manifold gulfs of the deep.

O stout north-easter,
Sea-king, land-waster,
For all thine haste, or
   Thy stormy skill,
Yet hadst thou never,
For all endeavour,
Strength to dissever
   Or strength to spill,
Save of his giving
Who gave our living,
Whose hands are weaving
   What ours fulfil;
Whose feet tread under
The storms and thunder;
Who made our wonder to work his will.

His years and hours,
His world's blind powers,
His stars and flowers,
  His nights and days,
Sea-tide and river,
And waves that shiver,
Praise God, the giver
  Of tongues to praise.
Winds in their blowing,
And fruits in growing;
Time in its going,
  While time shall be;
In death and living,
With one thanksgiving,
Praise him whose hand is the strength of the sea.

LECTURE III.

BALLADS OF NORTHUMBERLAND.

Ballads have quite a peculiar interest of their own; indeed, I might truly say, interests, and many of them. They have their value as literature, but they are more precious as showing the social condition of the people at the time to which they belong. They help us to realise what our forefathers of certain periods were really like when they were not good or sitting for their portraits. At times they have had a distinct political power and value. They do not belong to any period, although their character alters as the centuries pass and the character of the people alters. They are the most widely diffused of all the poem family. We meet them so soon as the English come over to England, and they have been with us through all the centuries since, and they are with us still if we know where to look for them. Upon the whole, they have all the time been fresh, pure, and simple : not infrequently they have a vigorous healthy coarseness about them; at times they are nasty and nothing else, and a man must be very learned to find out any insufficient reason (even) why they should be preserved at all. But, upon the whole, they are good and wholesome, and are worthy of grave and careful consideration, for they have ever had a wide influence upon the people of our land. Fletcher of Saltoun said with some truth, as much probably as an epigrammatic saying can hold, " Let me write the ballads of a nation, and I care not who writes their laws."

The division between the poet and the ballad-singer was soon made in this country. The poet, the maker, was called by our old English forefathers the 'scop,' the shaper. They knew, as the old Greeks and Romans knew, that, though you cannot manufacture a poet—he must be born with the divine faculty—yet he can, must, and does manufacture his poetry. When I was young we were always told that poetry was the result of inspiration, and were led to imagine that poems leaped fully formed out of the brains of their creators, where they had grown in some mysterious way to perfection during disturbed nights. But we were also told that *Paradise Lost* was one of the greatest of English poems, and we came, in the sixth book, to the invention by the infernal powers of cannon and gunpowder, which, though no doubt an inspiration, did not quite lend itself to the idea of inspired verse. And we learned how in the case of the greatest master-poet, Shakespere himself, he wrote, re-wrote, wrought carefully and minutely, was a cunning craftsman and thus a supreme poet.

The scop was the poet, the glee-man was the ballad-singer. "Gly" in Old Norsk was joy, mirth, laughter : in old English " glig " was music, sport, joke. The glee-man was one who made mirth or music for other men. He was a story-teller who sang his tales. Ballads are therefore narrative poetry. When there were no books, no letters, no newspapers or magazines, the glee-man or ballad-singer had a wide, nearly an universal field before him. From the Wanderer's Song, which I mentioned in my last lecture as probably brought over by the English from the mainland, we learn that a singer who could well uplift the song, whilst loud to the voice the harp resounded, was welcome everywhere and was well assured of many gifts, and we further find that the members of the profession were numerous.

After the Norman Conquest we lose the glee-man and come to the minstrel. As early as the eighth century the French had used the word *menestrel*, applying it to musicians, but calling the makers and singers of songs *jongleurs*. A minstrel with us might be a jester or mimic ; a dancer ; a tumbler ; a man who played tricks with cup and ball ; a Sandow ; one who sang songs which had been handed down or which he made ; one who played upon divers instruments without singing at all ; in short, the term included all men, who lived by making sport for other men. He still wandered from place to place, welcome alike in the cottage of the poor or the castle of the rich. Indeed, the great lords had harpers attached to their houses and, in the case of the lion-hearted king, at all events, his minstrel went with him to the holy war. In many Border towns the town-piper was as regular an institution as was the town-crier when some of us were boys, and our fore-bears marched to meet the Scots to the inspiring strains of the Northumbrian small pipes, which, even to-day, we find so soul-stirring. In the duke of Northumberland's piper we have still a relic of this custom, but if we want ballad-singers nowadays, we must look for them on a Saturday in the Bigg Market. Printing of books, and the learning to read on the part of men generally, killed minstrelsy. In the thirty-ninth year of Queen Elizabeth an Act of Parliament was passed, declaring that "minstrels wandering abroad " should be classed amongst "rogues, vagabonds, and sturdy beggars," and be punished accordingly.

But some of their ballads survive. Thousands must have vanished altogether, and those which remain have been sadly knocked about. It is not too much to say that we have not one which has not suffered from injudicious and futile attempts at emendation. The ballads which I shall speak of to-night are those which belong to what I may call the middle period of our history. I much regret that I have not time to speak about that marvellous epical romance, "Beowulf," which, if not written in Northumbria, was certainly altered and re-edited here, and which stands alone in value as the first true non-religious poem in the old English language. I have to leave unnoticed the burst of poetry which the North awakened into towards the end of the thirteenth and the beginning of the fourteenth centuries. Yet there is some interest in the fact that some of our finest ballads go back to this period. It is rather difficult to speak of "our ballads," for, excepting in the case of distinctly historical ballads, we find that the good ones have really rarely "a local habitation." It is not possible to say with any certainty whether many of the romantic and legendary or semi-historical ballads belong to the north or south of the Tweed. They are found in both parts and nearly in the same words. But there is surely no great difficulty in seeing that this, in the very nature of things, must be so. The ballad-singer was not a fixture but a peripatetic. The ballad which he sang was heard both by Scotch and English lords, and local colouring could be given, if required, by the slight alteration of names. "False Northumberland" is not a foot longer than "Traitorous Scotland."

There is nothing simpler : it is done nowadays quite unblushingly. An eminent poet, who has lectured to this society, read to me the ode which he had sent in to the Crystal Palace authorities in competition for the prize offered at the time of the Burns' centenary for the best ode upon the most glorious of Scotchmen ; there was a grand passage about the Palace itself, and the marvellous effects produced upon it by the sunshine. "If I don't get the prize" he said "I shall still publish the ode, but I shall put 'ocean' in the place of 'Palace ;'" the old trick of the ballad-singer, the same yesterday and to-day. In reading Tennyson's life, I find that he turned an old poem on "Armageddon" into "Timbuctoo" by a little alteration of the beginning and the end, and to his utter astonishment won the Cambridge medal with it. I do not, of course, mean for a moment to deny that there are plenty of ballads, both historical and romantic, which can, at once, be assigned their true locality. Such speak for themselves. I mentioned, in my first lecture, that, when we came to consider the ballads of our county, we should find them, as a rule, inferior in poetic merit, to those whose certain home is north of the Tweed. We have nothing quite to compare with "Annan Water," or "Fair Annie of Lochroyan," or the "Border Widow's Lament," or "Sir Patrick Spens," or the host which make the Yarrow a stream sacred to the poetic muse. But we hold our ground better in this department than in more serious verse.

Even in the historical ballad you must not look for minute accuracy of detail. We are not told which of Sir Hugh Wytheryngton's stumps were smitten off first, nor, in the older version of the ballad, are we satisfied as to the knotty point involved in which knee he kneeled upon, or is the yet greater difficulty involved in the feat of kneeling at all when his legs had been hewn in two fully cleared up. In the Romantic Ballads, of course, this is carried much further, and the "Gay Goss-hawk" is quite an admirable conversationist. But this is a great part of the good and glory of the whole business. What matters it to any one of us how the gallant Widdrington did this thing? We know that he did do it, and that is surely enough for any reasonable person. And for the "Gay Goss-hawk." Birds don't talk, you say. And what has that to do with it? Now they don't, but they did then, for their conversation is preserved for us, and, if you do not believe it, I am sorry for you. Why, if it could not carry on a conversation, we should not have had that reply of "the fairest flower of England," which is one of the rarest gems which our ballad poetry can boast. The goss-hawk speaks :

> Ye're bidden send your love a send.
> For he has sent you three ;
> And tell *him* where he can see *you*,
> Or for your love he'll dee.

And she replies :—

> I send him the rings from my white fingers,
>   The garlands aff my hair,
> I send him the heart that's in my breast,
>   What would my love ha'e mair ?
> And at the fourth kirk in fair Scotland,
>   Ye'll bid him meet me there.

I have always been convinced that this was and must be a Northumbrian ballad. The colouring and spirit are Northumbrian throughout. It is at all events about a Northumberland girl. The heroine must have been taken away soon after her apparent death, as soon as the necessary arrangements could be made; but nine days were few enough to complete these, and to make the funeral journey from North Northumberland into Scotland; the first of the four churches was undoubtedly Jedburgh or Kelso, the second Dryburgh, the third Melrose, and the fourth St. Mary's Kirk at the foot of sweet St. Mary's Loch. The Scotch, with patriotic acquisitiveness, call it a Scotch ballad. We admire them for it: it is quite like them to do so. Professor Child shows us that there is a very similar story in the French, " Belle Isamburg," and in many other French popular chansons; that it is found in Germany, the Netherlands, Scandinavia, and Spain. That is quite natural: the story is one of facts which may have frequently occurred, or other lands may have borrowed it from us: but Professor Child gives us six versions of our ballad which agree in the most important particulars, the last having evidently been worked upon by some antiquarian pedant, who has substituted a parrot as a more likely bird than a goss-hawk: save the mark!

Probably you all know the ballad, but as you may not have seen it lately, and as it has been a favourite of mine through life, you will, perhaps, forgive me for reading it to you.

THE GAY GOSS-HAWK.

" O well is me my gay goss-hawk,
   That ye can speak and flee;
For ye shall carry a love-letter
   To my true-love frae me."

" O how shall I your true-love find,
   Or how should I her knaw?
I bear a tongue ne'er wi' her spake,
   An eye that ne'er her saw."

" O well shall you my true-love ken,
   Sae soon as her ye see,
For of a' the flowers o' fair England,
   The fairest flower is she.

" And when ye come to her castle,
   Light on the bush of ash,
And sit ye there, and sing ye there,
   As she comes frae the mass.

" And when she goes into the house,
 Light ye upon the whin;
And sit ye there, and sing ye there,
 As she gaes out and in."

Lord William has written a love-letter
 Put it under the wing sae grey;
And the bird is awa' to southern land,
 As fast as he could gae.

And when he flew to that castle,
 He lighted on the ash,
And there he sat, and there he sang,
 As she came frae the mass.

And when she went into the house,
 He flew unto the whin;
And there he sat, and there he sang,
 As she gaed out and in.

" Come hitherward, my maidens a',
 And prie the wine amang,
Till I go to the west-window,
 And hear a birdie's sang."

She's gane into the west-window,
 And fainly aye it drew,
And soon into her white silk lap
 The bird the letter threw.

" Ye're bidden send your love a send,
 For he has sent you three;
And tell him where he can see you,
 Or for your love he'll dee."

" I send him the rings from my white fingers,
 The garlands aff my hair,
I send him the heart that's in my breast,
 What would my love hae mair?
And at the fourth kirk in fair Scotland,
 Ye'll bid him meet me there."

She's gane until her father dear,
 As fast as she could hie,
" An asking, an asking, my father dear,
 An asking grant ye me!
That if I die in merry England,
 In Scotland you'll bury me.

" At the first kirk o' fair Scotland,
   Ye'll cause the the bells be rung ;
At the neist kirk o' fair Scotland,
   Ye'll cause the mass be sung.

" At the third kirk o' fair Scotland,
   Ye'll deal the gowd for me ;
At the fourth kirk o' fair Scotland,
   It's there you'll bury me."

She has ta'en her to her bigly bower,
   As fast as she could hie ;
And she has drappèd down like deid
   Beside her mother's knee ;
Then out and spak' an auld witch-wife,
   By the fire-side sate she.

Says,—" Drap the het lead on her cheek,
   And drap it on her chin,
And drap it on her rose-red lips,
   And she will speak again ;
O meikle will a maiden do,
   To her true-love to win ! "

They drapt the het lead on her cheek,
   They drapt it on her chin,
They drapt it on her rose-red lips,
   But breath was nane within.

Then up arose her seven brothers,
   And made for her a bier,
The boards were of the cedar wood,
   The plates o' silver clear.

And up arose her seven sisters,
   And made for her a sark ;
The claith of it was satin fine,
   The steeking silken wark.

The first Scots kirk that they cam' to,
   They gar'd the bells be rung ;
The neist Scots kirk that they cam' to,
   They gar'd the mass be sung.

The third Scots kirk that they cam' to,
   They dealt the gowd for her ;
The fourth Scots kirk that they cam' to,
   Her true-love met them there.

"Set down, set down the bier," he said,
　"Till I look on the dead;
The last time that I saw her face,
　Her cheeks were rosy red."

He rent the sheet upon her face,
　A little abune the chin;
And fast he saw her colour come,
　And sweet she smiled on him.

" O give me a chive of your bread, my love,
　And ae drap o' your wine;
For I have fasted for your sake,
　These weary lang days nine !

" Gae hame, gae hame, my seven brothers;
　Gae hame and blaw your horn !
I trow ye wad ha'e gien me the skaith,
　But I've gied you the scorn.

" I cam' not here to fair Scotland,
　To lie amang the dead;
But I cam' here to fair Scotland,
　Wi' my ain true-love to wed."

Of course, thoroughly to enter into the full delight of ballads,
you must be brought up on them as children, and you must know the
habitat of each ; you must walk through our glorious Border-land,
ballad-book in hand, and read them in their own homes, and know
all that can be known about the *loci in quo*. Great will be your
reward.

Wills't den Dichter du verstehen ?
Musst im Dichter's Lande gehen.

You should, of course, visit both sides of the Border, for we must
always bear in mind that part of it, at all events, was debateable land;
and that the peoples on either side were closely akin to each other,
and therefore hated each other with the intense hatred peculiar to
close relationships. And so the man who hails from Northumberland
is always in Scotch ballads a southron loon, and the man from the
Lowlands in Northumbrian ballads is a fause Scot, and, in either case,
surliness, treachery, cruelty, every manner of iniquity, is to be
expected. We must take all the ballads, Scotch and English alike,
with a good big pinch of salt.

But they agree in the strange picture they give us of that old-
world life,. so gay, so fierce, so cruel ; when men's passions were under
less apparent constraint and the sword was a weapon more easily

wielded than the pen. Our romantic ballads are tales of a wild and
unsettled time, when witchcraft was of daily occurrence; when fairies
still danced upon the green; when men and women followed their
natural inclinations without much regard to social conventions ; when
life was held of small account. " Fair Mary of Wallington " is a sad
and eerie story, telling the legend of the dread fate which was alleged
to overtake the mothers of the heirs of the Fenwick race. "The
Laidley Worm of Spindleston Heugh " is a ballad so carefully and
extensively touched up that it reminds you of a modern photographic
portrait, in which there is " neither spot, or wrinkle, or any such
thing," and which bears small resemblance to its origin, as every
characteristic has been carefully eliminated. You get a picture when
you want a portrait. It is a kind of " Beauty and the Beast " ballad,
and is, no doubt, founded upon an old and widespread tradition; but
the existing version is, as Mr. Justice Grantham would say, quite " too
artistic." You have a witch stepmother turning a beautiful princess
into a laidley worm, as rapacious as the worm of Lambton, and being
herself afterwards turned into a loathsome, spiteful toad of monstrous
size. You have witch-wives despatched to sink the ship of the
delivering prince, the Lohengrin of the ballad, but foiled by rowan
wood. And you have the poisonous worm restored to her lovely
womanhood by gallant kisses three. It is a capital story, but sadly
spoiled in the telling. Imagine an old ballad-singer saying :—

> His absence and her serpent shape
> The king had long deplored ;
> He now rejoiced to see them both
> Again to him restored.

That is the bleat of the Norham Lamb, not the voice of an old
singer.

Young Beichan was delivered from prison in Turkey by his captor's
only daughter, under the promise :—

> O I've got houses and I've got land,
> And half Northumberland belongs to me ;
> And I will give it all to the fair young lady
> As out of prison would let me go free.

The daughter replies :—

> O in seven long years, I'll make a vow
> For seven long years, and keep it strong,
> That if you'll wed no other woman,
> O I will wed no other man.

But, when she reaches young Beichan's castle seven years and fourteen days afterwards, with all her gay clothing,

> The fairest young lady
> As ever my two eyes did see,

in the words of the porter;

> She has got rings on every finger,
> And on one finger she has got three;
> With as much gay gold about her middle
> As would buy half Northumberlee;

he, for whom she has gone through so much, has just taken his young bride home.   But, whether it were the visible wealth or his conscience that moved him, the bride is sent back, and for the fair Turk another marriage is prepared.   In another ballad, we hear how, when the lord is from home, Long Lonkin visits his tower near Whittle Dene, and, by the treachery of a maidservant, creeps in at a little window, which has been forgotten when the others were penned in, and murders the lady with barbarous ferocity.   In another, Johnny Faa, the king of the gipsies, so bewitches a northern earl's lady with his glamours that, in her "high-heeled shoes, made of the Spanish leather," she goes off with him, and when the earl overtakes her, and reproaches her, she answers:—

> O what care I for houses and land?
> Or what care I for money?
> So as I have brewed so will I return:
> So fare you well, my honey.

But, whatever came of *her*, fifteen blithe and bonny gipsies were hanged in a row for Johnny Faa's ill deeds.

When I was a child, the strange Egyptian folk played much part in our young lives.   Before the time of railways in the North, seldom did we drive along a country road without coming upon an encampment of these swarthy wanderers.   About Rothbury they were rife, and my earliest angling lessons, more than half a century ago, were given me by a grand old gipsy, by name Bill the Tinner.   They were great days, those of early childhood.   There was a romance in life then which has long since gone for ever.   What legends we heard; what songs and ballads we listened to; how we longed to join the free and careless folk.   When I last visited Esther Faa, the gipsy queen, at Kirk Yetholm, where her people had learned to live in houses, how good it was to have memories of the olden time revived, and how proud the old queen was of her position and her ancient lineage.   And

well might she be. Had not James V. of Scotland, in 1540, recognised Johnnie Faa's right and title as lord and earl of Little Egypt,
and issued letters to his officers to assist that potentate "in execution
of justice upon his company and folks, conform to the laws of Egypt,
and in punishing of all them that rebels against him." She was proud,
too, of what she thought the higher morality of her people than that
of their Border neighbours. She questioned me about the gipsies of
Seville, of whom I had seen much, and told me how, when the
Hungarian gipsy band were at Paris, several of them had travelled
over to pay their respects to her, and that they could hold much converse with her in Romany. And the gipsy days are not yet quite
over, for, as I write, the daily papers tell of how the southern magis-
trates have held it to be unlawful for them to camp out on commons,
and how the gipsies have defied such laws.

But to come back to our romantic ballads : one of the most
charming is "The Fair Flower of Northumberland."

> It was a knight in Scotland born,
>   Follow, my love, come over the strand,
> Was taken prisoner and left forlorn,
>   Even by the good Earl of Northumberland.

Whilst he pined in the prison, where "he could not walk or lay
along," the earl's sweet daughter passed by like an angel bright.
To her he appealed for pity, but she asked him how she could pity a
foe to her country.

> "Fair lady ! I am no foe," he said,
> . Follow, my love, come over the strand,
> "For thy sweet love here was I stay'd,
>   For thee, Fair Flower of Northumberland !"

> "Why should'st thou come here for love of me,"
>   Follow, my love, come over the strand,
> "Having wife and children in thy country,
>   And I the Fair Flower of Northumberland ?"

But he swears, by the blessed Trinity, that he has neither wife nor
child, and that, if she will set him free, he will marry her in fair
Scotland, where she shall be a lady of castles and towers, and sit like a
queen in princely bowers.

. She gives way before the voice of love ; takes two gallant steeds
from her father's stables, and rides off with the prisoner whom she
has freed. They swim the Tweed :

From top to toe all wet was she ;
  "Follow, my love ! come over the strand,
This I have done for love of thee,
  And I the Fair Flower of Northumberland."

And she rode through the winter's night, until they came in sight of "Edinborough, the fairest town in all Scotland." Then he turned to her, and told her to get home to Northumberland, for he had there a wife and children five ; but he would take her horse, and she should go back on foot.

She prayed him to draw his sword and end her shame, but he took her off her horse, which he stole from her, and left her in extreme need. Happily two gallant knights came riding by, and had pity upon her. They took her up behind them, and brought her to her father again, and she was soon forgiven. Her mother smiled gently on her, with the reflection "She is not the first that the Scots have beguiled,"

But she's still the Fair Flower of Northumberland.
She shanna want gold, she shanna want fee,
  Although that her love was so easily wan ;
She shanna want gold to gain a man wi',
  And she's still the Fair Flower of Northumberland.

The version of the ballad from which I have chiefly quoted ends with this sage reflection,

All you, fair maidens ! be warned by me,
  (Follow, my love, come over the strand ?)
Scots never were true, nor ever will be,
  To Lord, nor Lady, nor fair England.

We may contrast this happily with the beautiful ballad of the "Nut-brown Maid," the heroine of which was Lady Margaret Percy, daughter of the earl of Northumberland, who accompanied King Henry VIII. to the Field of the Cloth of Gold. You may remember how the lover explains to his lady-love that he is an outlaw and condemned to die, so

I must to the green-wood go
  Alone, a banished man.

But she will go with him, for, of all mankind, she loves but him alone. He paints to her all the hardships, trials, dangers, and difficulties of the life she would have to lead, but not a whit is she dismayed. She will risk all, bear all,

Shall never be said the Nut-brown Maid
  Was to her love unkind ;

and he at length confesses that he has but tried her, that he is the earl of Westmoreland's son, and will marry her. He was Henry Clifford, who succeeded as eleventh Baron Clifford, and was afterwards made earl of Cumberland, but he had led, in his young days, an outlaw's life in the dales of Yorkshire and Westmoreland.

Sir Walter Scott's beautiful ballad, "Jock o' Hazel-dean," is founded upon an old one which tells much the same story, but whereas the great poet's version makes the lady leave the youngest son to fly "o'er the Borders and awa' wi' Jock o' Hazel-dean," in the old verses it is John of Hazel-green who is the youngest son, and, when the father conveys the lady to his castle, the lovers are brought together to their mutual surprise and delight.

But it is time that I turned to our important historical ballads, for, in these, our side of the Border is especially rich. They are nearly all connected with one phase or another of the fierce warfare which was waged, with varying fortunes, between the north and the south for centuries. When I was a boy the feud was by no means extinct. Some Hawick lads had a bad time of it at "Bruce's," because they boasted of how, each year, there was a procession in that staid Border town with bands and banners to commemorate some victory over the English, which we believed that correct history had forgotten. The historical ballads can scarcely be relied upon for accurate information ; they catch the true spirit of the events which they describe, but they distort the facts. And the spirit is the main thing, after all. It is very difficult, at any time, to know what is really happening when war is going on. The bulletins put forth by the French government after Sedan were not unfairly summed up in the supposed despatch :— " Another glorious victory over the Germans who are thirty miles nearer Paris." When living in Paris during those troublous times we could get no inkling of what was going on until the English newspapers arrived, and even they were frequently wrong. The actual truth only came out afterwards, when Von Moltke digested the reports from the staff officers of the several armies and published them, that the mistakes, as well as the successes of the leaders, should be fully known, so that instruction might be gained from both alike. We must not, therefore, ask for too much accuracy in songs which celebrate warlike events at a time when there were no newspapers, no special war correspondents, and, frequently, an eager desire, on the singer's part at least, that the exact truth should not be known.

I must make some exception for the fine batch of war songs in which Lawrence Minot, a North country poet, described the victories of Edward III. from Halidon Hill to the capture of Guisnes Castle. They are of some real historic worth, for they give a succession of narratives of the stirring events of great battles with the Scotch and French which were really fought, and are by one living at the time of their occurrence. They are simple, direct, with many details which bear the impress of truth, and the versification is remarkably good, when their early date is considered.

I should choose the grand old ballad of "Chevy Chase," in one of its numerous versions, as the best representative which I could find of this class of historical ballads, were it not that it is so well known. It has ever been the delight of all who could appreciate true song. Sir Philip Sidney, in his *Apologie for Poetry*, says, "Certainly I must confess my own barbarousness, I never heard the old song of Percy and Douglas, that I found not my heart mooued more than with a trumpet; and yet it is sung but by some blind Crowder, with no rougher voyce than rude stile." Rare Ben Jonson declared that he would rather have written it than all his works, and Bishop Percy truly says "the fine heroic song of 'Chevy Chase' has ever been admired by competent judges. Those genuine strokes of nature and artless passion which have endeared it to the most simple readers have recommended it to the most refined, and it has equally been the amusement of our childhood and the favourite of our riper years."

And truly, it is a noble song, and it does, even in these days, rouse us as with the fierce delight of war, and we can feel that it was true for each foe that

> As, with a shout of triumph, they rushed on to the fight,
> All the battle-glory made their faces bright.

What a cheery gleam of honour and high-minded chivalry is cast upon those dark old days when we read of the deep and tender sorrow of the Percy over his fallen foe. How forcibly the deadly character of the hand-to-hand Border warfare is set forth in the concluding lines:—

> This battle began in Cheviat
> An hour before the noon,
> And whanne even-song belle was rang
> The battle was not half done:
> They toke on, on ethar hond,
> By the licht of the mone:
> Many had no strength for to stonde
> In Cheviat the hills aboon.

Of fifteen hundred archers of England
  Went away but fifty and three ;
Of twenty hundred spearmen of Scotland,
  But even five and fifty.
There was never a time on the March partés,
  Sen the Percy and Douglas met,
But it was marvele an the red bluid roun not
  As the rene doys in the strete.

Our local historical ballads divide themselves into two classes : those which treat of battles between large forces of men, either raised by great Border chiefs like the Douglas, the Percy, or the bold Buccleuch, or led by generals (as we should call them) appointed by one or other monarch, or called out by the Warden of the Marches to execute summary vengeance or rude justice such as Belted Will Howard well understood. We have many of these. In addition to "The Hunting of the Cheviot," "The Battle of Otterburn," and "Chevy Chase," of which I have already spoken, I may name "Flodden Field," "The Rising in the North," "The Raid o' the Reidswire," "The Battle of Neville's Cross," "Hamildon Hill," and so forth. This class has been sufficiently alluded to already in what I have said about "The Hunting of the Cheviot."

But the other class demands a more special notice, for it reveals to us much more closely the kind of life which Borderers led in those fierce old times, when for a Northumbrian to take a lowlander's cattle, or for a few Scots to harry and ravage a part of the southern Borders, was of habitual occurrence. We have an interesting account of the feelings aroused by the rumour of a foray in the account which Æneas Sylvius Piccolomini (afterwards Pope Pius II.) gives of his adventurous journey from Edinburgh to London in 1435. He had taken twelve days to sail from Holland to Dunbar, and refused to have further transactions with the stormy North Sea ; so he disguised himself as a merchant, and set forth on his scarcely less perilous land journey. As he travelled across the barren Northumbrian plain, he had to spend a night amongst the barbarous people who dwelt upon it. At night the cattle were driven into the peel tower, whither the men also repaired, whilst the traveller and his attendants were left round a watch-fire with a multitude of women and children. The men refused to take Æneas Sylvius with them, as he would be safe enough with the women folk, whom the Scots, if they crossed the Border, would not hurt. In the night, an alarm was given that the Scots were at hand, and the women fled to the woods, but Æneas Sylvius managed to take refuge in a stable. However, the invading troop turned out to be friends : it was a false alarm : or we might possibly have known at first hand what a Border raid was really like, or the history of the popes might have had a strange variation.

Æneas Sylvius speaks of the great delight which it gave the Scots to hear the English roundly abused. The English seem to have found enjoyment in a similar pastime. The "Death of Parcy Reed" begins :—

> God send the land deliverance
> From every reiving, riding Scot :
> We'll sune hae neither cow nor ewe,
> We'll sune hae neither staig nor stot.

It was probably six of one and half a dozen of the other.

There is still shown at Hesleyside, the residence of the old Charlton family, the spur which, at meal-times, was discovered in the dish when the good wife uncovered it, and which told the hungry laird and his hungry retainers that the larder was empty, and they must "boot, saddle, to horse and away," that, by killing game or lifting cattle, it might be replenished. The scene of such a discovery is admirably depicted in one of the Wallington pictures. Another relic of those old days is also shown in the same place and tells a very similar tale, the sword of the duke of Buccleuch taken by the Charlton of the day in some fierce fight. The duke appealed to Henry VIII., and Cardinal Wolsey commanded the North Tyne squire to return it. "If he wants it, he must come and take it," is said to have been the stout reply, and the sword is still at Hesleyside. In 1498, Don Pedro de Ayala, the Spanish minister to the Scotch court, reported of the people of Scotland to Ferdinand and Isabella, "They spend all their time in wars, and, when there is no war, they fight one another." That might have been truly said of either side of the Border.

It must not be forgotten, when we speak of the Borders, that England held territory within the present bounds of Scotland nearly down to the sixteenth century. This territory was won for Scotland by petty local strife, not by war between the two nations. Burton says, "There was a natural feeling that what was thus acquired belonged to the victors by a title more independent than a feudal holding of the crown. On either side, the royal writs, whether coming from the chancery of England or Scotland, met with scant respect. There was little of nationality on either side. The English wardens took care that if those they were set to watch were to go a-plundering, it should be rather in Scotland than in England ; and the Scots wardens reciprocated this policy. But except that it was safer to pillage on the other side than among their own countrymen, there was hardly a sense of nationality. At Flodden the English Borderers pillaged the English army as readily as the enemy's." The good Scotch historian does not point out that, on that occasion, the Scotch army offered rather more facilities for plunder.

Of all the Border potentates, the Armstrongs were the chief. They held sway over much territory, the greater part of which belonged to neither kingdom, but was known as the Debateable Land. When the English government applied to that of Scotland in 1528 for the release of certain English subjects who were known to be imprisoned within their territory, the Scots reply was that "they would endeavour themselves, for so much as in them is, that the said prisoners should be freed and go at large."

These prisoners had been captured by the Armstrongs, and any allegiance which was paid by the Armstrongs to the Scottish king was so paid from policy and not as an acknowledged duty. The chief of the Armstrongs came to look upon himself rather as an inde- pendent potentate who was an ally of the Scotch monarch than as his subject. Indeed it not infrequently happened that the Armstrong foray was carried out in Scottish territory altogether.

In 1528, Sym Armstrong, the laird of Whitlaugh, told the earl of Northumberland that he and his men had laid waste sixty miles in Scotland, and destroyed thirty parish churches, and that there was not one in the realm of Scotland dare remedy the same. In the same year, Lord Dacre, the English warden of the West Marches, tried, at the head of 2,000 men, to surprise and conquer these redoubtable foes, but his attempt was defeated. At this time it was said that the Armstrongs could put 3,000 horsemen into the field. Liddesdale was their realm, and Mangerton House their central stronghold, until Johnnie built Gilnockie Tower on the Esk. They also held the castle of Langholm, and they ruled over Eskdale, Ewesdale, Wauchopedale, and Annandale. Our balladry teems with tales of these great free-booters. To them escaped the desperadoes who were too bad for either England or Scotland. Yet we should gather from the ballads that there was a rough love of fairplay and justice, absolute courage, and a certain dignity of command about these lairds of Liddesdale. "Hobbie Noble," "Jock o' the Side," "Johnnie Armstrong," "The Raid o' the Reidswire," "Jock o' the Cow," are amongst the best of these ditties, and two, at least, of them are supremely good. "Johnnie Armstrong" tells how, at length, James V. of Scotland determined, in 1530, that he would put an end to this competitive power in his own kingdom, and how he caught the Armstrongs by guile. He invited 1,200 lords and gentlemen to meet him at the Meggat-water (ostensibly) for a great deer-hunting, but he proceeded southward with an army of 8,000 men, until he came near Langholm, when he wrote with his own hand a loving letter to Johnnie Armstrong, asking him to join them. Johnnie called his followers together, prepared a feast at Gilnockie for the king, and set out in high feather for the interview, but their ladies, with women's finer wit, seem to have had a presage of coming evil, for they wished "God bring our men weel back again."

The king received Johnnie with ironical courtesy, moving his bonnet to him, but when the chief made his duty to him, asking grace for himself and his men, the king called him a traitor and declared his life forfeit. Johnnie pleaded gently with him, offering him many great gifts if his life were granted; but, when he proved obdurate, and still called him "traitor," the Border chief's patience was exhausted, and he burst forth :—

> "Ye lied, ye lied, now, king!" he says,
> "Although a king and prince ye be;
> For I lo'ed naething in a' my life,
> I will daur say't, but honestie.
>
> Save a fleet horse, and a fair woman,
> Twa bonnie dogs to kill a deer;
> But England should have found me meal and malt,
> Gif I had lived this hundred year.
>
> She should have found me meal and malt,
> And beef and mutton in all plentie;
> But ne'er a Scots wife could have said
> That e'er I skaithed her a poor flea.
>
> To seek het water beneath cauld ice,
> I trow it is a great follie:
> I have asked grace at a graceless face,
> But there is nane for my men and me.
>
> But had I kenn'd, or I cam frae hame,
> How thou unkind wad'st been to me,
> I would have kept the Border-side,
> In spite of all thy peers and thee."

Johnnie Armstrong was splendidly attired, with a gold girdle round his waist, and nine targets or tassels in his hat, each worth three hundred pounds, and this seems to have further incensed King James, who asked:—

> "What wants that knave a king should have
>   But the sword of honour and the crown ?
>
> "O whair gat ye these targats, Johnnie,
>   That blink sae brawly abune thy bree?"
> "I gat them in the field fighting,
>   Where, cruel king, thou durst not be!
>
> Had I my horse and my harness good,
>   And riding as I wont to be,
> It should have been tauld this hundred year
>   The meeting of my king and me!"

How our hearts go with the brave old Borderer, but now come the verses which the gentle Goldsmith loved. In his essays he says:— "The music of the finest singer is dissonance to what I felt when our old dairy-maid sung me into tears with Johnny Armstrong's 'Last Good Night, or the Cruelty of Barbara Allen.'" Johnny first takes leave of his brother, and then goes on :—

> And God be with thee, Christy, my son,
>   Where thou sits on thy nurse's knee:
> But an' thou live this hundred year
>   Thy father's better thou'll never be.
>
> Farewell, my bonny Gilnock-ha',
>   Where, on the Esk, thou standest stout:
> Gif I had lived but seven years mair,
>   I wad hae gilt thee round about.
>
> Johnie murdered was at Carlinrigg,
>   And all his gallant companie ;
> But Scotland's heart was ne'er so wae,
>   To see sae mony brave men dee :
>
> Because they saved their country dear
>   From Englishmen : nane were sae bauld ;
> While Johnie lived on the Border-side
>   Nane of them durst come near his hauld.

I must end my tale of our old ballads by reading you one which many of you probably know, but which I always find fresh and fine after half a century's close acquaintance. I am delighted to see that Prof. Child, in that splendid collection of English and Scottish Popular Ballads, for which we can never be too grateful to him, says that "Jock o' the Side" is "one of the best (ballads) in the world, and enough to make a horse-trooper of any young Borderer, had he lacked the impulse."

King James V. had not killed off the Armstrongs, for this tale of "Jock o' the Side" is certainly to be dated towards the end of the 16th century. The "Side" seems to have been a cottage on the Liddel, opposite Mangerton House. It has an historical interest, for it carries us back to the time when the strong differences between the Catholic North and the Protestant South of England resulted in the great Rising of the North, which had for its object, as the earl of Northumberland said, "the reformation of religion and the preservation of the Queen of Scots." Protestanism had small hold in the North, where it was held in contempt, and Mary Queen of Scots had, during her captivity at Bolton and elsewhere, by her beauty and her wiles turned the heads of the entire youth of these parts. The rebellion might have been of real danger ; the people turned out in great numbers ; on the 14th November, 1569, Durham Cathedral was ransacked and all signs of the reformed faith were destroyed ; but the rebels were badly led and soon lost heart, and, in five weeks, all danger was over without any blood being spilled until the executioner got to work. After the Rising in the North had failed, the earls of Northumberland and Westmoreland, who had been the leaders, fled to Liddesdale, and Sussex writing to Cecil on the 22nd December, 1569, says that they left the countess of Northumberland, who was worth a dozen of such poor creatures as her husband and his friend put together, "at John of the Syde's house, a cottage not to be compared to any dog-kennel in England. . . . . My lord of Westmoreland changed his coat of plate and sword with John of the Syde, to be the more unknown." Of the other characters in the ballad, "the Laird's Jock" was probably a son of Thomas Armstrong of Mangerton, the elder brother of Gilnockie. He is not infrequently mentioned in existing documents. Hobbie Noble was a native of Cumberland, who took refuge with the Armstrongs when his irregularities caused him to be banished from Bewcastle.

JOCK O' THE SIDE.

Now Liddesdale has ridden a raid,
  But I wat they had better hae staid at hame ;
For Michael o' Winfield he is dead,
  And Jock o' the Side is prisoner ta'en.

For Mangerton house Lady Downie has gane,
  Her coats she has kilted up to her knee ;
And down the water wi' speed she rins,
  While tears in spaits fa' fast frae her e'e.

Then up and spoke our gude auld laird—
  " What news, what news, sister Downie to me ?"
" Bad news, bad news, for Michael is kill'd,
  And they hae taken my son Johnie."

" Ne'er fear, sister Downie," quo' Mangerton,
  " I have yokes of owsen, twenty and three ;
My barns, my byres, and my faulds a' weel fill'd,
  I'll part wi' them a' ere Johnie shall die.

" Three men I'll send to set him free,
  A' harness'd wi' the best o' steel ;
The English loons may hear, and drie
  The weight o' their braid-swords to feel.

" The Laird's Jock ane, the Laird's Wat twa,
  O Hobbie Noble, thou ane maun be !
Thy coat is blue, thou hast been true,
  Since England banish'd thee to me."

Now Hobbie was an English man,
  In Bewcastle dale was bred and born ;
But his misdeeds they were sae great,
  They banished him ne'er to return.

Laird Mangerton them orders gave,
  " Your horses the wrang way maun be shod :
Like gentlemen ye maunna seem,
  But look like corn-cadgers ga'en the road.

" Your armour gude ye maunna show,
  Nor yet appear like men of weir ;
As country lads be a' array'd,
  Wi' branks and brecham on each mare."

Sae their horses are the wrang way shod,
  And Hobbie has mounted his gray sae fine ;
Jock his lively bay, Wat's on his white horse behind,
  And on they rode for the water of Tyne.

At the Cholerford they all light down,
  And there wi' the help of the light o' the moon,
A tree they cut, wi' fifteen nogs on each side,
  To climb up the wa' of Newcastle toun.

But when they cam' to Newcastle toun,
  And were alighted at the wa',
They fand their tree three ells ower laigh,
  They fand their stick baith short and sma'.

Then up and spak' the Laird's ain Jock :
  "There's naething for't ; the gates we maun force."
But when they cam' the gate untill,
  A proud porter withstood baith men and horse.

His neck in twa the Armstrangs wrung ;
  Wi' fute or hand he ne'er play'd pa !
His life and his keys at anes they hae ta'en,
  And cast the body ahint the wa'.

Now sune they reach Newcastle jail,
  And to the prisoner thus they call :
"Sleeps thou, wakes thou, Jock o' the Side,
  Or art thou weary of thy thrall ?"

Jock answers thus, wi' dulefu' tone ;
  "Aft, aft, I wake—I seldom sleep ;
But whae's this kens my name sae weel,
  And thus to ease my wae does seek ?"

Then out and spak' the gude Laird's Jock,
  "Now fear ye na, my billie," quo' he ;
"For here are the Laird's Jock, the Laird's Wat,
  And Hobbie Noble, come to set thee free."

"Now haud thy tongue, my gude Laird's Jock,
  For ever, alas ! this canna be ;
For if a' Liddesdale were here the night,
  The morn's the day that I maun die."

"Full fifteen stane o' Spanish iron,
  They hae laid a' right sair on me :
Wi' locks and keys I am fast bound
  Into this dungeon dark and dreirie."

"Fear ye nae that," quo' the Laird's Jock ;
  "A faint heart ne'er won a fair ladie ;
Work thou within, we'll work without,
  And I'll be sworn we'll set thee free."

The first strong door that they cam' at,
  They loosed it without a key ;
The next chain'd door that they cam' at,
  They gar'd it a' to flinders flee.

The prisoner now upon his back,
　　The Laird's Jock has gotten up fu' hie ;
And down the stair, him, irons and a',
　　Wi' nae sma' speid and joy brings he.

" Now, Jock, my man," quo' Hobbie Noble,
　　" Some o' his weight ye may lay on me."
" I wat weel no !" quo' the Laird's ain Jock,
　　" I count him lighter than a flee."

Sae out at the gates they a' are gane,
　　The prisoner's set on horseback hie ;
And now wi' speed they've ta'en the gate,
　　While ilk ane jokes fu' wantonlie :

" O Jock I sae winsomely's ye ride,
　　Wi' baith your feet upon ae side ;
Sae weel ye're harness'd, and sae trig,
　　In troth ye sit like ony bride !"

The night, tho' wat, they did na mind,
　　But hied them on fu' merilie,
Until they cam' to Cholerford brae,
　　Where the water ran like mountains hie.

But when they cam' to Cholerford,
　　There they met with an auld man ;
Says—" Honest man, will the water ride ?
　　Tell us in haste if that ye can."

" I wat weel no," quo' the gude auld man ;
　　" I hae lived here thirty years and three,
And I ne'er yet saw the Tyne sae big,
　　Nor running anes sae like a sea."

Then out and spoke the Laird's Saft Wat,
　　The greatest coward in the companie :
" Now halt, now halt, we needna try't ;
　　The day is come we a' maun die !"

" Puir faint-hearted thief I" cried the Laird's ain Jock.
　　" There'll nae man die but him that's fey ;
I'll guide ye a' right safely thro' ;
　　Lift ye the prisoner on ahint me."

Wi' that the water they hae ta'en,
　　By ane's and twa's they a' swam thro' ;
" Here are we a' safe," quo' the Laird's Jock,
　　" And puir faint Wat, what think ye now ?"

They scarce the other brae had won,
　　When twenty men they saw pursue ;
Frae Newcastle toun they had been sent,
　　A' English lads baith stout and true.

But when the land-serjeant the water saw,
  "It winna ride, my lads," says he;
Then cried aloud—"The prisoner take,
  But leave the fetters, I pray, to me."

"I wat weel no," quo' the Laird's Jock;
  "I'll keep them a'; shoon to my mare they'll be,
My gude bay mare—for I am sure,
  She has bought them a' right dear frae thee."

Sae now they are on to Liddesdale,
  E'en as fast as they could them hie;
The prisoner is brought to's ain fireside,
  And there o' his airns they mak' him free.

"Now, Jock, my billie," quo' a' the three,
  "The day is com'd thou was to die;
But thou's as weel at thy ain ingle-side,
  Now sitting, I think, twixt thee and me."

I do not mention the many admirable ballads which have been written in later days, but I may say a word about Robert White, the historian of the battles of Otterburn and Flodden, himself a ballad writer, and the indefatigable collector of songs and ballads. Professor Child mentions specially how much he was indebted to him for valuable information and assistance. Many of us remember, with affection and respect, the gentle and kindly face which was so often to be seen in this room, for he was, for many years, an active member of the committee of this society. I may be allowed to say, too, how proud his family are of my father's well-known ballad, "The Legend of the Lambton Worm," which made its first appearance in *Tait's Edinburgh Magazine* in 1833, and has been and still is constantly reprinted. But the best of all the modern ballads which come closely home to the members of this society is by one who was once our assistant librarian, and who is still among us, my honoured friend, Joseph Skipsey. His ballad "The Hartley Calamity" is of the true type. In it a singer, who has himself passed the greater part of his life in the coal mine, tells of the terrible calamity which befell the men at work in the Hartley pit on January 16th, 1862. His simple and touching lines recall to those of us who were privileged to take some part in the consolation of the survivors the awful days of fruitless endeavour, the agony of hopeless hope, which so stirred the whole of our land during six days of weary waiting. This ballad will not die, and with Joseph Skipsey's name I appropriately close my sketch of the simple poetry of which we Northumbrians may well be proud.

LECTURE IV.

RIDLEY AND THE REFORMATION.

We were talking last week about our ballads, and the stir and unrest upon the Borders which they revealed. Those of which we spoke cover a long period of time—two centuries and a half, at least—reaching from the middle of the fourteenth nearly to the end of the sixteenth century. These centuries were of vast importance in the political and social history of our country. They saw parliamentary government passing through many a peril but firmly established at last. They saw the people become conscious of their existence as a power in the State. They saw the loss of many possessions on the continent of Europe, to the great gain of England ; and they all but saw the union with Scotland an accomplished fact. The early part of this period saw a North-country man from the banks of the Tees beginning a mighty movement in that least moveable of all matters, religious belief, and advocating reforms which are even yet only partially obtained, and upon some of which there is still wide diversity of opinion. So far as any one man can be pointed to as the originator of any vast intellectual revolution, John Wyclif was the forerunner of the great religious Reformation which produced the Protestant Church. In every direction he broke boldly through the traditions of his time. He taught the belief in immediate communication between man and God without the intervention of the priesthood. He urged the clergy to abandon their accumulated wealth, and to become poor as in the earlier and purer days ; and he taught that, for the needs of the nation, church property might be seized and employed like any other. He, first amongst Englishmen, appealed openly by sermon and by tract to the great body of the people. He translated the Bible into the people's tongue, and almost the last act of his life was the denial of the temporal power of the bishop of Rome, although he still called him the chief vicar of Christ upon earth. His learning, courage, deep conviction and power of convincing others, the vast, original, and brave work which he did, the amazing breadth and depth of his intellectual power, the far-reaching influence which his teaching exerted over his own and other lands and centuries, place him in the forefront of great religious Reformers.

So much I may say of this noble North-country man, but it is with the later work of Reformation which sprang from the seed which he had sown that I must deal to-night, and we thus move forward to the early years of the sixteenth century. The world was awakening then to a new life. " The old order " was changing, "yielding place to new " in all directions of thought. Few historical considerations can be of greater importance than that of the chain of events which led to the outburst of free thought, free research, and, ultimately, free speech. The Crusades, with their unlooked-for result of awakening the minds of multitudes of untutored men by the potent and manifold influences of travel, and their undesired result in the Mohammedan conquest of Constantinople and the consequent dispersion of the intellectual wealth of ancient Greece ; the determination of Dante to follow the example of Ulfilas, Charlemagne, and our own Cædmon and Cynewulf, and to give his best to the safe-keeping of the people's tongue ; the new departure of Art upon the path which Natural Science bravely followed, and, led by Niccola Pisano from the very cathedral in which Galileo Galilei two centuries afterwards, watched the swinging of a lamp, to what purpose you all know ; the bold preaching and teaching in matters of religious faith of John Wyclif and his disciples in other lands ; the disturbance of Eastern trade which sent Columbus, Vasco de Gama, and the heroic Magellan forth on those voyages of discovery which produced so many unexpected fruits, not in commerce alone ; the invention of the telescope, disclosing worlds of light undreamed of in the visions of the most advanced observers ; the discovery of printing by moveable types, by which the results of all discoveries might be spread more widely in a year than centuries would previously have sufficed for, and by which the reading world were at once made " heirs of all the Ages' gain ; " and, lastly, the patient working out of the great truths of astronomy, which, in no mere phrase but in very truth, were to give to men " new heavens and a new earth ; " these are amongst the chief events which led up to and formed the new birth of the intellectual world which produced such momentous effects upon our country in the reign of Henry VIII. and his immediate successors.

The stirring of new life just bursting into being was felt strongly in England. During the whole of the fourteenth century there had been a wide revival of interest in what used to be called polite literature, as distinguished from the barbarous productions of native tongues. For centuries the latter had been held in the contempt which is the legitimate offspring of ignorance. There had always been a few persons in our land who had learned and loved Greek, but, speaking generally, it was for many centuries a lost tongue. At an early date there had been a serious attack made in the name of religion upon the cultivation of the intellect at all, and during three centuries at least students who wished to become learned had to find their way to the cities of southern Spain, where the Moors kept alive the lamp of truth with munificent catholicity. We have only to realise that Gerbert, afterwards Pope Sylvester II., was a student at Cordova to understand the vast debt which the whole of Europe is under to the Mohammedan rulers of the great Spanish peninsula. But in the fourteenth century, led by the scholar and poet, Francis Petrarch, there began a general revolt against the imprisonment of the mind, and the intellect of man was recognised to be his glory, not his shame. Everywhere was there the search for manuscripts of the great Greek and Roman writers ; was there patient and devoted copying of such as were discovered ; was there a passionate thirst for deep and full knowledge of the grand old tongues and their splendid fruits. When the fifteenth century opened, the love of classical learning had grown, in Italy, into an absorbing passion. The great families vied with each other in their costly collections of splendid manuscripts. Greek scholars were the most welcome of guests at many a brilliant and enlightened court. And then came the discovery of the art of printing with moveable types, and within half a century Aldo Manuzio had, in Venice, carried that art to a perfection which has never since been attained.

England felt this outburst of new and vigorous intellectual life, but it was slow to reach our shores. Yet it came to us direct from that land of Italy with which we English have been more closely bound, intellectually and spiritually, than with any other all through our history ; that land which has held a strange and subtle sway over the minds of our greatest poets through all the centuries down to the present day ; and which, though physically so different from our own, has a curiously friendly feeling to the traveller from our shores. The earliest of our scholars to seek the new learning in Italy whom I can name was Grocyn (the best and most honourable man who ever lived in England, according to Erasmus), who probably reached that land in 1485, and who was delivering Greek lectures in Oxford in 1491. Then came Linacre, who was the first president of the College of Physicians founded by Henry VIII. in 1518, and who took part in the academy founded by Aldo Manuzio at the end of the fifteenth century in Venice for discussing the several manuscripts of the great Greek and Latin authors and deciding the readings which were to issue from his unrivalled press. Erasmus was a member of this academy some ten or twelve years later.

But the greatest of our young scholars who went to Italy to feel the full force of the new birth of learning was, undoubtedly, John Colet, the founder of St. Paul's School, which we may call the parent of the numerous grammar schools which sprang into existence in the reign of Henry VIII. and Edward VI. But John Colet was far more than the father of secondary education for our land, he was a great religious reformer of quite a new type. Of deep learning himself, and with a passion for imparting his knowledge to others, with direct simple eloquence, earnest and vigorous, his lectures at once aroused wide attention. He cast aside as worthless the vain and windy disputations of the schoolmen, and went directly to the gospels for his inspiration. To him the mere form was a mere convenience which, in the very nature of things, must perish : the spirit was all. Why waste precious time in the dreary mazes of musty theological dissertations, when the plain and simple words of the New Testament were open to you ? To his young students, Colet's advice was "keep to the Bible and the Apostles' Creed ; and let divines, if they like, dispute about the rest."

Here was indeed a new and a grand departure, and around him Colet had great allies. Erasmus, whose name is a synonyme for ripe and profound scholarship, being too poor at the time to visit Italy, came to Oxford that he might study Greek under Grocyn. Here he found a group of men who were to do great things for England. This was in 1499, and he says, " I have found in Oxford so much polish and learning that now I hardly care about going to Italy at all, save for the sake of having been there. When I listen to my friend Colet it seems like listening to Plato himself. Who does not wonder at the wide range of Grocyn's knowledge ? What can be more searching, deep, and refined, than the judgment of Linacre ? When did nature mould a temper more gentle, endearing, and happy, than the temper of Thomas More ? "

The influence of such a group of men extended far beyond Oxford. Modern England was making at this time. The new spirit was springing into active life. The sister university of Cambridge soon awakened to the fresh work, and in 1511 Erasmus himself was settled

NICOLAVS RIDLE
EPISCOPVS ROFFENSIS
ISCOPVS LONDINENSIS & Aqu
MARTYRIO CORONA

BISHOP RIDLEY.

there as its professor of Greek. In 1516 he writes, of the result of discarding the old formal learning for the new knowledge of the great men of Greece and Rome, "the university is now so flourishing that it can compete with the best universities of the age." Fresh scholars arrived from Italy to carry on the work. There was fierce opposition on the part of the old professors and their followers, but the young king and his great adviser, Cardinal Wolsey, with Fox, the bishop of Winchester, and Fisher, the bishop of Rochester, threw their mighty influence upon the side of the new learning, and the students were filled with the spirit of anxious, earnest, self-sacrificing work. It was indeed a marvellous time this of the outburst of new intellectual life.

I do not know of any record of the number of students actually attending either of the universities at this time, but old Latimer stated, in 1550, that there were then 10,000 fewer in attendance than was the case twenty years previously. He alluded to both Oxford and Cambridge.

Amongst the men who came up to Cambridge to share in the benefits of this new birth was a young man from a remote part of Northumberland, Nicholas Ridley, who was to become one of the chief actors in the reform of religion which was to spring from this revival of learning : "himself not least, but honoured of them all."

He was born at the old peel tower of Willimoteswick in Tynedale, " not far from the Scotch borders in Northumberland, as he himself informs us," says his biographer, the Rev. Gloucester Ridley, who published a life of him in 1763. The Ridley family was one of the oldest and best known on the Borders, and it is still famous amongst us. Many houses in the neighbourhood of Willimoteswick belonged to them, notably Hard-riding and Unthank and Ridley Halls, and some doubt has been expressed as to the martyr's actual birthplace. But his biographer further gives as his authority for mentioning Willimoteswick, Ridley's countryman and fellow collegian, Dr. Turner, and I see no reason for disputing the point. The date of his birth is unknown : it was " towards the beginning of the sixteenth century."

You may see the farmhouse which now occupies the site of his birthplace, as you approach or leave the Bardon Mill Station on the Newcastle and Carlisle Railway. It stands on the south bank of the South Tyne, and a slightly sloping field lies between it and the river. Of the old castle itself, the actual seat of the Ridley family for many generations, but little now remains except a massive tower through which the farmyard is entered, and from which we may gather that the old house partook much of the character of the customary Border peel tower built to defend man and his herds and flocks from the "ranting, reiving Scots." A pleasant walk behind the house takes you up a gentle hill-side, with a few trees and a little dene, and, when you gain the summit, you come out upon the moors which stretch away, almost without a break, until they reach the broad plains of Yorkshire.

I sometimes have thought of the subtle but potent influence which these moors must have had upon the mind of the Northumberland lad who was one day to be a martyr. I often wonder if we of the North country are sufficiently proud of and thankful for our moors. There is nothing like them : their beauty is their own. The moors are always glorious, but they reveal their full beauty only to those who love them and patiently search it out. You do not know them unless you are familiar with their every aspect. In the early morning when the dew-drops sparkle like gems of the first water at the earliest glint of the arising sun, and the sea of purple heather stretches away around you on every side into space without a breath of life but yours to break the charm : beneath the full moon's rays at midnight, when all things lie hushed in the mimic death of sleep, save the beasts of the forest which creep forth, and the distance which the eye seems able to travel over the vague surface, and the indefiniteness of all surrounding objects, and the clear mystery of the moonlight, awaken in your mind a feeling of infinitude akin to awe. Under the weird influence of the driving storm, when the hurrying mists drift across the wastes of bracken and heather in wild, strange shapes, and your range of vision is limited and ever-changing, and the look of everything is other, and beauty is gone but grandeur and wonder are everywhere : not the mild wonder of the moonlight but the bewildering wonder of the tempest : and, above all, the spirit of man rises in the fierce delight of stern struggling with adverse circumstances.

The moors have been fitly sung by a Northern poet, who says :—

> The moors—all hail! ye changeless, ye sublime,
>   That seldom hear a voice, save that of Heaven !
> Scorners of chance, and fate, and death, and time,
>   But not of Him, whose viewless hand hath riv'n
>   The chasm, through which the mountain stream is driven !
> How like a prostrate giant—not in sleep,
>   But listening to his beating heart—ye lie !
> With winds and clouds dread harmony ye keep:

Ye seem alone beneath the boundless sky ;
Ye speak, are mute—and there is no reply !
Here all is sapphire light, and gloomy land,
    Blue, brilliant, sky above a sable sea
Of hills, like chaos, ere the first command,
    "Let there be light!" bade light and beauty be.

But I must apologise for this digression, and return from the moors with Nicholas Ridley who was sent to Newcastle to receive the early part of his education. About the year 1518 he was removed to Pembroke Hall, Cambridge. It was a critical time. Martin Luther had nailed his Theses on the sale of indulgences to the door of the Wittenberg church in the preceding year. Sir Thomas More was in the service of Henry VIII.: Colet, now dean of St. Paul's, was broken in health, and had but a year to live : Erasmus was ill at Basle : Wolsey was archbishop of York and papal legate, and had begun to set Parliament aside : Henry was still the learned and popular monarch, with a taste for the new learning, and zealously put to death men who let it be known that they were infected with the heresies of Martin Luther. Nicholas Ridley reached Cambridge when the thirst for reform had begun to turn attention towards the need for religious reformation, although all movement in that direction was as yet in secret. The king was still to be named Defender of the Faith ; even Hugh Latimer had not so far left the teaching of the Fathers for that of the New ·Testament.

Little is known about Ridley's life at this time, excepting what his contemporaries, Bishop Grindal, who was afterwards his chaplain, and Bishop Bale, relate. Bishop Grindal says that, as a child, he learned his grammar with great dexterity at Newcastle, and that, "at Cambridge, in a short time he became so famous that, for his singular aptness, he was called to higher functions and offices of the university, by degrees attaining thereunto." Bale tells us, " He was a gentleman by his birth, and remarkable for an ingenuousness of mind, not only pious in his youth, but even then studiously applying himself to the acquiring of the learning then most in repute. With which view he repaired to Cambridge, to Pembroke Hall, where his attainments in Greek and Latin are particularly mentioned "

This good character is fully borne out by the few facts which have come down to us respecting his undergraduate life at Cambridge. He seems to have given much time to scholastic philosophy and theology, and to have gained considerable reputation for his attainments in them. His biographer says:—"The very walls of the garden at

Pembroke Hall bore testimony of his studies there, a walk under them being called Ridley's walk to this day, where he was accustomed to learn and repeat, without book, St. Paul's Epistles, in Greek."

He took his Bachelor's degree in 1522, and was offered a Fellowship in University College, Oxford, in 1524, but refused to accept it. Such an offer could only have been made to a man who had already distinguished himself, but his own college, in his own university, knew his value, and made him a Fellow in the same year. In 1525, he took his Master's degree, and in the next year he was appointed general agent for the college in all causes relating to several of their churches.

I have not mentioned that Nicholas Ridley was indebted to his uncle, Dr. Robert Ridley, "a little man but a great divine," says Cavendish, for his education at Cambridge, and the eminent canonist seems to have been well satisfied with his nephew's attainments, and to have desired to equip him, as thoroughly as might be, as an authority in divinity. It is possible that, having been the bishop of London's assessor in several cases of heresy, he was a little alarmed at his nephew's proficiency in Greek and Latin, and wished him to come under influences which were strongly conservative in religious matters. He sent him, in 1527, to study in Paris amongst the doctors of the Sorbonne, which had attained a European reputation as a faculty of theology, and thence he went to the university at Louvain, then considered the first university in Europe, and being especially distinguished as a school of Roman Catholic theology. It had no less than forty-three colleges, and its students coming from all countries, were 6,000 in number. He seems to have passed three years on the Continent, and to have returned to Cambridge in 1530, when he was chosen junior treasurer.

I may here quote part of the account which was given of Nicholas Ridley to Fox (when he was collecting materials for his *Book of Martyrs*) by William Turner, himself a native of Northumberland, and afterwards physician to the Lord Protector Somerset's family, and dean of Wells. After sketching his early career, and stating (as I have already said) that he was born at Willimontswick, now Willowmont, in the Northumbrian language signifying "the Duck of the Rocks," and explaining that he can tell more about him and more certainly than others, "being born in the same country with him, and for many years his collegian in Pembroke Hall, and his opponent in theological exercise," he proceeds :—

"Concerning his memory, and his manifold knowledge of tongues and arts, although I am able to be an ample witness (for he first instructed me in a further knowledge of the Greek tongue), yet, without my testimony, almost all Cantabrigians, to whom he was sufficiently known, will and can testify. How able he was in confuting or overthrowing anything, yet without any boasting or noise of arms, not only I, but all with whom he disputed, easily perceived; unless he understood that they thirsted more after glory than was fit : for those he set himself more vigorously to crush. His behaviour was very obliging, and was pious without hypocrisy, or monkish austerity : for very often he would shoot in the bow, or play at tennis with me. If there were no other witness of his beneficence to the poor, I will testify this to all, that before he was advanced to any ecclesiastical preferments, he carried me along in company with him to the next hospital, and when I had nothing to give to the poor beside what he himself, according to his estate, liberally gave, he often supplied me that I might give too. While he was himself in prison, what aid he sent out of England to us in our exile in Germany, that learned man, his faithful Achates, Dr. Edmund Grindal, now bishop of London, can testify ; and many others who were assisted by his liberality."

I think that Mr. Turner must have seen Nicholas Ridley's power of crushing the vain-glorious in full operation upon a strange but notable occasion in 1532. There was then what Archbishop Tenison calls a *duellum religiosum*, between two young Oxonians and five chosen champions of Cambridge, of whom Ridley was one. The school-doors were broken down by the crowd of students who pressed eagerly to hear the debate, but it did not come to much. The first question upon which the Oxford disputants had prepared themselves and had challenged Cambridge was "Whether the civil law was more excellent than medicine ?" but Throgmorton, who took this for Oxford, was hard pressed, lost his head and never recovered himself. So his fellow-combatant, Ashwell, who had to express the Oxford view of the great question, "Whether a woman, condemned to death, being twice tied up, and the cords both times breaking, ought to be hanged the third time," being in much fear, feigned sickness and so avoided the fight. Oxford expelled the two hot-headed and weak-minded challengers, but I have never been able to understand why a man of Ridley's standing bothered himself at all about so foolish a business.

But whilst Ridley was studying at the Sorbonne and Louvain, and patiently working away at Cambridge, there was great work going on at home and abroad. The years from 1520 to 1535 are perhaps the most momentous in the history of England. I do not allude to our foreign relations, although now, for the first time, we began systematically and generally to interfere in foreign affairs. But, at home, the greatest changes in society, in politics and in religion, were going rapidly forward. We had a king who was popular, for he was a big, handsome fellow, with more pretensions to a little learning and those more justifiable than most English monarchs have had : with also a strong belief in the Roman Catholic faith, and entering, on its behalf, the lists with Luther himself, not perhaps with conspicuous success : a king by nature despotic, wayward, passionate : like many men who are not kings, good-humoured enough when not crossed, and, like them also, best out of his own house. For he was a man who was selfishness itself, and who aimed at the gratification of his own desires at whatever cost to others, even when they were bound to him by the closest ties.

A young friend of mine, being asked at a school examination what was Henry VIII.'s principal occupation, promptly replied "Henry VIII.'s principal occupation was attending to the beheadment of his wives." This is putting the point somewhat more generally than the facts of the case quite justify. Henry's great apologist, Froude, told me that he once overheard a conversation upon the subject between a learned and brilliant lady and Thomas Carlyle. The lady was attacking Froude's conception of the character of the king, but failed to evoke much response from the sage until she brought her denunciations to a head with "Ah, then, Mr. Carlyle, think : he had six wives !" "Ay ! puir faller" was the unexpected and unwelcome reply.

But that is scarcely the last word upon the matter. We English folk gained enormously by it, but Henry's treatment of Catherine of Aragon, after having been married to her for twenty years, and having had many children by her, was as base and bad as her conduct was dignified and noble. What a pathos there is in her words, as reported by her examiners : "She knewe herself the kynge's trewe wief ; she sayde that she hath alwaies demeaned herself well and truly towards the kynge, and if it can be proved that other in wryting to the pope or to any other she hath other styrred or procured any thyng against hys grace or hys realme, she is content to suffer for it. For she sayde that she had done England lytel gode, and the loother she wolde be to do hyt any harme."

The proud king had a proud minister who aimed at making England foremost amongst European powers, and who hoped to bind the king to him by procuring him the divorce from Catherine which he so eagerly desired as his eye was already upon her successor. I shall not dwell upon this unsavoury bit of history. The attempt cost Cardinal Wolsey dear, as indeed was but right. But he was a great statesman, the first of our great statesmen, and he nearly succeeded in destroying our constitutional government. Happily he promised Henry that he would obtain a divorce for him from the pope himself, and was not able to perform his promise.

It was not an unnatural mistake, for, at this time, divorce was very much in the air, and dispensations were not always difficult to obtain. Henry had, of course, obtained one which enabled him to marry his brother Arthur's widow. But both of his sisters had curious matrimonial experiences. The elder of them, Margaret, when her first husband, James IV. of Scotland, died, married a married man, the earl of Angus, whom she shamefully deceived, and from whom she was afterwards divorced and married Harry Stewart, a son of Lord Evendale, who became Lord Methuen, and ill-treated her, and from whom she obtained a divorce. The younger sister, Mary, had married Louis XII. of France, and, almost directly he died, married her old lover, Sir Charles Brandon, afterwards duke of Suffolk, who, being engaged to Mrs. Ann Brown, broke his troth and married Lady Mortimer, but was divorced from her and then returned to Mrs. Brown, who died in time for him to marry the widowed Queen Mary. Well might brave Hugh Latimer warn poor little Edward VI. : " For the love of God, take an order for marriages here in England. For here is marriage for pleasure and voluptuousness, and for goods ; and so that they may join land to land, and possessions to possessions, they care for no more here in England. And that is the cause of so much adultery, and so much breach of wedlock in the noblemen and gentlemen, and so much divorcing. And it is not now in the noblemen only, but is come to the inferior sort. Every man, if he have but a small cause, will cast off his old wife, and take a new one, and will marry again at his pleasure ; and there be many that have done so."

The fall of Wolsey brought the elevation of Thomas Cromwell to power as the king's adviser, and he it was who engineered the Reformation in England as a revenge for the pope's refusal of a divorce. Henry, the Defender of the Faith, was to deny the supremacy of the pope, to declare himself the head of the Church, and to obtain a divorce from his own courts. And this was done. The Parliament, which Wolsey had thrust aside, was now regularly summoned : it supported Henry's every move, and in 1534, passed the Act of Supremacy, by which the king became "on earth Supreme Head of the Church of England."

Nicholas Ridley had his own part to play in these matters. He was senior proctor of the university when the question of the king's supremacy came before it to be examined upon the authority of Scripture. It was thoroughly discussed, and the decision signed on the 2nd May, 1534, in the name of the university by the vice-chancellor and the two proctors, was " That the bishop of Rome hath no more authority and jurisdiction derived to him from God in this kingdom of England, than any other foreign bishop." It is worth noting that the university of Paris had come to a similar conclusion.

You will at once see how far-reaching this breach with Rome must immediately become. Whenever two bodies which have been in close communion separate, it is as when two ships are lying side by side moored to a quay, and one is loosed from its moorings. For a few seconds it lingers, as though regretfully, by its companion ; for a few minutes there may be hurried communications between their passengers or crews, and then a great gulf separates them for ever.

All was changed when the pope ceased to have authority. Men's minds had long been troubled about many matters of religious belief. The king had no wish for more alterations in that direction than were absolutely necessary for his purpose. Persons who rashly presumed to express what he chose to look upon as heretical doctrines were burned by this arch-heretic himself without the least compunction. Nothing in the history of religion is more instructive than the tendency which the persecuted have usually shown to become the persecutors so soon as they got the chance. Nothing in the history of England is more extraordinary than the way in which an imperious monarch and devoted son of the Church became against his will the instrument for destroying the authority of that Church when it stood in the way, not of his power, not of his political aims, but of his inclination. But he was to be as arbitrary in matters of religion as in all others. He promoted the suppression of the monasteries, and benefited largely by the confiscation of their goods ; he permitted the publication of the Bible in English, and commanded that there should be a copy in every parish church ; but when the Protestants presumed upon his altered attitude, and pushed changes roughly, rapidly, and rudely forward, he soon showed them where he really was. So late as 1539 he had the famous Six Articles Act carried through Parliament, which enforced the chief points which the men of thought were troubled about, under the penalties of forfeiture of property for the first offence of speaking or writing against them, and of death for the second offence.

The first of these Articles is perhaps the only one which I need particularise, for it was upon that that the battle between Catholics and Protestants was ultimately fought out, or it might be better to say that it furnished the test which was the most readily applied to supposed unbelievers, and contained the doctrine which cost many good men their lives in Henry VIII.'s reign as well as in Mary's. This Article enacted " that the natural body and blood of Jesus Christ were present in the Blessed Sacrament," and that " after consecration there remained no substance of bread and wine, nor any other but the substance of Christ."

But, at the time of which we are speaking, this was yet in conformity with the belief of most religious men. It expressed the accepted belief, and the punishment of death was the accepted short way with unbelievers. And there was great discontent in many parts of the country, especially in the North, with the rupture with Rome and the religious reforms introduced. This culminated in 1536, in the rising known as Pilgrimage of Grace in which the whole nobility of the North united, and which was crushed out with relentless severity. Even some of the men to whom we now look as leaders in the English Reformation had, as yet, given but little real consideration to this and kindred matters. Let us see the position which Nicholas Ridley took, and how he came to assume it.

He had become public orator and chaplain to the university in 1534. Hugh Latimer had filled the office of chaplain at a somewhat earlier period. He and Ridley must have been well acquainted, although there is no record of any special friendship between them in those days. Latimer began life as an earnest Roman Catholic and an opponent of the new learning, attacking Luther and Melancthon with much vigour. But, when of mature years, he had come under the influence of Thomas Bilney, who was a learned man and a zealous reformer, and who was burned for his advocacy of the new doctrines in 1531. He now, to use his own words, " began to smell the word of God, and to forsake the school of doctors and such fooleries."

Latimer is, to my mind, the most interesting character of the

English Reformation. He had much learning, great courage, and, as a preacher, had that rare gift of plain speaking and racy homely illustration which has always given its possessor the art of finding his way directly to the hearts of his hearers. He had, too, the dangerous gift of irony, and was original and eloquent, but his great power lay in his simple earnestness. Ridley was more of the finished scholar : Cranmer was the statesman, and with something of the man of the world. In personal character Ridley was as high as Latimer, as pure, as true, as firm, as loyal to conviction. Cranmer's personal character was on a lower plane altogether. He had much wider opportunities, and played a more conspicuous part, showing, from time to time, remarkable firmness and even courage. But he had the statesman's love of power and desire to win, and, statesmanlike, would endeavour to adapt principles to circumstances, instead of compelling circumstances to give way to principles.

Ridley was brought into close contact with Cranmer, for, in 1537, he was appointed one of the archbishop's chaplains, and speedily became one whom he delighted to honour. And, indeed, our good Northumbrian scholar must have been a truly lovable man. His gentle and refined countenance, his manly carriage, his deep learning, his purity and piety, his power as a disputant, and his simple eloquence, soon won for him a great reputation as a preacher, and it is said that people came from great distances in such numbers to hear him that the surrounding churches were all but deserted.

At this time it is possible that he was less of a Reformer than either Latimer or Cranmer, but, when the Act of the Six Articles was passed, and in spite of the severity of its penalties, Ridley preached against it from his pulpit. The archbishop had made him vicar of Herne in East Kent. Cranmer himself opposed the Bill stoutly in the House of Lords and was well supported by Latimer, who, when it passed into law, resigned the see of Worcester to which he had been appointed four years previously, and soon afterwards he was cast into the Tower of London where he lay for six years.

When, in Edward VI.'s brief reign, the Council would have restored him to his bishopric, he refused, because in his old age he would not be entangled with the cares and honours of the world.

Ridley remained in his parish of Herne for two years, and then took the degree of Doctor of Divinity, being shortly afterwards elected the Master of his old college, Pembroke Hall, " a notable, remarkable, and precious college, shining wonderfully amongst all the other places of the university," as Henry VI.'s charter declares ; "an ancient and religious house " as it was styled upon Queen Elizabeth's visit. Its new Master, in the touching farewell which he penned when he was sentenced to death, says of it : " Thou wert ever named since I knew thee, to be studious and well learned, and a great setter forth of God's true word. So I found thee, and blessed be God ! so I left thee indeed. In thy orchard (the walls, butts, and trees, if they could speak would bear me witness) I learned without book almost all Paul's Epistles, and the canonical epistles too, save only the Apocalypse. Of which study, although in time a great part did depart from me, yet the sweet smell thereof, I trust, I shall carry with me into heaven : for the profit thereof I think I have felt in all my lifetime ever after. And of late (whether they abide there now or no, I cannot tell) there were, who did the like. The Lord grant that this zeal and love toward that part of God's word, which is a key and true commentary to all Holy Scripture, may ever abide in that college, so long as the world shall endure."

Honours now came rapidly to Ridley. The king made him one of his chaplains, and he became a prebend of Canterbury and afterwards of Westminster. But with honours came troubles. Looking at the spirit more than at the letter, Ridley had reached the conclusion that, when people met to pray to God and to sing to His praise, it might not be undesirable that they should know what they were about. He had translated the " Te Deum " of S. Ambrose for the use of his own congregation at Herne, and he now maintained that prayer should be made in a language which the people understood, and not in an unintelligible tongue, "for so it were but babbling." He warned his hearers against ceremonies, " beggarly ceremonies " as he called them, and, whilst he held that confession was useful as enabling one who had transgressed to obtain secret and faithful counsel, he openly said that he could find no warrant in Scripture for its being necessary to salvation.

These things may seem to us strangely retrograde for an advanced thinker, but we must always bear in thought what a tremendous thing even a little change of belief is to the religious mind, and how much we are influenced in all such matters by early training, prejudice, and prepossessions, and by the mental atmosphere by which we are surrounded. I have small patience with the habit of treating as petty puerilities beliefs which have been earnestly entertained by the wise and good of many centuries, and, although to us they may seem impossible, yet we must give credit to those who hold them for the like honesty and integrity which we claim for ourselves. It was at a time when change in these matters meant peril, persecution, and very possibly death; when the great, the wise, and the enormous majority were on the other side, that Ridley dared to go past the traditions of the Fathers and appeal to " Cristes lore and his Apostles twelve."

He was, in fact, in great danger by so doing. The king had for some time adopted the plan of playing off the supporters of the old learning, and those of the new learning, against each other. Gardiner, the bishop of Winchester, who had beaten Cromwell, was anxious also to beat Cranmer, and resolved to strike at him through his friend and chaplain, Nicholas Ridley, Dr. Lancelot Ridley, his cousin (who was a preacher at Canterbury Cathedral), and two others. So articles were preferred to the justices in Kent, alleging against Nicholas Ridley his wicked views on confession, ceremonies, and the use of Englished hymns; and, in due time, with a book of charges against the arch-bishop, they were laid before the king.

"The king put the Book of Articles into his sleeve, and went to divert himself upon the river; ordering the bargemen to row towards Lambeth." There he called the archbishop into the barge and showed him the Book of Articles against him and his chaplains. Cranmer boldly acknowledged that he was still opposed to the Six Articles, but had done nothing against them. Then the king asked him if his grace's bedchamber could stand the scrutiny of that Act ? He frankly confessed that he had a wife: but that he had sent her to Germany upon the passing of that Act. This pleased the king, who saw through the malicious design of the accusers, and he appointed a commission to examine into the matter, but particularly to sift out who was at the bottom of the accusation. The archbishop himself was chief com-missioner. The whole facts of the shameful conspiracy were ascer-tained; the accomplices were punished; and Gardiner obtained practical understanding of the text—"The wicked hath digged a pit, and hath fallen into it himself." During the remainder of Henry's reign, Ridley was left at peace.

But he was always learning, always thinking, always searching the Scriptures, and was about to step forward as the leader of reformed religion upon the most important question of transubstantiation. He retired in 1545 to his vicarage in Kent, apparently to meditate upon this matter, which was, at the time, occasioning warm and bitter controversy upon the continent of Europe amongst Catholics and

Protestants alike. Luther himself held the Catholic or traditional view. Cranmer had advocated it so recently as 1538. Zuinglius had differed from Luther, and, in 1524, published his views at Zurich. He and his followers declared that, whilst distinguishing between the signs and the things which they signified, they meant not to separate the reality from the signs : but believed that all, who by faith embraced the promises then offered to them, did spiritually receive Christ with his spiritual gifts.

It was a thorny and a dangerous subject to meddle with, but Ridley thought it out, saw reason to leave the views which he had held upon the matter, and then, probably in 1546, bravely brought his position before Cranmer, who, knowing the true-hearted, pious, and deeply-learned man he had to deal with, and having had good reason to respect his sincerity and sound judgment, went into the whole matter with the greatest care, and was convinced that Ridley was right. In the following year, he brought brave old Bishop Latimer to a similar conclusion.

This was the turning-point of the English Reformation. That year of quiet retirement at Herne ; the perusal of a little work written on the subject by Bertram, a monk of Corbey, about 840, at the instigation of the king of France, Charles the Bald ; and deep meditation upon the Scriptural writings, and those of the early Fathers ; had led Ridley to change his belief. He himself, when brought, in after years, to trial for his faith, said of this change, "plainly to confess the truth of these things ye now demand of me, I *have* thought otherwise in times past than now I do, yet (I call God to witness I lie not) I have not altered my judgment, as now it is, either by constraint of any man or law, either for the fear of any dangers of this world, either for any hope of commodity, but only for the love of the truth revealed unto me by the grace of God (as I am undoubtedly persuaded) in His holy word, and in the reading of the "ancient Fathers."

The end of Henry VIII.'s long reign was rapidly drawing near. He had set forces in motion which he was, with all his despotic authority, powerless to control. The great mass of the nation probably disliked most of the changes which had been slowly introduced, and was quite satisfied with the better understanding of that which they heard at church. Even this may be going somewhat far. Tennyson expresses that which was a widespread feeling then, and is so still, in his " Northern Farmer " :—

An' ah hallus comed to's choorch afoor moy Sally was dĕad,
An' 'eerd un a bummin awaay loike a buzzard-clock, ower may yĕad,
An' ah nivver knawed what n mĕaned, but ah thowt a 'ad summat to sǎay,
An' ah thowt a sǎaid wot a owt to a said, an' ah coomed awǎay.

But the Reformers were learned, able and resolute, and, though they
made many mistakes, they had to go through tribulations which
hallowed their cause, and made it certain of success.

Henry VIII.'s death was a powerful relief to them. His successor was a sickly boy of nine years of age, who, as he grew older,
showed the Tudor firmness (which in a subject would have been called
obstinacy) and held the curious charm of kingship which places it
above the necessity of knowledge. Yet, when the mists of courtier
adulation are cleared away, we find in this boy, who died at fifteen,
observation and thoughtfulness beyond his years. He was intensely
Protestant. One of the first acts of his reign was to have a Royal
Visitation throughout the kingdom which was divided into six circuits,
visitors being specially chosen for each, to be attended by some eminent
preacher who should expound the principles of religion. The northern
circuit included the dioceses of York, Durham, Carlisle, and Chester,
and Ridley was the preacher appointed for it.

Among the things enjoined upon clergymen were the teaching and
preaching in English ; the giving up of processions, and the use of
candles ; the doing away with the disposal of livings by simoniacal
pactions ; and the taking down of images. Ridley was in advance
of us.

He was made bishop of Rochester on the 25th September, 1547,
and was raised to the see of London and Westminster (then united for
the first time) in 1550, his patent being for life instead of, as was
usual, during the king's pleasure. Let me read you what his manner
of life at this time was. We are told that—" He, using all kind of
ways to mortify himself, was given to much prayer and contemplation ;
for duly every morning, so soon as his apparel was done upon him,
he went forthwith to his bed-chamber, and there upon his knees prayed
the space of half an hour ; which, being done, immediately he went to
his study, if there came no other business to interrupt him, where he
continued till ten of the clock, and then came to the common prayer,
daily used in his house. The prayers being done he went to dinner,
where he used little talk, except otherwise occasion by some had been
ministered, and then it was sober, discreet, and wise, and sometimes
merry, as cause required.

" The dinner done, which was not very long, he used to sit an hour or thereabouts, talking or playing at the chesse ; that done, he returned to his study, and there would continue, except suitors or business abroad were occasion of the contrary, until five of the clock at night, and then would come to common prayer, as in the forenoon : which being finished, he went to supper, behaving himself there as at his dinner before. After supper recreating himself in playing at chesse the space of an hour, he then would return again to his study, continuing there till eleven of the clock at night, which was his common hour to go to bed, there saying his prayers upon his knees, as in the morning when he rose.

" Being at his manor of Fulham, as divers times he used to be, he read daily a lecture to his family at the common prayer, beginning at the Acts of the Apostles, and so going through all the Epistles of St. Paul, giving every man that could read a New Testament" (a costly gift in those days), " hiring them beside with money to learn by heart certain principal chapters, especially Acts xiii." (where Paul and Barnabas go to the Gentiles), " reading also unto his household often-times Psalm ci." (which begins " I will sing of mercy and judgment"), " being marvellous careful over his family that they might be a spectacle of all virtue and honesty to others. To be short, as he was godly and virtuous himself, so nothing but virtue and godliness reigned in his house, feeding them with the food of our Saviour, Jesus Christ."

I should mention that, just about this time, one of those events occurred which show that the persecution to death of so-called heretics was not confined to Roman Catholics. A Kentish woman, Joan Bocher, was tried for rejecting an express article of the creed, that Christ was born of the Virgin Mary, and was delivered over to the secular arm, the euphuism employed for the sentence of being burned to death. Archbishop Cranmer and Hugh Latimer were two of the parties to this evil judgment. To his honour be it told that King Edward could hardly be induced by the archbishop to sign the sentence. Cranmer tried hard to persuade Joan to recant. Bishop Ridley took her to his own house, and pleaded earnestly with her but in vain, and so she was burned. It is a melancholy story, but one which may not be concealed. I cannot hold Ridley guiltless in this matter, and it certainly weakens the force of the condemnation with which we visit the dreadful persecution to which Queen Mary after-wards subjected the Protestants who, indeed, in their time of triumph committed many deplorable excesses.

But we next see Bishop Ridley in a much more favourable light. Soon after he became its bishop, London was visited by the dreaded plague: multitudes fell a prey to the fell disease; weeping and lamentation were everywhere to be heard. The rich and powerful who might, by timely attention to the simplest sanitation, have done much to avert the calamity, fled headlong from the scene of danger and death. Ridley stuck bravely to his post, expostulating with such of his clergy as feared to do their duty, and stimulating them to act worthily by his own faithful and well-directed labours.

"Never," says Foxe, "was good child more singularly loved of his dear parents, than he of his flock and diocese. Every holy day and Sunday he preached in some one place or other, except he were otherwise letted by weighty affairs and business: to whose summons the people resorted—swarming about him like bees, and courting the sweet flowers and wholesome juice of the fruitful doctrines which he did not only preach, but showed the same by his life, as a glittering lanthorn to the eyes and senses of the blind, in such pure order and chastity of life . . . that even his very enemies could not reprove him in any one jot thereof."

All this time the reformed doctrines were making steady progress, and the bishops were hard at work upon the Anglican liturgy, which they at length brought nearly into its present condition, when, in spite of imperfections, it must be admired by men of all creeds for felicity of expression, simplicity and beauty of thought, and the spirit of earnest faith and piety which it breathes throughout. The form of Common Prayer was confirmed by Act of Parliament in 1552, and it came into use on the 1st of November, when Bishop Ridley expounded it at Paul's Cross to a great audience, of whom the lord mayor and corporation of London formed part. The fact that his address lasted five hours and a half speaks volumes for the ability of the preacher and the exemplary patience of his audience.

In this year the bishop had a peculiarly interesting interview with the Lady Mary at her house at Hundsdon. She was pleased with his civility, and entertained him with very pleasant discourse for a quarter of an hour, telling him that she remembered him at court, when he was chaplain to her father, and mentioning a sermon which he had preached, and which had apparently impressed her. After dinner she sent for him again, but, when he asked her permission to preach before her on the next Sunday, she entirely refused. They had a long discussion, during which she became angry, and at length dismissed him with the words, "My lord, for your civility in coming to see me I thank you : but for your offering to preach before me I thank you not a whit."

The young king, early in 1553, fell sick, and his sickness could not be subdued. I cannot but think that he had to listen to far more preaching than was good for him, but one sermon which Ridley preached to him bore excellent fruit. In it the bishop took occasion to enlarge on the beauty of true charity, and upon the bounden duty of men in high places to be eminent in good works. "The same day the king sent for the bishop privately into the gallery at Whitehall, where he caused him to sit in a chair by him, and would not permit him to remain uncovered :" but, thanking him for his counsel, he begged him to direct him how he might best discharge his duty in this respect. The good bishop was greatly delighted and much affected by this entreaty, and, after consulting the lord mayor and several of the leading citizens of London, he proposed to the king that he should found three institutions : first, a home for young fatherless children ; second, an asylum for the sick and wounded ; and, third, a workhouse for the deliberately idle and thriftless. This the king gladly carried out, giving, for the education and maintenance of the first class, one of the most famous buildings in London, the Grey Friars' Church, near Newgate Market, with all the revenues thereunto belonging ; for cure and relief of the second class, he gave St. Bartholomew's, near Smithfield ; for correction of the third, he appointed "his house at Bridewell, the antient mansion of many English kings." He added 750 marks yearly out of the rents of the Savoy, and filled in with his own hand the blank left in the charter, for "lands to be afterward received in mortmain to a yearly value," with the words "four thousand marks by year." And so we got the Blue Coat or Christ's Hospital, St. Bartholomew's and St. Thomas's Hospitals, and Bridewell ; the first of which has just taken a new lease of life, and the second yet flourishes, both being monuments of the goodness of Edward and the enlightened wisdom of Ridley.

About this time, although he was not actually appointed, Ridley was named to succeed to the bishopric of Durham. But the end of Edward's brief reign had come, and the charters of his new and noble institutions were scarcely dry, when "this excellent young prince" breathed his last. There is much which is false and fulsome in the panegyrics which were poured out upon him, both during his life and at his death, but there can be no doubt that this youth who had just attained fifteen years of age had really great parts, and was innately of a true kingly disposition.

His death was a terrible blow to the Reformers, who vainly tried to keep Mary from ascending the throne. Ridley was one of Lady Jane Grey's stoutest supporters, and preached at Paul's Cross in her favour, but was listened to with impatience. The people wanted Mary, although she soon found out that the popular views about religious heresy were widely different from hers. It was on the 6th July, 1553, that Edward died, on the 19th Mary was proclaimed queen, and Bishop Ridley, who was one of the four persons specially exempted from the general pardon which she extended to all others, was conveyed as prisoner to the Tower of London on July 26th. . He was followed there, within two months, by Latimer and Cranmer.

There was an idea abroad in the minds of some of the leading Catholics that Ridley could be brought round to their views upon transubstantiation, and he was treated with much civility whilst in the Tower. He had learned arguments with the chief justice, the dean of St. Paul's, and others, but what were of prime importance were the meetings which he had with his brother prisoners, but especially with grand old Latimer, at which they strengthened each other in the faith, bringing forward and carefully sifting their advanced opinions so that they might be more completely prepared to confound their adversaries when the day of fierce searching came. The three men who were to be martyred also spent much time in reading the New Testament together, John Bradford joining them, and, by searching the Scriptures, they armed each other in defence of the truth. His biographer well says : " In short, all through his life,. never man used more serious industry to acquaint himself with the truth, than this truly Christian bishop did, and when assured, no man ever showed more resolution in maintaining it."

In March, 1554, Ridley, Cranmer, and Latimer were taken to Oxford, where they were confined in the loathsome prison called Bocardo. An ecclesiastical commission was formed to try the prisoners for heresy, and Ridley was brought before it on the 12th April. Three questions were framed by convocation to be disputed on this occasion :—1st, Whether the natural body of Christ was really in the sacrament; 2nd, Whether any other substance did remain, after the words of consecration, than the body and blood of Christ ; and, 3rd, Whether in the mass there was a propitiatory sacrifice for the sins of the dead and living ? There were thirty-three commissioners; nine appointed by convocation, the chancellor, vice-chancellor, professors, and doctors of the university of Oxford, and the vice-chancellor (who had succeeded Ridley as the head of Pembroke Hall), and six other representatives of Cambridge. Each of the so-called heretics was questioned, in the first place, what he thought of the doctrines alleged by the questions, and, when he declared that they were false, a day was appointed for a solemn disputation upon them. Old Latimer was brought in, with a handkerchief and two or three caps on his head, his spectacles hanging by a string at his breast, and a staff in his hand, and told them that he was so old and infirm that he was as meet to be captain of Calais as to dispute; but he had read the New Testament, which he held in his hand, seven times over deliberately, and yet could find no mass in it, neither the marrow-bones nor the sinews of it.

The disputation, when it came off, was a one-sided affair. Ridley had fourteen disputants opposed to him, and he was hardly treated by them. Ridley himself compared them to stage-players in interludes or disorderly students of the Sorbonne, " which, at Paris, I have seen in times past." Those who sat as judges "gave worst example, and did, as it were, blow the trumpet to the rest, to rave, roar, rage, and cry out." The disputants all spoke together, shouted opprobrious taunts, hissed and clapped their hands, and overwhelmed Ridley with hissing, shouting, and reproaches, when he protested that such outrageous disorder little became grave and learned men. He himself wrote of it: " That no person of any honesty could, without blushing, abide to hear such things spoken by a most vile varlet against a most wretched ruffian." And these were thirty-three religious and scholarly men, the chosen of the Church and the universities, trying one who had been the head of a college and a bishop, the chosen adviser of his king, and upon charges which aimed at his life!

Of course, these three good men and true were condemned as heretics, and taken back to prison, where they were treated with the greatest rigour. Ridley spent most of the remaining time he had upon earth in writing to his relatives and friends, to the public bodies with which he had been connected, and to his brother Reformers, both those in prison at home and those who had escaped to the Continent. Books, and, at length, pens, ink, and paper were denied him, but he cut the lead of his prison windows into pencils, and wrote on the margins of such books as he had.

The courage, simplicity, and unselfishness of these letters are only equalled by their wisdom and the beauty of their language. To John Bradford, who was lying in Newgate and hourly expecting the call of the executioner, he wrote: "Brother Bradford, so long as I shall understand thou art in thy journey, by God's grace I shall call upon our heavenly Father to see thee safely home ; and then, good brother, speak you, and pray for the remnant who are to suffer for Christ's sake, according to that thou shalt then know more clearly."

From time to time his mind turns to the home of his childhood, which I think he must have frequently revisited. "In Tynedale, where I was born, not far from the Scottish borders, I have known my countrymen watch night and day in their harness, such as they had, that is, in their jacks, and their spears in their hands (you call them northern gads), especially when they had any privy warning of the coming of the Scots. And so doing, although at every such bickerings some of them spent their lives, yet by such means like pretty men they defended their country." Again, in almost the last letter which he wrote, he says : " Ye know, who be my countrymen dwelling upon the Borders, where (alas !) the true man suffereth oftentimes much wrong at the thief's hand, if it chance a man to be slain of a thief (as it often chanceth there) who went out with his neighbour to help him to rescue his goods again, that the more cruelly he be slain, and the more stedfastly he stuck by his neighbour in the fight against the face of the thief, the more favour and friendship shall all his posterity have for the slain man's sake of all them that be true, as long as the memory of his fact and his posterity doth endure." These surely are precious little peep-holes, as it were, into that lawless Border life which we spoke of in the lecture upon our ballads.

This letter begins : "As a man minding to take a far journey, and to depart from his familiar friends, commonly and naturally hath a desire to bid his friends farewell before his departure ; so likewise now I, looking daily when I should be called for to depart hence from you, O all ye my dearly beloved brethren and sisters in our Saviour, Christ, that dwell here in this world, having a like mind towards you all ; and also, blessed be God for this ! such time and leisure, do bid you all, after such manner as I can, farewell."

And then follow such sweet and gentle leave-takings : " My dear brother George Shipside, whom I have found in the time of my cross most friendly and stedfast, and in God's cause ever hearty : my dear sister Alice, his wife, to whom God hath given a godly and loving husband : my well-beloved brother, John Ridley of the Walltown, and you my gentle and loving sister Elizabeth ; your daughter Elizabeth whom I love for the meek and gentle spirit which God hath given her : my well-beloved sister of Unthanke, with all your children, my nephews, and nieces : since the departure of my brother Hugh, my mind was to have been unto them in the stead of their father, but the Lord God must and will be their Father, if they will love Him and fear Him : my well-beloved and worshipful cousins, Master Nicholas Ridley of Willimontswick, and your wife." And then he addresses Cambridge, his loving mother and tender nurse, and Pembroke Hall, " of late mine own college, my cure and my charge," Herne, his first cure, Canterbury and Westminster, of the sees of which he was once a member ; Rochester, once his cathedral see, and then "Oh, London, London ! to whom now may I speak in thee, or whom shall I bid farewell ? " The whole of this lengthy and touching epistle is worthy of careful perusal.

The sentence which had been passed upon the three bishops was void, as the pope's authority in England had not been revived at the time, so they were to be tried over again. In the meantime Ridley and Latimer were removed from the horrible dungeon of Bocardo to the houses of civic dignitaries, Ridley being taken possession of by no less a personage than the mayor. Here, however, he was little better off. He writes the reason for his being more closely confined than the others to his former chaplain, Grindal, who had fled to Frankfort, and who has left on record how liberally, even when himself in prison, Bishop Ridley assisted the exiles. This part of his letter is in Latin for obvious reasons, but we may give it in English, as we have no reason to fear the curiosity or anger of Mrs. Irish. "I am kept most strait, and with least liberty, either because in the house where I am kept the wife rules the husband (although he is mayor of the city)"— Bishop Ridley was a bachelor—"a morose and most superstitious old woman, and who thinks it for her credit that it should be said of her that she guards me with the utmost caution and restraint : but the man himself, by name Irish, is obliging enough to every body, though truly much too obsequious to his wife. . . . . Either this is the cause, or the higher powers have ordered it ; which is what they tell me when I complain of their excessive severity."

Philip of Spain seems to have read the English character better than his poor, bitterly conscientious, hard-natured spouse, surely one of the most pathetic characters in our history. He was himself an adept in religious persecution, but had the good policy to check it in Mary's case, so long as he remained with her. When his hopes of a happy issue of the marriage died, and he wearied of her and left her, she gave Cardinal Pole *carte blanche*, and, in September, 1555, he issued a commission to the bishops of Gloucester, Lincoln, and Bristol, " to cite, examine, and judge Master Hugh Latimer and Master Dr. Ridley, pretended bishops of Worcester and London, for divers erroneous opinions held by them, and maintained in open disputations had in Oxford in 1554." The trial was held on the 30th of September and 1st of October, but the result was certain from the first. Nicholas Ridley was condemned as an heretic ; adjudged presently both by word and deed to be degraded from the degree of bishop, from priesthood, and all ecclesiastical orders ; declared to be no member of the Church, and therefore committed to the secular powers, of them to receive due punishment according to the tenor of the temporal laws ; and he was further excommunicated by the great excommunication. But he was never tried by the secular powers, and this was his death-sentence, and the only sentence ever passed upon him.

The bishop of Lincoln, who had taken the leading part in the trial, had dealt on the whole gently with Ridley, and, for a fortnight afterwards, great exertions were made to win him back to the church of Rome. His friends, too, tried hard to save him, Lord Dacres, his kinsman, offering Queen Mary ten thousand pounds if she would preserve so valuable a life, and some of the chiefs of his family, probably Lord Dacres himself and his granddaughter Mabyl, who had married Nicholas Ridley of Willimontswick, urged him to save himself. But he was not made of such stuff, and wrote his beloved cousin, gently condemning those who " for fear of trouble, either for loss of goods, will do in the sight of the world those things that they know and be assured are contrary to the will of God." And it was at this time that he wrote also the touching farewell to his friends which I have already described.

On the 15th October the good bishop was degraded from the priestly office with considerable violence and many threats. We must not unduly blame those who treated their noble victim with such harshness. They had done what they could to change him, and his perseverance in the right seemed to them, no doubt, sinful obstinacy. Nor am I inclined to blame the Roman Catholic faith, but rather the system which still obtains amongst Protestants and Catholics alike, of treating that from which we differ in religious matters as error which must be put down and punished, if not now by law, by social ostracism, which for many men is more potent than law.

Ridley and Latimer were to be executed on the following day, the 16th October. Ridley, ever mindful of others, sent a petition to the queen for divers poor men, to whom he had given leases, which his successor, Bishop Bonner, had cancelled. He read this petition to the bishop of Gloucester, and came to this passage : " I have also a poor sister, who came to me out of the North, with three fatherless children, whom, for her relief, I married after to a servant of mine own house : I beseech that her case may be mercifully considered." Here, for the first and only time, his tender affection overcame him, and, for a little space, he could not speak for weeping, but he soon recovered himself, saying, " This is nature that moveth me : but I have now done ; " and then he continued to read his petition.

This all happened in the mayor's house, and, so soon as the company were gone, the good bishop began to prepare himself for his marriage, as he called it, and, at supper, he was so cheerful that even Mrs. Irish shed tears. But he comforted her, saying, " O, Mrs. Irish, you love me not now, I see well enough. For, in that you weep, it doth appear you will not be at my marriage, neither be content therewith. Indeed you be not so much my friend as I thought you had been. But quiet yourself, though my breakfast shall be somewhat sharp and painful, yet I am sure my supper shall be more pleasant and sweet." His brother wished to sit up with him but he would not suffer him, for he said he was minded (God willing) to go to bed, and to sleep as quietly that night as ever he did in his life.

On the fatal morning, he dressed himself in his robes, and walked to the stake between the mayor and one of the aldermen. Being the first to arrive, he engaged in prayer, and, when Latimer came, he ran to him and said, " Be of good heart, brother, for God will either assuage the fury of the flame, or else strengthen us to abide it." They then kneeled down and prayed together. When they rose, Dr. Smith began a sermon to them on the text : . " Though I give my body to be burned and have not charity, it profiteth me nothing." Ridley was not permitted to reply to him, so he made himself ready, giving his clothes among the gentlemen who stood by weeping bitterly. " Happy was he who might get any rag of him." He then stood on a stone, and lifting up his hands towards heaven, he prayed " O heavenly Father, I give unto Thee most hearty thanks for that Thou hast called me to be a professor of Thee, even unto death. I beseech

Thee, Lord God, take mercy upon the realm of England, and deliver it from its enemies."

Then the smith brought an iron chain around the waist of each martyr, and, as he was driving in the staple, Bishop Ridley shook the chain and said to him, "Good fellow, knock it in hard, for the flesh will have its course." His brother wished to tie a small bag of gunpowder round his neck, but this he would not allow until it was also done to Latimer. Ridley, even at such a moment mindful of others, now asked Lord Williams, who was superintending the execution, to urge upon the queen the claims of the poor men to whom he had given leases. A faggot, ready kindled, was next brought and laid at his feet, and then did brave old Latimer say to him, "Be of good comfort, Master Ridley, and play the man. We shall this day light such a candle by God's grace in England as I trust shall never be put out." Ridley cried with an exceeding loud voice, "Into Thy hands, O Lord, I commend my spirit," Latimer praying as earnestly, "O Father of heaven, receive my soul." He received the flame as if embracing it, and soon died with little appearance of pain.

Not so Ridley. On his side, so great a quantity of faggots had been piled upon the furze, that the flame could not get through but burned fiercely beneath. In his agony, he prayed the onlookers to let the fire come to him, but his poor brother, not seeing what was really the matter, quite covered him with more wood, so that, before the fire could touch the vital parts, his lower members were consumed. Yet, in this fierce torment, he continued to pray : "Lord have mercy upon me : let the fire come to me : I cannot burn"; and, at last, a by-stander, with his bill, pulled off the upper faggots, and the tortured martyr writhed into the flames which sprang up to meet him, and he was at rest.

Thanks be to God, the candle that day lighted burns amongst us still.

MARK AKENSIDE.

LECTURE V.

MARK AKENSIDE.

I observed, in my first lecture, that our county has never since the old English days produced a poet of the first rank. But a poet was born to us towards the beginning of last century who gained a certain place amongst the bards of that somewhat unpoetical age, and whom we must spend some time over, although he is more interesting because of the questions which the place he occupies gives rise to than because of his own merits.

Mark Akenside was born at the Butcher Bank in Newcastle, on the 9th November, 1721. The house of his birth has been pulled down, and the Butcher Bank of his and our youth is now Akenside Hill. He was a Grammar School boy for some time, but received the most of his primary education at a private school. His father wished to see him "wag his head in a pulpit," and, by the aid of admiring friends, sent him to Edinburgh University where he might obtain the requisite learning. But Mark Akenside had already dallied with the muses, and now deserted the pulpit for the pill-box. He became a medical student, medicine being more congenial to poetry than divinity—at all events at the beginning of the 18th century.

> And why should this be thought so odd?
> Can't he write rhymes who cures a phthysic?
> Of poetry though patron god,
> Apollo patronizes physic.

When Akenside returned to Newcastle in 1742, he was a surgeon, and it is said that he practised here for two years, but he was busy with the first cast of his chief poem, *The Pleasures of the Imagination*, which he succeeded in selling to Dodsley for £120 in 1743, and that celebrated publisher brought it out in the following year.

It is a portentous title and a portentous poem, but, before I speak of it in any detail, let us see how such a poem became possible.

For each age has its own way of singing, its own poetic method, and one age's poetic meat is another's poison. A didactic poem has about as much chance of finding readers in this society to-day as a singer who chanted an incident of the Chitral war in sixty-eight four-lined verses would have of finding a Town Hall audience to listen to him. But there was a time, and a time of thought and action, when no other form of poetry had much of a chance. Let me add that there is little advantage to be gained by discussing whether the poems produced at that time were poetry at all or not. Such discussions have no end. Each reader must be his own judge in all matters of this kind. He pays his money for the book he wants, and takes his choice of it.

I need scarcely say that I speak of poetry which is purely and simply didactic, the end, aim, and object of which is the giving of instruction or appearing to give it. In one sense, all true poetry is didactic, but the teaching is in the poetry itself as the sap is in the living tree : in the didactic poetry of which I speak, there is no sap— only the cut and dried wood.

The didacticism to which I refer was the attempt to reduce the efforts of the imagination to fixed rule, and thus the ancient classical writers became the standard for the altered state of poetic endeavour.

I might, if time permitted, go back to a very early date and show how didactic poetry was evolved from the love-songs of the troubadours, but time happily does not allow it, and I should only have started then *in medias res* after all. But I may safely begin with the influence which the French writers of the classical Renaissance had upon English verse, for we can trace this influence directly. The revival of classical learning had, in France, the effect of making the form of greater consequence than the spirit of poetry. The men who wrote verse thought more of the way in which a thing was said than of what they had to say. They set before themselves as models the great classical writers, and dreamed that they could make their own language conform to the rules which those writers had observed. This movement began in the middle of the sixteenth century with a group of seven authors, who received the name of the "Pléiade" after the well-known constellation, Ronsard being the brightest star of the constellation. They were nothing if not artificial. They were "the padded men who wore the stays," and the stays and padding destroyed all natural movement and freedom for them and for those who followed them for nearly two centuries.

Rare Ben Jonson saw through the folly and danger of such writing. How refreshingly he lays down the true doctrine : "Nothing is lasting that is feigned ; it will have another face than it had ere long. As Euripides saith, no lie ever grows old."

Not when we look at the life of the literary world, but, as the lives of men go, a good many lies attain to quite a respectable age before they are found out.

Ronsard had great merit, and the best of his followers was Du Bartas, a Gascon, whose *Création du Monde* has been described by Henri Van Laun as "the marriage-register of science and verse, written by a Gascon Moses, who, to the minuteness of a Walt Whitman and the unction of a parish-clerk, added an occasional dignity superior to anything attained by the abortive epic of his master." He came to England, and James I., who was one of his translators, tried hard to keep him at his court. Joshua Sylvester became briefly famous or notorious chiefly because of his translations of Du Bartas' verses ; and John Dryden writes : "I remember, when I was a boy, I thought inimitable Spenser a mean poet in comparison of Sylvester's Du Bartas, and was wrapt into an ecstasy when I read these lines :—

> Now, when the winter's keener breath began
> To crystallize the Baltic ocean ;
> To glaze the lakes, to bridle up the floods,
> And periwig with snow the bald-pate woods.

But there soon sprang up in France men who saw the absurdity of the extravagances to which this love of words for their own sake led : men like Molière who lashed the fashionable blue-stockings, *Les Précieuses*, with merciless satire, and, above all, his friend Boileau, who, fighting fiercely against the degradation of taste, still fastened faster the classical shackles upon French and English poetry alike. His *Art of Poetry*, indeed, attacked the petty puerilities to which I have alluded, but it was to the writers of Greece and Rome that he turned as the great examples of what good poetry must be, even for other days and other lands.

The French didactic school began its work nearly two centuries before ours. Dryden was greatly influenced by it, but it was Pope who first came fully under its sway. The trivialities of that school found an echo in smaller men ; our poet, Akenside, was strongly influenced by the classicism preached by Boileau. In his account of the design of *The Pleasures of the Imagination*, he expressly says that "he had two models ; that antient and simple one of the first Grecian poets, as it is refined by Virgil in the 'Georgics,' and the familiar epistolary way of Horace. . . . Yet, after all, the subject before us, tending almost constantly to admiration and enthusiasm, seemed rather to demand a more open, pathetic and figured style. This, too, appeared more natural, as the author's aim was not so much to give formal precepts, or enter into the way of direct argumentation, as by exhibiting the most ingaging prospects of nature, to enlarge and harmonize the imagination, and by that means insensibly dispose the minds of men to a similar taste and habit of thinking in religion, morals, and civil life."

I scarcely know how to describe the *Pleasures of the Imagination*, that long and wearisome poem which Dr. Johnson declared that he had never been able to read through. But it achieved a remarkable popularity. It went through many editions, and was translated into French and Italian. Akenside's French critics, indeed, had an amazingly high opinion of his style. One of them speaks of the poem as "un des plus beaux monuments de la poésie Anglaise," though he adds, "il est cependant moins lu qu'il n'est admiré." But he goes on to say, "Il est écrit en vers blancs, comme la poème de Milton ; et Akenside a peut-être mieux connu que Milton même l'harmonie propre à ce genre de poésie." There is much virtue in that "peut-être." .

In the first book of 604 lines, he introduces his subject, and speaks (with truth) of the difficulty of dealing with it poetically. He then treats of the divine mind, the origin of every quality pleasing to the imagination ; the natural variety of constitution in the minds of men, with its final cause ; the idea of a fine imagination, and the state of the mind in the enjoyment of those pleasures which it affords.

> For as old Memnon's image, long renown'd
> By fabling Nilus, to the quivering touch
> Of Titan's ray, with each repulsive string
> Consenting, sounded through the warbling air
> Unbidden strains ; even so did nature's hand
> To certain species of external things,
> Attune the finer organs of the mind :
> So the glad impulse of congenial powers,
> Or of sweet sound, or fair proportion'd form,
> The grace of motion, or the bloom of light,
> Thrills through imagination's tender frame,
> From nerve to nerve : all naked and alive
> They catch the spreading rays : till now the soul
> At length discloses every tuneful spring,
> To that harmonious movement from without
> Responsive.

He goes on to show that "all the primary pleasures of the imagination result from the perception of greatness, or wonderfulness, or beauty in objects. He describes the pleasure which springs from each of these, with its final cause ; applies the connection of beauty with truth and good to the conduct of life ; invites to the study of moral philosophy ; describes the different degrees of beauty in different species of objects, colour, shape, natural concretes, vegetables, animals, and the mind ; passes to the sublime, the fair, the wonderful ; and the connexion of the imagination and the moral faculty ; and ends with an invocation of the genius of Ancient Greece."

I give you this account almost in Akenside's own words. In the second book, he goes on to lament the separation of the works of imagination from philosophy, and the cause of their abuse among the moderns, with the prospect of their re-union under the influence of public liberty. He enumerates accidental pleasures,—those of sense, particular circumstances of the mind, the discovery of truth, the perception of contrivance and design, and the emotion of the passions, —which increase the effect of objects delightful to the imagination. He ends by an allegorical vision, exemplifying in sorrow, pity, terror, and indignation, that all the natural passions partake of a pleasing sensation. The last sixty lines of this book are perhaps the finest amongst the 1,949 of the poem. There are certain of them which deserve to be remembered, *e.g.* :—

> Ask thy own heart ; when at the midnight hour,
> Slow through the studious gloom thy pausing eye
> Led by the glimmering taper moves around
> The sacred volumes of the dead, the songs
> Of Grecian bards, and records writ by fame
> For Grecian heroes, where the present power
> Of heaven and earth surveys the immortal page,
> Even as a father blessing, while he reads
> The praises of his son. If then thy soul,
> Spurning the yoke of these inglorious days,
> Mix in their deeds and kindle with their flame ;
> Say, when the prospect blackens on thy view,
> When, rooted from the base, heroic states
> Mourn in the dust, and tremble at the frown
> Of curst ambition ; when the pious band
> Of youths who fought for freedom and their sires,
> Lie side by side in gore ; when ruffian pride
> Usurps the throne of justice, turns the pomp
> Of public power, the majesty of rule,
> The sword, the laurel, and the purple robe,

To slavish empty pageants, to adorn
A tyrant's walk, and glitter in the eyes
Of such as bow the knee ; when honour'd urns
Of patriots and of chiefs, the awful bust
And storied arch, to glut the coward rage
Of regal envy, strew the public way
With hallow'd ruins ; when the Muse's haunt,
The marble porch where wisdom wont to talk
With Socrates or Tully, hears no more,
Save the hoarse jargon of contentious monks,
Or female superstition's midnight prayer ;
When ruthless rapine from the hand of time
Tears the destroying scythe, with surer blow
To sweep the works of glory from their base ;
Till desolation o'er the grass-grown street
Expands his raven wings, and up the wall,
Where senates once the price of monarchs doom'd,
Hisses the gliding snake through hoary weeds
That clasp the mouldering column ; thus defac'd,
Thus widely mournful when the prospect thrills
Thy beating bosom ; when the patriot's tear
Starts from thine eye, and thy extended arm
In fancy hurls the thunderbolt of Jove
To fire the impious wreath on Philip's brow,
Or dash Octavian from the trophied car ;
Say, does thy secret soul repine to taste
The big distress ?   Or would'st thou then exchange
Those heart-ennobling sorrows for the lot
Of him who sits amid the gaudy herd
Of mute barbarians bending to his nod,
And bears aloft his gold-invested front,
And says within himself, " I am a king,
And wherefore should the clamorous voice of woe
Intrude upon mine ear ?"   The baleful dregs
Of these late ages, this inglorious draught
Of servitude and folly, have not yet,
Blest be the Eternal Ruler of the world !
Defil'd to such a depth of sordid shame
The native honours of the human soul,
Nor so effac'd the image of its sire.

Now, that is undoubtedly a fine passage : good things well said ;
for a young man of two and twenty years, a remarkable performance.
The metre is perfect : each line is smoothness itself : there are ideas.
It is Mark Akenside at his best.

In the third book, he speaks of the charm of observing the temper
and manners of men, even when they are vicious or absurd ; and of the

origin of vice from false representations of the fancy, producing false opinions concerning good and evil. Then he takes up ridicule, and considers its proper use. Upon this, that big bully Bishop Warburton fell foul of him, as he did of every one whom he came across, but found that in the limping, pedantic butcher's son he had caught a Tartar who was able to give him as good as he got. He next describes the operations of the mind in the production of works of imagination, and, after considering the nature and conduct of taste, he concludes with an account of the natural and moral advantages resulting from a sensible and well-informed imagination.

When we look at this poem as a whole we find that, although it abounds in common-place thought expressed in a multitude of high-sounding words, Akenside really had a message to give, and that there is an impressive dignity in the manner in which he gave it. Could he have thrown aside his classical models and been true to himself, he might have done fine work of a certain kind. But he, in common with the best of our didactic poets, danced in fetters which, though he proudly made them for himself, were none the less incumbrances, and " cabined, cribbed, and confined " him at every turn. He forgot that the gods, who form so important a part of the machinery of the great poems of antiquity, were really believed in by the men who wrote them ; that, to them, they were actual entities with power over mankind for good or evil. He replaced them with cold, lifeless, impossible intellectual abstractions, deliberately invented for the special occasion, but not for an instant believed in by the poet or his readers : "indulgent fancy," "genius of human kind," "memory divine," and the like. To him, Shakespere and Waller were almost kindred powers. I think that you will feel how far he fell below the men who, in the same century, did return to nature, if you will patiently consider the lines in which he speaks of the stars of heaven, and of the deeply poetic fact that, since some of these first burst into being, their light has been ever journeying towards us but has not reached us yet, with those in which the true poet, William Cowper, treats of the same theme. Akenside speaks of

> The empyreal waste, where happy spirits hold,
> Beyond this concave heaven, their calm abode ;
> And fields of radiance, whose unfading light
> Has travelled the profound six thousand years,
> Nor yet arrives in sight of mortal things.

Whilst Cowper, in the fifth book of his admirably performed *Task*, breaks forth :—

> Tell me, ye shining hosts,
> That navigate a sea that knows no storms,
> Beneath a vault unsullied with a cloud,
> If from your elevation, whence ye view
> Distinctly scenes invisible to man,
> And systems of whose birth no tidings yet
> Have reach'd this nether world.

They speak two different tongues : one the calm, frigid language of the schools ; the other the speech which men use when they meet in homely converse. The first scarcely moves the reason, the other touches the heart.

In later life Akenside began to re-write his long poem, and completed the first and second books, and the first part of the third and fourth also, but he did not live to finish them. We need not linger over this work of reconstruction, always a difficult and seldom a successful operation. But certain lines near the beginning of the fourth book I must quote, both because they show a timorous approach to actual nature, and because they furnish pleasing evidence of the poet's recollection, in advancing years, of the scenes dear to boyhood.

> Would I again were with you ! O ye dales
> Of Tyne, and ye most ancient woodlands ; where,
> Oft as the giant flood obliquely strides,
> And his banks open, and his lawns extend,
> Stops short the pleased traveller to view
> Presiding o'er the scene some rustic tower
> Founded by Norman or by Saxon hands :
> O ye Northumbrian shades, which overlook
> The rocky pavement and the mossy falls
> Of solitary Wensbeck's limpid stream ;
> How gladly I recall your well-known seats
> Belov'd of old, and that delightful time
> When all alone, for many a summer's day,
> I wander'd through your calm recesses, led
> In silence by some powerful hand unseen.

Akenside wrote a number of odes of considerable merit, as such things go. Indeed, although Dr. Johnson lumped them in one severe condemnation, I am surprised that some of them have not lived and become English classics. Let me bring a few verses of one or two of them before you. In one, on "The use of Poetry," he declares that the award of the bard is more lasting and his rule wider than that of hero or legislator : and compares Lycurgus, the Spartan law-giver, and Pompey, who gave universal sway to Rome, with Homer, whose "reverend page holds empire to the thirtieth age, and tongues and climes obey." Then he comes home to England :—

> And thus when William's acts divine
> No longer shall from Bourbon's line
>   Draw one vindictive vow ;
> When Sidney shall with Cato rest,
> And Russel move the patriot's breast
>   No more than Brutus now.
>
> Yet then shall Shakespeare's powerful art
> O'er every passion, every heart,
>   Confirm his awful throne :
> Tyrants shall bow before his laws ;
> And freedom's, glory's, virtue's cause,
>   Their dread assertor own.

We must make some allowance for the peculiar use of such adjectives as "awful" and "dread" in such connection. At this time, mountains were "horrid piles," and, sometimes, "hideous excrescences." The poet used "awful" then as freely and inappropriately as young people use it now.

Perhaps the finest of his odes is that addressed to the earl of Huntingdon. The following verse has always been a favourite of mine :—

> Mark, how the dread Pantheon stands,
> Amid the domes of modern hands :
> Amid the toys of idle state,
> How simply, how severely great !
> Then turn, and, while each Western clime
> Presents her tuneful sons to Time,
>   So mark thou Milton's name ;
> And add, "Thus differs from the throng
> The spirit which inform'd thy awful song,
> Which bade thy potent voice protect thy country's fame."

The conclusion of the ode is really noble.

> Be thou thine own approver.   Honest praise
>   Oft nobly sways
>   Ingenuous youth ;
> But, sought from cowards and the lying mouth,
> Praise is reproach.   Eternal God alone
> For mortals fixeth that sublime award.
> He, from the faithful records of his throne,
>   Bids the historian and the bard
>   Dispose of honour and of scorn ;
>   Discern the patriot from the slave ;
>   And write the good, the wise, the brave,
> For lessons to the multitude unborn.

Akenside had the lack of humour which is, and has always been, characteristic of our county. I do not wish to argue this point at indefinite length, or to go into the nice distinctions which have been drawn between "wit" and "wut" and humour. I do not think that we have ever had much of either to boast of. We are a serious folk. True, we have plenty of funny stories, but the fun is in the circumstances of the story, not in the story itself. I can best explain my meaning by illustration and contrast. Take the tale of the pitman, who "wasna fou but just was canty," and who got upon the line between Howdon and Percy Main one Saturday night. A train coming up on the same line, and the engine-driver seeing the trespasser when it was too late to stop, the whistle was blown and steam shut-off, but Geordie held on his way and was knocked over the embankment. So soon as the train could be pulled up, every one hurried back to pick up the remains, and when he was lifted on his feet, and had shaken himself, he stammered out : " Eh ! hinnies, diven't tak us up : if ah've hort the injun, ah'll pay for 't."

Now compare this with the angry Scotch maid whose mistress said to her, "Dear me, Tibbie, what are ye so snappish about that you go knocking the things about as ye dust them ? " "Oh, mem, it's Jock." "Well, what has Jock been doing ? " "Oh, he was angry at me, an' mis-ca'd me, an' I said I was just as the Lord had made me, an'——" " Well, Tibbie ? " " An' he said the Lord could ha' had little to do when he made me."

Or take the all-round compliment which the car-driver paid to Lady Zetland when she and Miss Balfour were in the West of Ireland. "Take care, my good man," she said, as he helped her into the car ; "I am not so young as I used to be." "Shure, an' whativer age your leddyship may be, you don't look it."

Remember I am speaking generally. Far be it from me to hint that there is any good thing which cannot be found, at least in samples, in Northumberland. Who has forgotten the brilliant fence between Mr. Justice Bigham and a Tynedale farmer on the trial of a certain election petition—"How long have you lived at Tyne Farm, Mr. Gwillim ? " " Oh ! ever since time immemorial." " What were you doing on the day of the poll ? " " Oh ! only bringing up candec-dates." " Well, that was your brother : where does your brother live now ? " Slowly and with Border pawkiness and caution combined : " Weel, ah doant exacly know : he's deed."

To return to Akenside : he has no humour ; no fun of any kind ;

he never gets off his high horse. We can readily believe that he was not a very pleasant man to meet; he was too conscious of his own superiority. Indeed, the successful literary men of the first half of last century were not conspicuous for sweet reasonableness. But there are many points in his life which tell strongly in his favour. When he determined to follow medicine as his profession, he repaid his father's friends the monies which they had subscribed to send him to Edinburgh as a theological student. When only nineteen years old he was elected a member of the Medical Society of Edinburgh, and became famous as an eloquent speaker. In every way he ripened early, the rapidity of his achievements being quite phenomenal. He went to Holland in April, 1744, and, after making a tour through it, he settled at Leyden for purposes of study, taking his degree as doctor of physic on May 16th of that year. In June he began practice at Northampton, but settled in London in the winter of 1745. He had made a valuable friend in Leyden, Jeremiah Dyson, afterwards clerk to the House of Commons, who generously settled £300 a year upon him, and fitted him up a house in Bloomsbury Square, but, if his friend's design was to afford him leisure for wooing the Muse, he must have been sadly disappointed. Dr. Akenside became a physician in considerable practice, and only occasional verses appeared thenceforward, and at considerable intervals. In 1753, he was made a Fellow of the Royal Society, and was given his doctor's degree at Cambridge ; the following year he became a member of the College of Physicians, giving the Gulstonian lectures before it in 1755, and the Croonian lectures in 1756, the first series being published in the Transactions of the Royal Society in 1757. In January, 1759, he was appointed assistant physician to Christ's Hospital, and chief physician two months later, but he was nearly dismissed from this post on account of his roughness and cruelty to the poor. In 1761, he was chosen one of the physicians to the queen, and became the fashion, but, when only forty-eight years and six months old, he died of putrid fever, after a brief illness.

"One leg of Dr. Akenside," says a contemporary, "was considerably shorter than the other, which was in some measure remedied by the aid of a false heel." I should explain that this lameness was occasioned in early childhood by a blow, accidental or otherwise, from a butcher's cleaver in his father's shop. "He had a pale, strumous countenance, but was always very neat and elegant in his dress. He wore a large white wig, and carried a long sword. He would order the servants (at Christ's Hospital) on his visiting days, to precede him with brooms to clear the way, and prevent the patients from too nearly approaching him." I cannot but think that Mark Akenside was altogether an artificial character, without nobility of disposition, and that the abiding dislike of his humble origin is accountable for much of the stiff priggishness of his character which colours the whole of his life's work.

In all of this he contrasts completely and unfavourably with the next Northumbrian of whom I shall speak, and who is, to me, *facile princeps* amongst the entire group of our modern Northumbrian worthies. As you enter Newcastle from Gateshead by the High Level Bridge, you are confronted, just below Amen Corner, and at the head of that narrow and crooked lane known as the Side, once the principal entrance to our city, by a high, square, brick house bearing the legend "Smoke Harvey's Hand-Spun Brown Twist." In this house (which had been rebuilt but a short time before) Cuthbert Collingwood was born on the 26th September, 1750, says his son-in-law Mr. Newnham Collingwood, following the inscription on the cenotaph in St. Nicholas' Church, but he was baptised on the 24th October, 1748, as the registers of St. Nicholas, quoted by John Clayton in a paper on Lord Collingwood in the thirteenth volume of the *Archæologia Aeliana*, declare.

He was sent to the Royal Grammar School for his education. The Rev. Hugh Moises was then the headmaster, and, amongst the scholars, were two brothers Scott, William and John, one of whom remembered the pretty and gentle boy who was destined, as they were, to achieve greatness. William Scott became Lord Stowell, the founder of the Admiralty law of the whole civilised world, and his decisions are as remarkable for their elegant, classical, and polished diction as for their broad grasp of great principles. John Scott, who was rather younger than Cuthbert Collingwood, became Lord Eldon, the great lord chancellor of England. Hugh Moises must have been a rare schoolmaster, one who could teach and, at the same time, inspire his pupils with confidence and affection. It is pleasant to find the noble admiral, Lord Collingwood, on November 7th, 1806, writing his father-in-law, Mr. J. E. Blackett, with a subscription of £20 "for the monument of my worthy master, Mr. Moises."

The "pretty and gentle boy" had not long to remain under the influence of his worthy master for, when only thirteen years of age, he was sent into the "Shannon" which was commanded by his uncle,

Captain (afterwards Admiral) Brathwaite, who was a kind and true friend to him and took a keen interest in directing his improvement in nautical knowledge. In after life the great admiral used to tell how, when he first joined his ship, as he was sitting alone, weeping for his separation from home, the first lieutenant, pitying the tender years of the poor child, spoke to him so kindly that, in the fulness of his gratitude, he took the officer to his box, and offered him a large slice of the plum-cake which his mother had given him.

When he had become famous, and was pressed for information about his life, he said that it had been a continued service at sea without anything which could be very interesting or entertaining to the public. In this he took too humble a view of his own deeds, but, throughout life, he was one of the rare men who never press their claims, content to do the work and caring little for the fame. He was made a lieutenant in 1775 for his services at the battle of Bunker's Hill. From an early date he and Nelson were close friends. In 1780, he was post-captain in the " Hinchinbroke," a 28 gun frigate, and had a terrible experience on an expedition to the Spanish Main, in which he succeeded Nelson who had fallen dangerously sick of the fever and had to return to England. Collingwood's constitution resisted many attacks, but, in four months, he buried 180 out of his crew of 200 men.

I do not propose to follow the details of his early life. It is from his own letters that I wish to give you a few glimpses of this remarkable man. There are no other letters in our language to be compared with them for simple and direct beauty. I think that Hugh Moises must have had a rare teaching secret, for no other headmaster has ever turned out two such stylists (using the term in its best and biggest sense) as Collingwood and Stowell, but the sailor bears away the palm. He must have been a minute and indefatigable student, and a careful and extensive reader. His brother officers held him even Nelson's superior in seamanship, and his moral character was as lofty as his intellectual ability. No wonder that he was looked upon as the man of all others to whom young men could be safely entrusted, and happy were those who came under that ennobling influence. Let me read you some extracts from a letter which he wrote to one of these in 1787 :—" You may depend on it, that it is more in your own power than in any one else's to promote both your comfort and advancement. A strict and unwearied attention to your duty, and a complaisant and respectful behaviour, not only to your superiors, but to everybody, will ensure you their regard, and the reward will surely come, and I hope soon, in the shape of preferment ; but if it should not, I am sure you have too much good sense to let disappointment sour you. Guard carefully against letting discontent appear in you ; it is sorrow to your friends, a triumph to your competitors, and cannot be productive of any good. . . . Let it be your ambition to be foremost on all duty. Do not be a nice observer of turns, but for ever present yourself ready for everything. . . . I never knew one who was exact not to do more than his share of duty, who would not neglect that, when he could do so without fear of punishment. I need not say more to you on the subject of sobriety, than to recommend to you the continuance of it as exactly as when you were with me. Every day affords you instances of the evils arising from drunkenness. Were a man as wise as Solomon, and as brave as Achilles, he would still be unworthy of trust if he addicted himself to grog. . . . Young men are generally introduced to this vice by the company they keep : but do you carefully guard against ever submitting yourself to be the companion of low, vulgar, and dissipated men : and hold it as a maxim, that you had better be alone than in mean company. . . . Read—let me charge you to read. Study books that treat of your profession, and of history. . . . Thus employed, you will always be in good company. Nature has sown in man the seeds of knowledge ; but they must be cultivated to produce fruit. Wisdom does not come by instinct, but will be found when diligently sought for ; seek her, she will be a friend that will never fail you. . . . Remember, Lane, before you are five and twenty, you must establish a character that will serve you all your life." Collingwood practised that which he preached : of all men he was the most diligent and the least self-assertive.

From 1786 to 1790 he was at home, and in June, 1791, he married Miss Sarah Blackett, daughter of John Erasmus Blackett, then mayor of Newcastle, whose wife was one of the ancient Northumbrian family of Roddam. You remember the rhyming grant, the seal whereof, to attest its truth, King Athelstan bit with his hollow tooth, and which ends :—

> While moor bears moss, and head grows hair,
> A Roddam of Roddam for evermair.

Collingwood made a happy choice. Throughout life he remained his wife's courtly and devoted lover, and his letters to her reveal a character of exquisite tenderness and perfect purity. I cannot too strongly recommend all who do not know them to make the close acquaintance of these beautiful letters.

Two daughters were born to them, Sarah in May, 1792, and Mary Patience in 1793. He saw but little of his children, but, as his letters show, his thoughts were constantly with them, and he watched over their education with loving care. He had settled in Morpeth, and devoted himself to gardening and the joys of domestic life, but, in eighteen months, war with France broke out, and he was appointed captain of the "Prince," Rear-Admiral Bowyer's flagship, removing with him to the "Barfleur," and in June, 1794, taking part in what he speaks of as "a battle unlike anything that perhaps ever happened before, for we had three days' hard fighting before we were crowned with victory, by the total defeat and flight of a fleet superior to our own, and sent out for the express purpose of destroying us." The letter in which he describes the engagement is written to Mr. Blackett, and in it he speaks of cruising for a few days "like disappointed people looking for what they could not find, until the morning of little Sarah's birthday." Then they found the French fleet, and the fighting began. The night before the final battle "was spent in watching and preparation for the succeeding day; and many a blessing did I send forth to my Sarah, lest I should never bless her more. . . . . I observed to the admiral that about that time our wives were going to church, but that I thought the peal we should ring about the Frenchmen's ears would outdo their parish bells."

Here you must allow me to say, once for all, that looking as I do upon all war as absolutely opposed to the spirit of Christ, I cannot understand how so good a man as Collingwood certainly was should entirely fail to see the almost ludicrous incongruity of thoughts like these.

In the rewards which followed this engagement Collingwood was passed over, but his admiral wrote that he did not know a more brave, or capable officer, or one better in all respects. His next engagement was at Cape St. Vincent on the 14th February, 1797, "perhaps the most brilliant action on record" at that time, and Nelson, whose ship, the "Captain," had been relieved by Collingwood in the "Excellent" at a critical moment, wrote him "'a friend in need is a friend indeed' was never more truly verified than by your most noble and gallant conduct yesterday in sparing the 'Captain' from further loss; and I beg, both as a public officer and a friend, you will accept my most sincere thanks."

In all his home letters he speaks of his longing for peace. He was now rear-admiral of the White, and had already gained the reputation, which time ever increased, of having the power of managing men. Lord St. Vincent was in the habit of drafting the most ungovernable spirits into the rear-admiral's ship. "Send them to Collingwood," he used to say, "and he will bring them to order." And Collingwood did this by decision, firmness, and kindness combined, without capital punishment, so common in other ships, and almost without corporal punishment at all.

Remember that the men he had to deal with had frequently been forced to sea by the press-gang, were unfitted for the work, and were often under a burning and abiding sense of the cruel injustice done them. Collingwood always disliked the press-gang, and appreciated the position of such men. But other officers did not ; and a sentence of a hundred lashes was looked upon as almost a light one. Collingwood strongly reprobated all such practices. When he felt that flogging must be resorted to he was always present himself, and for hours after was silent and melancholy. He kept an exact account in his own handwriting of every punishment, and the number of lashes inflicted varied, as a rule, from six to twelve. His abhorrence of the system grew with advancing years, and more than a year often passed away without his once resorting to it. For the degrading and soul-souring cat he substituted watering the grog, exclusion from mess, and the like. He kept his men amused in many ways : "My wits are ever at work," he writes, "to keep my people employed, both for health's sake and to save them from mischief. We have lately been making musical instruments, and have now a very good band. Every moonlight night the sailors dance ; and there seems as much mirth and festivity as if we were in Wapping itself. One night the rats destroyed the bagpipes we had made, by eating up the bellows ; but they suffer for it, for in revenge we have made traps of all constructions, and have declared a war of extermination against them." He visited his sick sailors daily and supplied them from his own table. He never trifled with the men, never used to them coarse or violent language, or allowed others to do so. He had not the view, which seems now to be prevalent, that profanity is a necessary adjunct of a naval officer. Stern but kind, exacting good work and implicit obedience but thoroughly understanding and appreciating the difficulties of its execution ; just, honourable, and considerate ; he was the idol of his crew ; and, when he changed his ship, the roughest and toughest old salts shed tears of regret. He was a seaman and a gentleman at once, and both in the superlative degree.

LORD COLLINGWOOD.

And now he began to exhibit his phenomenal gift of intuitive perception. Of all men, he was the most able to appreciate and enter into the designs of his enemy, however skilful or intricate, and thus be prepared or prepare others to frustrate his designs.

After a weary time of cruising off the French and Spanish coasts, Collingwood arrived at Spithead, on December 9th, 1798, but could not leave his ship until well on into the following January. He writes : " Last night I went to Lady Parker's Twelfth-night, where all the gentlemen's children of the town were at dance and revelry ; but I thought of my own, and was so completely out of spirits that I left them in the middle of it. My wife shall know all my movements, even the very hour in which I shall be able to come to you. I hope they will not hurry me to sea again, for my spirit requires some respite from the anxieties which a ship occasions. Bless my precious girls for me, and their beloved mother."

But they did hurry him to sea again. In a few weeks he was made rear-admiral and joined the Channel fleet, but was speedily despatched to the Mediterranean. Again he had a long and weary period of cruising about, and the illness of his beloved wife at home added to Collingwood's other troubles. Not until December, 1800, did he once more reach England, and then he had to stay at Plymouth, conducting the fitting out of the fleet. As he could not go North, Mrs. Collingwood resolved that she would take the long and difficult journey to him, and that her little Sarah should accompany her. But, before she could reach him, his ship was lying completely ready, and would sail on the least motion of the enemy. His wife was expected to reach Plymouth on a Tuesday, but, at two o'clock on that day, Collingwood received express orders to go to sea immediately with all the ships that were ready. He was presiding at a court-martial, and could not leave until the next morning, and, when, after the duty was over, he was dining with Lord Nelson, her arrival was announced. "I flew to the inn where I had desired my wife to come, and found her and little Sarah as well after their journey as if it had lasted only for the day. No greater happiness is human nature capable of than was mine that evening ; but at dawn we parted and I went to sea." He described the evening in a letter to a friend thus : " How surprised you would have been to have popped into the Fountain Inn, and seen Lord Nelson, my wife and myself, sitting by the fireside eating, and little Sarah teaching Phillis, her dog, to dance." A month afterwards he writes : " It is grief to me to think of it now ; it almost broke my heart then. After such a journey to see me but for a few hours, with scarce time for her to relate the incidents of her journey, and no time for me to tell her half that my heart felt at such a proof of her affection ; but I am thankful that I did see her and my sweet child. It was a blessing to me, and composed my mind, which was before very much agitated." Soon after this, peace seemed to be at hand, but it was not until October that the actual news came, and then Collingwood wrote : " I cannot tell you how much joy the news of the peace gave me. The hope of returning to my family, and living in quiet and comfort among those I love, fills my heart with gladness." The treaty of Amiens was signed in March, 1802, and the admiral speedily returned to Morpeth. Here he was at rest and peace, superintending the education of his daughters, studying diligently, drawing and gardening, but especially planting acorns. This was his chief hobby : he never went for a walk without having his pockets full of them. and dropping them as he went along, and he urged all his friends to do likewise. Iron ships were undreamed of, and it was by great growth of oak that the wooden walls of old England were to be secured perpetuity.

But rest and peace were never to be his for any prolonged period, greatly as he loved them. War was declared with France in 1803, and in the early spring he left his wife, children, and home, never to see them again. His work was still that of watching the French, to whom the Spaniards were now joined. In August, 1805, he succeeded with four ships in blockading Cadiz, where the combined fleet was "as thick as a wood." He worked and watched from morning to evening, and frequently all night, and he so manœuvred when he was reinforced as, to Nelson's great admiration and delight, to compel the enemy to come out, and thus he brought about the battle of Trafalgar, which was fought on the 21st October. Nelson and he had been for some time in constant communication, and Nelson sent Collingwood his plan of attack on October 9th. He wrote : " They surely cannot escape us. I wish we could get a fine day. I send you my plan of attack, as far as a man dare venture to guess at the very uncertain position the enemy may be found in ; but, my dear friend, it is to place you perfectly at ease respecting my intentions, and to give full scope to your judgment for carrying them into effect. *We* can, my dear Coll., have no little jealousies ; we have only one great object in view—that of annihilating our enemies, and getting a glorious peace for our country. No man has more confidence in another than I have in you ; and no man will ever render your services more justice than your very old friend, Nelson and Bronte."

There is no need that I should enter into details of the great sea fight which all Englishmen are familiar with, and which did so much for Europe. We all remember how Collingwood, in the "Royal Sovereign," far outstripped the rest of the fleet, and, as he bore down alone, and under a crowd of sail, upon the foe ; how he exclaimed : "What would Nelson give to be here !" at the very moment when Nelson on the "Victory" said to his officers : "See how that gallant fellow, Collingwood, takes his ship into action;" how, for three hours, the fight was muzzle to muzzle, yards locked, no flinching or running on either side ; and how, in the hour of victory, his last fight over and won, Nelson fell.

In the despatch home giving the official account of the battle, a despatch remarkable alike for clearness of detail and modesty of expression, Collingwood says : "I have not only to lament, in common with the British navy and the British nation, in the fall of the commander-in-chief, the loss of a hero whose name will be immortal, and his memory ever dear to his country ; but my heart is rent with the most poignant grief for the death of a friend, to whom, by many years of intimacy, and a perfect knowledge of the virtues of his mind, which inspired ideas superior to the common race of men, I was bound by the strongest ties of affection—a grief which, even the glorious occasion in which he fell, does not bring the consolation which perhaps it ought."

The value of Collingwood's services was fully acknowledged. He became Baron Collingwood of Caldeburne and Hethpoole ; he took command of the Mediterranean fleet ; he received the thanks of both houses of Parliament, and the freedom of almost every British city ; the king wrote him an autograph letter of thanks ; the duke of Clarence sent him a sword, similar to those which, in the hour of victory, he had given to Nelson and to Lord St. Vincent. And not only did our island ring with his praise, but, by an act worthy of the best traditions of the noblest chivalry, the offering to the commander of the Spanish fleet, the wounded Spanish prisoners, he roused in southern Spain a perfect ferment of gratitude and admiration.

And now his true greatness began to show itself. He had no longer simply to take part in or direct naval manœuvres ; he had to take upon him the nicest diplomatic duties, to enter into friendly relations with kings, sultans, deys, and other potentates, to reconcile

conflicting interests, to endeavour to foresee and frustrate the crafty
designs of Napoleon, and to keep the home government advised of all
movements, all beliefs, all observations, and of all the multitude of
matters which it only could attend to or upon which it expected to
be consulted. The wisdom, foresight, and strength disclosed by his
vast political correspondence are amazing, and justice has never been
done to this quiet, resolute, but self-sacrificing man who contributed
so largely to the destruction of the Napoleonic scheme of a universal
European monarchy.

The first difficulties with which he had to deal were those
occasioned by the foolish conduct of the king and queen of Naples,
who had been expelled after the peace of Pressburg in 1805,
Napoleon's still more foolish brother Joseph being made king by him
in their stead. They retired to Palermo, whence the queen continued
alternately to breathe defiance to France and to court its alliance ;
and thus to give Lord Collingwood much cause for anxiety. " The
king," he wrote, " is a cipher." The queen was not a cipher.
" There is a king who should reign and a queen who will." The
morality of the court, which was notoriously low even at that
intensely immoral period, gained little from the example of the
imperious, impracticable, and dissolute queen.

Both king and queen wrote Collingwood repeatedly, begging him
to be to them " ce que a été le respectable Milord Nelson, notre ami,
protecteur, et défenseur." His replies were models of respectful
caution : " I beg your majesty to consider me as an officer devoted
to the service of his country. The allies of my sovereign and the
patrons of my friend Lord Nelson, whose noble character obtained for
him the regard of your majesty, will be ever dear to me : and if my
humble service shall aid in giving tranquillity to your kingdoms, and
happiness to your majesty, the pleasure I shall receive from it will be
amongst the blessings of my life." But he wrote home to point out
the difficulties of the case : "There is nothing left for Naples but by
negotiation to endeavour to deprecate the vengeance of Buonaparte ;
though I think it is scarce to be expected that his mercy will be less
ruinous than his wrath." At the same time, Collingwood took
measures to protect Sicily, and urged upon the monarchs to prepare in
every way for stubborn defence ; he visited the island and advised
upon the methods to be adopted ; and he continued successfully,
through the remainder of his career, at a great expenditure of time
and trouble, to guard Sicily from the French.

It was indeed a critical time, and one in which wisdom, foresight, and courage, were demanded from all men in authority. Napoleon was at the very height of his power. He had overrun mid-Europe, and reduced it everywhere to apparently perfect subjection. Spain was his willing, Russia his unwilling, ally. All his mind was now given to the humiliation of England. His threatened invasion of her had collapsed, thanks in a great measure to Collingwood's marvellous power of penetrating into the most secret designs. His attempt to combine the navies of Europe against her had been shattered to pieces by Nelson at Copenhagen and Trafalgar. His cajoleries and lying overtures had been cast contemptuously aside by Canning. But now he would seize upon Spain and Portugal and add their navies to his own, so as with those of Russia and Turkey, which he was scheming to combine also with his, to make a naval force which should be irresistible. He was idolised by the Spanish people. He had reduced the classes throughout Europe to subjection, and the willingness with which they hugged their chains was degrading in the extreme. He was just the kind of figure to captivate the democracy of Europe at the first glance and for a time ; strongly self-assertive, noisy, aggressive, and wonderfully successful.

But it was the democracy which was to hurl him from his high estate when its eyes were opened. It was his hatred of England which was to seal his doom. It was his mad rush into Spain which was to be the beginning of the end for him and his ambitious designs, and Wellington on land was to perfect the work which Collingwood began at sea. It was British patience, stubbornness, and courage, guided by consummate military and naval wisdom, which saved Europe from what, at the time of which I write, seemed to be its inevitable fate. But it was the rising of the peoples of the European nations, and first and foremost the people of the Spanish peninsula, which made the downfall of Napoleon certain. A nation whose people are fully roused may often be defeated, but will never be conquered.

Collingwood had been wounded at Trafalgar in the leg by the splinter of a shell, whilst his back had been injured by the wind of a great shot. He made little of these mishaps, and tells Lady Collingwood that : "With my losses, and breakings, and movings, I have scarce a knife or fork left, and, indeed, am very ill-off for everything. . . . I hope you told my darling how delighted I was with her French letter : she must converse when she has an opportunity, and remember not to admire anything French but the language." And again, "My soup is served in a tin pan, and I have borrowed a pewter teapot for my breakfast." And yet again, "I shall never have any good prospect 'till I can get my darlings about me, and then, perhaps, I shall be almost blind and not able to see them.

"Pray do not talk about the wound in my leg, or people may think that I am vapouring about my dangers. We are to have the medals for the last action, and I do not despair of getting another soon. I am the only officer in the service with three. How can I bless you as I love you? Not in words—they have not the power—and I must refer you to your own heart."

At this time all looked dark. The Spaniards were preparing a very fine squadron at Cadiz which Collingwood looked forward to fighting; the French were mustering a great armament in every part of the Adriatic; Turkey refused to renew her alliance with us, even when the admiral himself visited the Dardanelles to persuade them;* the entire power of Europe was opposed to us; most kings were Napoleon's thralls; "the poor king and queen of Prussia in an apothecary's shop, and unable to get their breakfast until the bed is made." But Napoleon carried his forceful policy too far, and poured 80,000 French troops into Spain in defiance of all treaties, forced both the Spanish king and his son to abdicate, and placed his brother Joseph on the throne, retaining, however, the reversion of it. And now the Spanish people rose against the usurper and to maintain the independence of their country. At once Lord Collingwood saw the inwardness of this rising, and was on the spot. Arrived at Cadiz on June 14th, a month before certain selected nobles had gathered at Bayonne to accept the nomination of Joseph as king, Collingwood writes to Don Thomas de Morla, the Governor-General of Andalusia, "It is from the energies of the Spanish people, and from the example of what a great country can do when unanimous, that the continent of Europe is to learn the means of repelling that usurpation which has bound so many states in a degrading dependence." The entire attitude of Spain was changed. Peace was declared with England. Collingwood writes: "We are doing everything for them that we can. Yesterday we supplied them with gunpowder for their army; and their cause and ours are now the same. . . . They consult

* Collingwood's despatch from the Dardanelles might have been written several times since: "I am afraid we shall never do any good in concert with the Russians; they hate the Turks, and the Turks detest them, which neither party is at any trouble to conceal. The Turks like us, and I am afraid the Russians are a little jealous of us."

with us on everything, and I do what is in my power for their aid and succour. . . . They say that Buonaparte has hitherto had only armies to contend with, but that now he has a nation, where every man is a soldier." In his home despatches he enters more fully into the details of the wise and far-seeing advice which he gave, and shows how the great movement is from the people, " irritated to the greatest degree against the French, and full of resentment at being robbed of their king." They "are raised to enthusiasm, and would do anything ; their councils, maintaining the gravity of their national character, would let this ardour cool and do nothing." I wish that time would permit me to lay these despatches and the declarations of those in power in Spain more completely before you, that you might the more fully realise the immense value which the services of our great Northumbrian were to Spain, to England, and to Europe, in giving direction and impetus to the movement which was ultimately to destroy the most unmitigated scoundrel who has mounted the throne in modern history.

When Collingwood landed at Cadiz, he had a more than royal reception. At the opera the audience clapped for a quarter of an hour when he went into the governor's box ; the streets were crowded by many thousands of people crying out welcome ; the volunteers, the soldiers, the officers from the surrounding district, vied with each other as to which should do him the greatest honour. They would fain have had him stay on shore, but "after a visit of three hours, and a collation at the governor's, I returned to my ship."

All this time he never ceased to give careful attention to things at home. A cousin had left him an estate at Chirton, near North Shields, and he wrote : " Whatever establishments may be found there for the comfort of the poor or the education and improvement of their children, I would have continued and increased. I want to make no great accession of wealth from it, nor will I have anybody put to the smallest inconvenience for me." When it was proposed to raise the rental of his colliery from £80 to £600, he wrote : " I would not, for all the collieries in Northumberland, be a party to such extortion. A fair increase of rent is allowable, but this is beyond all bounds."

One of the most beautiful of his letters was written to his wife on the 16th June, 1806, the anniversary of their marriage. To abbreviate it is almost a crime, and yet I must content myself with a few extracts from it. " If ever we have peace," he says, " I hope to spend my latter days amid my family, which is the only sort of happiness I can enjoy. After this life of labour, to retire to peace and quietness is all I look for in the world. Should we decide to change the place of our dwelling, our route would of course be to the southward of Morpeth ; but then I should be for ever regretting those beautiful views which are nowhere to be exceeded, and even the rattling of that old waggon that used to pass our door at six o'clock in a winter's morning had its charms. The fact is, whenever I think how I am to be happy again, my thoughts carry me back to Morpeth, where, out of the fuss and parade of the world, surrounded by those I loved most dearly and who loved me, I enjoyed as much happiness as my nature is capable of. Many things that I see in the world give me a distaste for the finery of it. The great knaves are not like those poor unfortunates who, driven perhaps to distress from accidents which they could not prevent, or at least not educated in principles of honour and honesty, are hanged for some little thievery ; while a knave of education and high breeding, who brandishes his honour in the eyes of the world, would rob a state to its ruin. For the first, I feel pity and compassion ; for the latter, abhorrence and contempt ; they are the ten-fold vicious.

Have you read—but what I am more interested about, is your sister with you, and is she well and happy ? Tell her—God bless her !—I wish I were with you, that we might have a good laugh. God bless me ! I have scarcely laughed these three years. . . .

How do the dear girls go on ? I would have them taught geometry, which is of all sciences in the world the most entertaining ; it expands the mind more to the knowledge of all things in nature, and better teaches to distinguish between truths and such things as have the appearance of being truths, yet are not, than any other. Their education and the proper cultivation of the sense which God has given them are the objects on which my happiness most depends. To inspire them with a love of everything that is honourable and virtuous though in rags, and with contempt for vanity in embroidery is the way to make them the darlings of my heart. . . . How would it enlarge their minds if they could acquire a sufficient knowledge of mathematics and astronomy to give them an idea of the beauty and wonders of the creation ? I am persuaded that the generality of people, and particularly fine ladies, only adore God because they are told it is proper, and the fashion to go to church ; but I would have my girls gain such knowledge of the works of the creation that they may have a fixed idea of the nature of that Being who could be the Author of such a world. . . .

"Tell me how do the trees which I planted thrive? Is there shade under the three oaks for a comfortable summer seat? Do the poplars grow at the walk, and does the wall of the terrace stand firm?"

The rest and peace which Lord Collingwood so coveted, and which he had so richly earned, were never to be his. In August, 1808, he told the home government how worn out and feeble he was, and how he doubted his capacity to discharge his duties properly, and begged to be released. But, in reply, he was told that he could not be spared, for "importance was attached to his continuance in a situation in which, through a variety of great and complicated objects, of difficult and delicate arrangements, of political as well as of professional considerations, he had in no instance failed to adopt the most judicious and best concerted measures." His simple and noble reply was that his best service was due to his country as long as he lived.

To his wife he wrote, "The impression which (t)his letter made on me was one of grief and sorrow : first, that with such a list as we have there should be thought to be any difficulty in finding a successor of superior ability to me ; and next, that there should be any obstacle in the way of the only comfort and happiness that I have to look forward to in this world. The variety of subjects, all of great importance, with which I am engaged would puzzle a longer head than mine. The conduct of the fleet alone would be easy ; but the political correspondence which I have to carry on with the Spaniards, the Turks, the Albanians, the Egyptians, and all the states of Barbary, gives me such constant occupation that I really often feel my spirits quite exhausted, and of course my health is much impaired : but if I must go on I will do the best I can."

And he did his best until the end. He continued to watch over and visit Sicily ; negotiated a peace with the dey of Algiers ; aided the English and the Spaniards in the early phases of the Peninsular war ; worked steadily from daylight to midnight with all his strength, often borrowing an hour or two of the next day, and with scarcely time to eat his scanty dinner ; watched the French fleets ; co-operated with the Austrians in the Adriatic, when they took the field against France ; established a system of recruiting which should obviate any necessity for the press-gang ; kept his own ship's crew in perfect health, and received the honourable title of the "sailor's friend ; " had a most successful engagement with the French in the Gulf of Lyons, the victory being obtained " without a hair in anybody's head being hurt, and almost without a shot being fired ; " but all the time suffering more and more.

It was more than seven years since he had sailed from England, and more than five years since he had slept on land. For seventeen months at a time he had never left his ship. Now, in February, 1810, he could scarcely walk across his cabin, and on the 3rd March he resigned his command to Rear-Admiral Martin, and at sunset on the 6th his ship, the " Ville de Paris," cleared the harbour of Port Mahon and sailed for England. When he knew that he was at sea he rallied, and said to his friends who were nursing him, " Then I may yet live to meet the French once more." It was rough on the 7th, and when Captain Thomas said that he feared the motion of the vessel would disturb him, he replied, " No, Thomas, I am now in a state in which nothing in this world can disturb me more. I am dying ; and I am sure that it must console you and all who love me to see how comfortably I am coming to my end." At times he spoke of the dear ones at home, and of the stern struggle in which his country was involved, but with perfect resignation, and after bidding his sorrowing friends a long farewell he passed quietly to his rest on the evening of that day, being nearly sixty-one years old.

We ne'er shall look upon his like again.

LECTURE VI.

Northumbrian Art and Song.

We have dealt in the preceding lectures with divers aspects or presentments of the Northumbrian mind, with the history of its vehicle of expression, and with different modes in which it has expressed itself, and I propose to consider to-night its principal characteristics. In doing so, I shall touch slightly upon one or two phases not yet noticed, but I must, because of the limitations of time, leave many others, perhaps of equal importance, quite unmentioned. It would be well worth the while of enthusiastic Northumbrians to work up the whole subject in careful detail. There is room for many courses of lectures dealing with such men as Alcuin, Duns Scotus, Laurence Minot, Bernard Gilpin ; with our great lawyers, as Eldon, Stowell, and Cresswell ; with our men of science, as Lord Armstrong, the Hancocks, the Stephensons, Buddle, Wood, Sopwith ; with our musicians, as Avison and Shield ; with our painters, as Duncan, Good, Harvey, Robson, Balmer, and, above all, old Tom Richardson : and this without touching what has been said of us in olden days by many travellers from this and other lands, and in our own day by Howitt, Stephen Oliver, White, and others ; and without mentioning living persons, of whom quite a multitude are doing good, and a select few great, work in literature, science, and art. I seem scarcely to have crossed the border-line of the beautiful land.

But let us enquire what, in that which we have talked over together, strikes us as the chief features which characterise the men and things of which we have spoken. I should place, first of all, simplicity. It is a high virtue ; one which all can understand who have not perverted their mental vision ; and one which, under all the constant change of circumstance, retains its value. It is refreshing because it demands no effort of thought although it richly repays prolonged and earnest contemplation. It is natural because it spares unnecessary effort. It is one of the few great virtues which is readily within the reach of all, and yet one which demands for true appreciation a certain amount of the homely wisdom which we call common-sense.

The men we spoke of in the earliest lectures were simple, for they lived in simple days and amongst simple folk, very close to nature. They preached simply to simple men. The ballads we next spoke of were simple from the very necessity of the case, because they were written for the multitude of men in an unlettered age. Bishop Ridley was a man of simple life, and, though of great learning, of simple mind. Mark Akenside was rather of the order of the exception which proves the rule, but |Lord Collingwood was simplicity itself, and turned away from courts and kings with delight to the simple charms of quiet little Morpeth. I shall take another example of this prominent characteristic of the best Northumbrian mind shortly ; but let us for a moment consider what is involved in it.

Directness, in the first place : that which is simple goes straight to its aim. Truth, in the second place : that which is simple is free from the essence of falsehood, the very idea of which is the not being that which you seem to be. Repose, in the third place : for simplicity avoids emphasis and unrest. "He speaketh as one having authority." This is what our inmost souls crave for ; what we acknowledge and glory in when we find it ; what we search for eagerly in thinking, in doing in whatever way, in saying by mouth or hand, pencil or pen : authority, that which is said or done with authority, and so once for all. The very essence of such authority is simplicity. "He spake, and it was done."

Now we have had, amongst us Northumbrians in these latter days, a man who strikingly exemplifies what I have been saying. I allude to Thomas Bewick, born in 1753 at Cherryburn, some twelve miles west of Newcastle, and in the lovely country on the banks of the Tyne. He was an artist from the earliest part of his life, as perhaps all true artists have been. Think of the Italian shepherd lad who was to do for painting what Nicholas the Pisan did for sculpture, and how Cimabue found him, the herd boy Giotto, drawing the figure of one of his sheep upon a bit of slate with a pointed stone ; of little Handel stealing up to the garret in the dead of the night to improvise on the ancient spinnet. The names of child artists are legion ; but they do not necessarily]become men artists. That depends upon many things, congenial and sympathetic surroundings being the chief : for the budding of art, "if in youth, too frost-nipt, it grow to flowers, will in manhood yield no fruit, but a prickly, bitter-rinded stone-fruit, of which the fewest can find the kernel."

Thomas Bewick went to a school at Mickley to acquire some knowledge of the three R's. He was very young, but he used to fill his slate, the margins of his school books, and every bit of paper he could get hold of, with representations of such objects as had struck his fancy ; and, when he got out of school, he ornamented the church porch and the gravestones with chalk drawings, although, as he says, "at that time I had never heard of the word 'drawing ;' nor did I know of any other paintings beside the king's arms in the church and the signs in Ovingham of the Black Bull, the White Horse, the Salmon, and the Hare and Hounds." He covered the floor and hearthstone of his father's house with similar designs to those he lavished upon the churchyard, and then was given some paper, upon which he painted with blackberry juice, or did pen-and-ink sketches. Even when at church he was hard at work "drawing figures upon the soft, painted book-board with a pin.".

This boy was to live until 1828, and he was to win a world-wide fame as the restorer of the fine old art of wood engraving. He was to be the earliest, and to remain *facile princeps*, amongst drawers and engravers upon wood.

And what was his secret ? He himself tells it in his delightful autobiography, and in the following words : " Had I been a painter, I never would have copied the works of 'old masters,' or others, however highly they might be esteemed. I would have gone to nature for all my patterns ; for she exhibits an endless variety not possible to be surpassed, and scarcely ever to be truly imitated. I would, indeed, have endeavoured to discover how those artists of old made or compounded their excellent colours, as well as the disposition of their lights and shades, by which they were enabled to accomplish so much and so well."

There, surely, is the whole case admirably stated in a few words. No nonsense about "art for art's sake ;" no preaching up of schools ; readiness to accept every manner of mechanical aid ; but when the subject to be dealt with is considered and the manner of its treatment, then entire independence, and that return to nature, the only true and inexhaustible fountain of artistic endeavour, which has been the distinguishing characteristic of every true artist whatever his medium of interpretation.

We who dwell in Newcastle have splendid and unrivalled facilities for the study of Thomas Bewick's work. In the marvellous museum of the Natural History Society at Barras Bridge, the south side of the central gallery contains many hundred specimens of the master's work. Just as you will find there the finest specimens of bird-stuffing in the world, the work of that unrivalled and artistic naturalist, John Hancock, so you will find, what you can find nowhere else, a great wealth of drawings in water-colour, ink, pencil, and sépia, by our greatest Northumbrian artist, as well as almost a complete series of the whole of his wood engravings.

But will you find them ? Will you take the trouble to look for them ? Few people do. The great majority of the people of Newcastle never dream of entering this, one of the most interesting and important buildings which the city contains. But if you will search out these drawings, and then patiently and lovingly search into them, you will reap a rich reward.

For we Newcastle folk have never yet discovered how great a man Thomas Bewick was. We have had men (and one or two of surpassing excellence) who have painted big pictures, and to them we do reverence ; but Bewick's art is so small in size, so great in quantity, so common amongst us, that we are apt to under-estimate it or overlook it altogether. And, yet, Thomas Bewick is far more than our Hogarth : he is the Robert Burns of the pencil. There is the same wide sympathy, the same love for simple beauty, the same fearless outspokenness, at times the same healthy coarseness, the same power of seeing into the very heart of all surrounding him, and drawing forth and depicting the innate beauty and hidden meaning of common things. All his work is true. He had thought deeply upon the questions which will always puzzle all who are interested in art, but he had found the true practical solution for the most prominent difficulties, and expounded this in the words which I have quoted. They were probably written in 1825 when John Ruskin was a boy of six years of age.

Let us take down our *Bewick* almost at random, and see what he has to say to us ; and we will content ourselves with one or two of those tail-pieces which are of so infinite a variety, although we might well have chosen some of the charming and appropriate back-grounds which give much value to his drawings of beasts and birds, although the figures of the creatures themselves, being copied from stuffed and badly stuffed specimens, in many instances are somewhat stiff and doubtful. I have chanced upon the " Animals," and am at once in rural Northumberland. Here are the streams which form so valuable a part of her scenery ; the dull country lane enlivened by a tattered gipsy on his bony old mare ; the quiet village with its church tower or spire ; the moor ; the ruined abbey ; the old keep or peel tower ; the sea shore when you

Might fancy that the mighty deep
Was even the gentlest of all gentle things;

or when it rises and beats upon the wave-worn cliffs in fierce rage,
and, in a night, destroys the pride and joy and hope of many a
sailor's home. Our county lies before us, in its beauty and its degradation; its strength and weakness, life and death. But there is much
more than this: there are lessons to learn as well as beauty to
admire. Look at those boys who are hanging a cat, or flogging a
donkey with hat and furze bush, whilst the gibbet in the distance
preaches "He that is cruel troubleth his own flesh." Or take the
thief staggering away through the night with his ill-gotten gain, his
burden increased by the weight of the devil who has mounted upon
his shoulders, and the gallows standing by again points the certain
moral. Then look at the tombstone with the legend "Sacred to the
memory of," but it has crumbled away and no longer tells to whom it
was inscribed: a sermon on "The vanity of human wishes," in a few
pencil strokes. Then there is the old horse, gaunt and weary, standing beneath a leafless and lifeless tree in the pitiless rain, and itself
waiting for death. What subtle dramatic force there is in the
thrilling tale of the careless nurse, who, having wandered with her
infant charge into the fields, has left it to amuse itself whilst she has
betaken herself to her lover beneath a distant hedge. The happy
child has toddled up to a horse grazing in the field, and is plucking
at its tail. The ears and eyes viciously thrown back portend terrible
disaster, which the terrified mother, who is rushing over the adjacent
stile, is probably too far off to prevent.

I find quite a special beauty in the tail-piece which depicts a poor
broken-down French prisoner of war chained in his stone cell; worn,
tattered, and sitting despairingly upon the straw with which the
floor is strewn. But the beam of sunshine which streams through
his window bars will surely bear to him a ray of hope. I can never
look at this touching little drawing without Beranger's *Hirondelles*
coming at once to mind. But, I hold first of all, the very master-
piece of Thomas Bewick's cunning hand and warm heart, the old
soldier who, the perils of war over, has tramped wearily many a long
mile towards his home, with all his small belongings on his back.
Eleven miles have still to be traversed when, in a pelting, pitiless
storm, he reaches a broad bay of the sea sweeping far inland, and
there is no house at hand to shelter him and no boat to ferry him
across. I do not need to hint at the infinite pathos in such a tale so
told.

In all of this work, in all of Bewick's work, we find the same direct, truthful, simplicity, and we recognise in the gentle old Northumbrian the first, in order of time as in order of merit, of all who have given our county its position in the realm of the Fine Arts. Let me once more point out his real place in relation to wood engraving in England. He stands in a similar position in reference to it as Hans Memling and the Van Eycks stand in relation to oil-painting in the Low Countries. His not only were the drawings to be engraved, but he restored or rather re-created, the art of engraving the drawing on wood, and invented the instruments with which he worked as well as the methods of his working. And the result of his labours is that his engravings are like our fine old ballads, direct, true, simple, and full of meaning to those who have eyes to see and hearts to feel. He is not the great master who compels admiration but dwells afar off as on the topmost peak; he is the cherished friend of daily life whom you welcome at all times to your own fire-side. Life would have been different to many of us without Thomas Bewick.

We have had in these latter days, and in quite another intellectual sphere, strong evidence of the simplicity which is the ruling characteristic of the best Northumbrian mind. I allude to our songs. Now, you may perhaps be inclined to say that is a matter of course. Songs must be simple. I grant you that good songs must be simple, but the simplicity of which I speak is to all men. There are numberless songs in all languages which are good and simple, but only to a select few. Special knowledge, special intuition, and special education is required for the full understanding of these. Granted that you have the clue, the riddle is easily read, but I am referring to the treasures which require no unlocking. No flower can be simpler or more beautiful than the *Narcissus poeticus*, but to find it greatly abounding you must travel to the Pyrenees; "the buttercup, the little children's dower," lies everywhere around us at home. Our songs are the buttercups and daisies of the great world of literature, and are appreciated best by those to whom they are the most common, by those to whom they are the best known. To them, as to our ballads to which I applied it in my third lecture, and, indeed, to all poetry, the truth applies closely :—

> Will'st den Dichter du verstehen
> Musst im Dichter's Lande gehen.

You may appreciate the songs of other lands from the intellectual or purely literary point of view by simply reading them, but you

Robert Roacha

must hear them sung in their own land before you can approximate to any real understanding of their true worth.

Now, in the world of song, Northumberland has won a distinct and foremost place in a region which is generally rather looked down upon as of small account. When we speak of a sporting song we expect words baldly expressive of the more patent facts of sport and nothing else, and we find more noise than melody when it is sung. But in the *Coquetdale Fishing Songs* we have quite a unique combination of sport and poetry, and of words truly descriptive of every aspect of the sport, the more hidden as well as the openly revealed, wedded to worthy music. It is worth our while to ascertain how this unusual state of affairs came about.

In 1767, Robert Roxby was born on the banks of the Reedwater, and he was thus an angler from his youth up. He spent the most of his life as a bank clerk in Newcastle. About 1803, he became acquainted with Thomas Doubleday, then (as he himself says) "a bashful, odd, and nervous lad" of thirteen years of age, but a most ardent votary of the gentle art, and they soon became fast friends. At first they began to dress flies together, but they soon learned that they had other tastes in common. Like all true anglers, they found much more in fishing than the sport. There are no fairer rivers on the earth than those which form the finest features of our Northumbrian landscapes, and these are intimately known to the fisher and to no one else. He, indeed, knows every stream and pool, every rock and cliff, every stone and tree, and knows them too in each of their constantly varied moods. I dare almost say that every true fisher is a potential poet. Our two friends certainly were. Roxby had already made essays in that gentle art. They both had a wide knowledge of good poetry, especially of lyrical work, and Doubleday had even translated some of Horace's odes into verse, and had his memory richly stored with Prior and Pope, but, most happily, with Burns and Shakespere as well. In 1807, they first fished the Coquet together, though both of them had previous knowledge of that glorious stream, and Doubleday then learned the extraordinary grace and delicacy with which his older friend could "thraw the flee." From this date, they made frequent fishing expeditions, and, at length, through Doubleday's influence, and, acting on Prior's principle that "who often reads will sometimes want to write," Robert Roxby ventured to attempt a fishing song.

And here these fishing songs are brought closely into connection with the Northumbrian worthy of whom I have already spoken this evening, Thomas Bewick. He also was an eager angler. In common with Roxby and Doubleday, he had a keen love of music, and, with every true Northumbrian, delighted in the gentle sounds of our sweet Northumbrian pipes. He joined his persuasions to those of other friends, and, in 1821, the first *Fisher's Garland* was written and published, Bewick lending one of his vignettes to adorn the print. From this time the Garlands appeared annually until 1845, although they were not always written by Roxby or Doubleday.

I think that the history of this first Garland, as told by Thomas Doubleday, is really that of all of them alike. He says :—"The spring of 1821 proved very uncertain and rough, even for the rude climate of Northumberland. Seduced, however, by the prevalence for some few days of westerly and south-westerly winds, with some sunshine, and a somewhat mild temperature of the air, we had, on the 28th of March, ventured over to the Coquet, to take our chance for a day's fly-fishing. On our arrival at Weldon Bridge in the evening, we fell in with Matthew Ferguson, an experienced angler, then resident within a short distance of our quarters, and he agreed to join us next day, let the weather be what it might. Matthew faithfully 'kept tryst ;' and, as is often the case with precarious ventures, our day's sport turned out favourably, far beyond any anticipations which we either indulged or had a right to indulge. The day proved to be a rude, boisterous, and changeable one in the extreme. The wind blew from the west all through, but in heavy gusts, with frequent lulls, most of the blasts being accompanied with flying showers of sleet, or even snow. As the clouds passed, however, we had intervals of bright sunshine, under which the half-frozen flakes that stuck to our jackets absolutely glittered. The result of the day's work was a dish of trout, including three salmon trout, such as for weight I have never seen equalled either before or since."

It will be readily conceived that, after a day's sport like this, those concerned returned home highly pleased with the result. This little excitement led to other and to better consequences. In a few days after "our return home, I received a note from my companion, begging me to call at his lodgings, as he had 'something to show me.' On calling, I had the satisfaction to find, fairly down upon paper, the first three stanzas of the first song of this series. I could not but perceive that the lines had that peculiar freshness of spirit and natural simplicity which are best suited to such a subject ; and I urged the author to complete a work so auspiciously begun. The answer was that, like Dominie Sampson, he was fairly 'stickit,' and that, if finished they were to be, I must do it. The world has the result before it."

I think that this gives us the true account of the authorship of the *Fisher's Garlands* or *Coquetdale Fishing Songs*. Some of them were undoubtedly entirely by Doubleday ; I doubt if there was one entirely by Roxby, who had indeed the poetic mind but lacked the power of poetic expression. Doubleday was a true poet : some of his sonnets are amongst the best in our language. He was, indeed, a man of singular versatility of genius ; a dramatist, a keen politician, and the author of learned economical and philosophical works. But it will be by his angling songs that he will be the longest remembered. They have been spoken of as "pleasing trifles," but that is a libel upon them. They are the only sporting songs that have ever yet been written which, whilst preserving exactly every detail and feature of the sport, are yet instinct with the true spirit of poetry.

Let us look at this rather more closely, and let me first instance a few cases which will illustrate the fact that the details of the sport are preserved. Perhaps I should apologise for dwelling upon this point, to an audience which may possibly include some who are so unfortunate as not to be anglers. But if not themselves of the gentle craft, they must have some interest in it. They can scarcely be Northumbrians, or even dwellers in Northumberland without such interest. And, first, as in duty bound, let us see one or two instances which treat of that all-important point, the weather. I have known ladies who have said that the weather is never right for fishing, and, truly, it very seldom is theoretically perfect. There is still much truth contained in the ancient fishing lines :—

> When the wind is in the north,
> The prudent fisher goes not forth :
> When the wind is in the south,
> It blows the bait in the fish's mouth :
> When the wind is in the east,
> It's neither good for man nor beast :
> But when the wind is in the west,
> Oh, then, it's at the very best.

And we find, accordingly, that the art of the favouring wind is often alluded to :—

> The sun-beams glint on Linden-Ha',
> The breeze comes frae the west.

Again,

> The farmer walks the field,
>   The seed he's casting steady,
> The breeze is blowing west,
>   Be ready, fishers, ready.

And again,

> The westlin breezes saftly blaw.

And, yet again,

> It's May-day this—the wale o' days—
> The westlin wind blaws saft an' free.

But the storm-wind, too, finds mention, and in a lovely picturesque verse :—

> Yestreen the clouds hung few an' mild,
>   An' saft as maidens when they weep !
> Or gently lay on Simondside,
>   Like bairns that cry themselves to sleep ;
> But, now, out owre the mountain tap,
>   They're sweepin' wi' an angry sky ;
> The veerin' blast blaws dead south-wast,
>   —We'se cheat them a', an' up the Wreigh !

Then the welcome disappearance of the snow, and the springing to life of the early flowers, are much dwelt upon. Thus we find :—

> The lambs they are feeding on lonely Shilmore,
> The breezes blow softly o'er dark Simondside ;
> The birds they are lilting in ev'ry green bower,
>   And the streams of the Coquet now merrily glide.
> The primrose is blooming at Halystane Well,
>   And the bud 's on the saugh and the bonny birk tree,
> The moorcocks are calling round Harbottle Fell,
>   And the snaw-wreaths are gane frae the Cheviot so hie.

And again,

> Tho' Cheviot's top be frosty still,
> He's green belaw the knee.

And then this verse filled with the very essence of the spirit of poetry :—

> O ! let it be in April-tide.
>   But one of April's best,
> A mornin' that seems made o' May,
>   In dews an' sunshine dressed ;
> Frae off the crags o' Simonside,
>   Let the fresh breezes blaw,
> And let auld Cheviot's sides be green,
>   Albeit his head be snaw.

Then to turn, for a brief space, to the pure technique of the gentle art, we find such passages as :—

> But gi'e to me the light midge flee,
>   When streams are rinnin' clearly,
> And a cast o' line "far aff an' fine,"
>   All in the mornin' airly.

Or,

> Still we can toddle, fit by fit,
>   To Brinkburn where the breeze hits fine ;
> The auld man's nae sae crazy yet
>   But he can thraw a winsome line.
> 'Gin there we fail, we'se no repine,
>   When smelts are eydent, trouts are shy ;
> And i' th' slack, by the dam-back,
>   We'se maybe raise a grilse forbye !

Every old fisher who hears me understands the wisdom and truth which lies in that line, that great line—

> When smelts are eydent, trouts are shy.

No one who was not an experienced fisherman could have written it, but every old fisher knows how vain it is to hope for more than a very exceptional trout when the smelts come eagerly at every cast.

And, lastly, for I must finish my quotations, not sheathing my sword for lack of argument, but because of the limits of time and patience, we have "The Auld Fisher's Advice," full of piscatorial wisdom. It has been a bright day without a breeze, and any fish which rose to the finest cast came shyly, but "we'se try him in the gloamin'."

> 'Twill no be lang or ere the sun
>   Shall set behind the Cheviot,
> An' thraw his latter rays upon
>   Clear Jed an' woody Teviot.
> 'Twill no be lang ere Simondside
>   Stands dim an' dark in shadow,
> An' mists frae Coquet's bosom glide
>   Ow're mony a haugh an' meadow.
>
> Then ye'se put on your best moth flee
>   When e'enin's dews are fallin',
> And, frae his screen in bush or tree,
>   The mellow throstle's callin' ;
> An' I'se put on my mennim gear,
>   When moonlight's just beginnin',
> An' to the streams, frae far and near,
>   The hungry trouts are rinnin'.

An' first we'se try a cast aboon,
   Just where the stream gaes birlin',
And sets the pool, aneath the moon,
   In mony a wrinkle swirlin'.
Then, gin ye fail, I'se tak a cast,
   E'en where the stream is foamin';
The mennim's sure his doom at last,
   We'se hae him in the gloamin' !

But I have detained you long, perhaps too long, over some of the
details of these exquisite songs ; but let us look at them now from a
more general point of view. There were not many of them. In
1852 they were published in what Mr. Doubleday called "a collective
form," at the expense of the Coquetdale Angling Club, and I recall
with pride that the author and editor records "that Mr. Joseph
Watson, the worthy secretary of the Coquetdale Angling Club, has
evinced that interest in the success of the volume which one literary
man only can feel for the work of another, and which constitutes,
perhaps, the most pleasing accompaniment of all such undertakings,
on whatever scale or of whatever character."

There are only sixteen songs in this collection, but it is scarcely
too much to say that each of them is a gem. Prefixed to each is
some account of its origin by Mr. Doubleday himself, as well as
frequently some critical observations by one who, from the plough,
became a literary man of more than local fame, a book-collector whose
library it was a great and, to some of us, no rare treat to overhaul,
and a critic whose opinions were always well worth listening to. The
preface and the conclusion are admirable, and should have careful
perusal. The preface speaks of the joys of fishing, and gently waves
aside some of the objections which are at times made, by those who
are ignorant of the subject, on the score of cruelty. I remember how
in the old days, when we met round the fire at famous Tibbie Sheil's
after the day's work to discuss the sport of the day, grand old
Dr. Guthrie used to sweep away the question of why, if fishes did not
feel, they performed such amazing gyrations, with the reply,
"Muscular contractility, ma'am, mere muscular contractility." But I
must avoid this topic, for, in common with all my brethren, I have a
great sheaf of instances which prove beyond the shadow of a doubt
that feeling, as we understand it, is not to be found amongst fishes.
But to return to the preface : it goes on to give a charming account
of the course of the Coquet from near the Carter Fell to the sea.
It ends with a sonnet which I must read you, as it seems to me to

justify the claim of Mr. Doubleday to a place amongst true poets. He has said that "the pursuit of the angler carries a moral with it, which may be useful to those to whom angling may have small charms and little of fascination." He expresses this moral thus :—

> Go, take thine angle, and with practised line,
>   Light as the gossamer, the current sweep ;
>   And if thou failest in the calm, still deep,
> In the rough eddy may a prize be thine.
> Say thou'rt unlucky where the sunbeams shine ;
>   Beneath the shadow, where the waters creep,
>   Perchance the monarch of the brook shall leap—
> For fate is ever better than design.
> Still persevere ; the giddiest breeze that blows
>   For thee may blow, with fame and fortune rife.
> Be prosperous ; and what reck if it arose
>   Out of some pebble with the stream at strife,
> Or that the light wind dallied with the boughs?
>   Thou art successful. Such is human life !

The conclusion gives a beautiful account of Robert Roxby, emphasising his love of the rod and the gun ; his delight in music, and especially in the simple Scotch airs, and our own pipes; his passionate love of nature ; his conscientious attention to the drudgery and details of business ; his intuitive faculty of poetic tact ; his singular warmth of heart, and strong (if somewhat impulsive) benevolence.

Of the songs themselves I must only mention one or two which are special favourites, although each has a charm of its own. The last verse of that written in 1822 is worth quoting and noting.

> Here's good luck to the gad, and success to each friend on't ;
>   If e'er pray'r of mine can have interest above,
> May they run their line smoothly, nor soon see an end on't,
>   And their course be as clear as the streams that they love !
> May the current of life still spread glitt'ring before them,
>   And their joys ever rise as the season draws nigh ;
> And if e'er—as 't will happen—misfortune comes o'er them,
>   Oh ! still may her dart fall as light as their fly !

This song goes to "They may Rail at this Life," but that with the greatest "go" of all, "The Old Angler's Triumph" has "Auld Sir Simon" for its tune, "a strange, wild, exultant rant," Doubleday calls it. It is the playful apotheosis of that invaluable fly, the red heckle. Let me quote you one or two verses :—

At Shilmore they're guid at the mennim;
 At Felton they're guid at the flee;
Lang Rothbury's streams for the brandlin';
 But Weldon, old Weldon, for me!
The Sharperton codgers are cunnin';
 At Thropton they're guid at a thraw;
But up wi' the bonnie red heckle—
 The heckle that tackled them a'.

．　．　．　．　．

There were some that went out in the gloamin',
 And some they got up wi' the lark;
Some poach'd wi' a net i' the mornin',
 Au' some they laid traps i' the dark:
But that for their meshin' and threshin'!
 Fish fair, or contrary to law;
Still, it's up wi' the bonnie red heckle—
 The heckle that tackled them a'.

．　．　．　．　．

There's wine i' the cellars o' Weldon,
 If ye ken the turn o' the key,
There's bonnie braw lasses o' Coquet,
 If ye ken the blink of their e'e;
There's braw yellow trouts up at Brinkburn,
 If ye ken the place where to thraw;
So here's to the bonnie red heckle—
 The heckle that tackled them a'!

Weldon Bridge has been the home of anglers for the greater part of a century, at all events. Its name occurs in many of the songs: "Our old home of Weldon," "Sweet Weldon Brig," "Weldon's frien'ly door," and the like. What a crowd of memories cluster round the dear old hostelry! How much travellers to Rothbury have lost since the opening of the railway! How thrilling was the descent of the long hill past Linden Hall to Weldon Bridge, with the first view of that best-loved of rivers, the Coquet! Was there ever such a sitting room as that bow-windowed parlour with its well-scratched panes, and the grand brown trout painted below the mantel-shelf by a member of that rare family of artists and anglers, the Crawhalls? And what a drive it was thence to the mountain-cup in which far-famed Rothbury stands: past "the green braes of Tod-stead, the pride of the vale;" past Brinkburn's "ruins grey," and the little hamlet of Pepperhaugh; and then past Crag-end and the crags and boiling waters of the Thrum, until the long street with its few well-grown trees burst on your view, and you drove up gladly to the hospitable Three Half Moons, and received a hearty welcome from Mr. and Mrs. Maxwell. It is fifty-seven years since she gave me a glass of her home-made ginger wine, but how good it was! Hosts and house alike are long departed.

There are few airs more sweetly pathetic than "Grammachree," and there are no words which seem more fitly wedded to it than those of "The Auld Fisher's Fareweel to Coquet." When that estimable painter, Edward Train, sang it to me in his studio in New Bridge Street, I thought, and still think, that we had truly, in this song, the setting of "perfect music unto noble words."

> Come bring to me my limber gad
>   I've fish'd wi' mony a year,
> An' let me hae my weel-worn creel,
>   An' a' my fishing gear;
> The sun-beams glint on Linden-Ha',
>   The breeze comes frae the west,
> An' lovely looks the gowden morn
>   On th' streams that I like best.
>
> I've thrawn the flee thae sixty year,
>   Ay, sixty year an' mair,
> An' mony a speckled troutie kill'd
>   Wi' heckle, heuk, an' hair;
> An' now I'm auld an' feeble grown,
>   My locks are like the snaw;
> But I'll gang again to Coquet-side,
>   An' tak' a fareweel thraw.
>
> O Coquet! in my youthfu' days
>   Thy river sweetly ran,
> An' sweetly down thy woody braes
>   The bonnie birdies sang;
> But streams may rin, an' birds may sing,
>   Sma' joy they bring to me,
> The blithesome strains I dimly hear,
>   The streams I dimly see.
>
> But, ance again, the weel kenn'd sounds
>   My minutes shall beguile,
> An' glistering in the airly sun
>   I'll see thy waters smile:
> An' sorrow shall forget his sigh,
>   An' age forget his pain,
> An' ance mair, by sweet Coquet-side,
>   My heart be young again.

Ance mair I'll touch, wi' gleesome foot,
   Thy waters clear and cold,
Ance mair I'll cheat the gleg-e'ed trout,
   An' wile him frae his hold ;
Ance mair, at Weldon's frien'ly door,
   I'll wind my tackle up,
An' drink "Success to Coquet-side,"
   Tho' a tear fa' in the cup.

An' then fareweel!—dear Coquet-side !
   Aye gaily may thou rin,
An' lead thy waters sparkling on,
   An' dash frae linn to linn ;
Blithe be the music o' thy streams
   An' banks, thro' after days,
An' blithe be every fisher's heart
   Shall ever tread thy braes.

The time did come when the Coquet could no more be visited by Robert Roxby or Thomas Doubleday. But, before that day, Doubleday had been heavily tried by financial ruin, at a time, too, when, in his own words, he had fallen into "the sere and yellow leaf," but whilst he still had a family depending upon his exertions. It was then that he composed the following touching lines, with which I shall close my account of the *Coquetdale Fishing Songs.* He calls them

THE AULD FISHER'S LAST WISH.

The morn is grey, and green the brae, the wind is frae the wast ;
Before the gale the snaw-white clouds are drivin' light and fast ;
The airly sun is glintin' forth, owre hill, and dell, an' plain ;
And Coquet's streams are glitt'rin', as they rin frae muir to main.

At Dewshill wood the mavis sings beside her birken nest ;
At Halystane the laverock springs upon his breezy quest ;
Wi' eydent e'e, aboon the craigs, the glead is high in air,
Beneath brent Brinkburn's shadowed cliff the fox lies in his lair.

There's joy at merry Thristleyhaugh the new-mawn hay to win ;
The busy bees at Todstead-shaw are bringing hinny in ;
The trouts they loup in ilka stream, the bird 's on ilka tree ;
Auld Coquet-side is Coquet still—but there's nae place for me.

My sun is set, my eyne are wet, cauld poortith now is mine ;
Nae mair I'll range by Coquet-side, and thraw the gleesome line ;
Nae mair I'll see her bonnie streams in spring-bright raiment drest,
Save in the dream that stirs the heart when the weary e'e's at rest.

Oh ! were my limbs as ance they were, to jink across the green ;
And were my heart as light again, as sometime it has been ;
And could my fortunes blink again, as erst when youth was sweet,
Then Coquet—hap what might beside—we'd no be lang to meet.

Or had I but the cushat's wing, where'er I list to flee,
And wi' a wish, might wend my way owre hill, an' dale, an' lea ;
'Tis there I'd fauld that weary wing, there gaze my latest gaze,
Content to see thee ance again—then sleep beside thy braes!

Now do you not agree with me that we Northumbrians have good right to be proud of our *Coquetdale Fishing Songs*. I have dwelt on them at length because they are our specialty ; no other county has anything of the kind to boast of.

And I think that we should show our pride in and gratitude to Thomas Doubleday in some more public way than we have hitherto done. We have no great street named after our most distinguished literary man ; no great public memorial of him : and yet his is a memory which we should keep alive amongst us for he has done great things for us. Those of us who had the privilege of knowing him and Robert Roxby personally are not likely to forget either of them, but Thomas Doubleday's real and wide merit surely demands public recognition of a lasting kind.

We have a rich store of local songs, many of which have a distinct merit of their own. They may be divided into two classes : those which have been written in the Newcastle dialect by men who know it, as we all do, by living in the city, but who do not habitually use it, and those which have, as it were, sprung from the soil. The first class have more finish, and are often admirable, but the latter are the more precious. They alike preserve our good old local speech ; they give us pictures of the actual life of our people ; they show how the changes which time has brought have struck the Newcastle folk ; they tell us of old ways and forgotten worthies ; and many a quaint custom, many a picturesque incident, many an odd character lives for us in these humble effusions. We find evidences of great changes in the songs themselves. Those of the last quarter of a century—I mean those which are still popularly sung—are gentler, more refined, give evidences of a social advance, which are, to a great extent wanting in the earlier ones, and they have not lost the truthfulness, the fun, or the high spirit which characterised their predecessors.

From time to time some of these songs seem to be lost. One which my father used to say to me when I was a child, I have never been able to recover. It described the earliest Polytechnic, first thought of, I believe, during the first meeting of the British Association in this city in the year 1838. That week of meeting was always popularly spoken of as " the Wise Week," and my father used to tell of how, when the brass band of a menagerie was heard in the Bigg Market on the Saturday before the Wise Week, a pit wife, who was purchasing her groceries in George Richardson's shop, rushed out into the street with the exclamation "Aa'se warnd its the wise folk cummin.'" The Polytechnic exhibition was opened in 1840. Only two verses of the old song have stuck in my memory. The first alludes, I believe, to the contributions of our respected and valued Vice-President, Dr. Embleton. It ran thus :—

> Great Dr. Dennis sent a case
> Containin' sparrows' byens, man ;
> Of monkeys' skeletons a brace,
> And lots o' boody stanes, man ;
> Frae Cullercoats he sent sea weeds ;
> Of bugs and butterflies a' breeds ;
> Cock robins' nebs and rattens' heeds,
> To grace wor Poly Technic.

The other refers to a picture of " Pan and the Bacchanals," by some old master, which was sent by Mr. John Gibson, a well-known house-painter and picture collector, whose gallery was thrown open during the Wise Week. It ran thus :—

> Poor painter Jack's gyen picture mad,
> His paintin', nobbut note, sirs ;
> A dirty-fyeced great lubbart lad,
> Cuddlin' a billy-goat, sirs !
> Get soap an' dook it i' the Tyne !
> And yet gowks call the daub divine !
> Not fit to be a pothouse sign,
> Or owt but Poly Technic.

The worst of songs which are filled with local allusions, and with references to passing characters and petty local incidents is that they lose their interest when the generation who knew the persons and shared in the incidents have passed away. If we take such an excellent specimen of its kind as "The Newcastle Props," we see at once how much of its fun and meaning are gone to us who never met, in the flesh, "Jacky Tate," nor even "Little Airchy Logan." Each verse deals with one or two of these "Props" of the good old town which seemed at the end of the first quarter of this century coming to pieces, as one after one of the slightly disreputable characters vanished.

> Oh, waes me, for wor canny toon, it canna stand it lang—
> The props are tum'lin ane by ane, the beeldins suin mun gan,

but even "the blythest iv the motley groop, an' fairly worth a score," Blind Willie himself is scarcely a name to the present generation.

You see the difference at once if you take the charmingly quaint, "Pitman's Courtship," which treats of matters of eternal and universal interest, however widely diverse the immediate application may be. I often wonder how such a song strikes a stranger. Take Lukey's comparison of Bessy when his courtship begins :—

> Ma granny liked spice singin' hinnies,
> Ma comely, aw like thou as weel.

Or the following verse :—

> Thou knaws, ever since we were littel,
>   Together we've ranged thru the wuds ;
> At neets, hand in hand toddled hame,
>   Varry oft wi' howl kites an' torn duds :
> But now we can taak aboot mairage,
>   An' lang sair for wor weddin' day ;
> When mairied thou's keep a bit shop,
>   An' sell things iv the huikstery way.

"Howl kites and torn duds" might possibly puzzle even some good Northumbrians. They are words of much interest. "Howl" is a contraction of "hollow," and is here equivalent to "empty." It is often so used. The winter quarter of the year is the howl quarter : to be howl is to be hungry. It has the "w" placed before the "l," as Chaucer places it immediately after. The clerk "looked holwe," or, as one text has it, "holwhe," or "holewɂ," as another manuscript says. We have "hol," in Dutch, first meaning a cave, a hole, and then applied to the sound, the blurred sound of noises in holes ; and then we get "holo," meaning anything which produces this blurred sound, and so anything which is empty.

Then we come to "kite," which means the belly : "howl kite" is equivalent to empty belly. "Kite" is really "cud" or "quid," the thing chewed, then that place where it is chewed. The ruminating animal throws the contents of its stomach up into the mouth for the purpose of being chewed again. So we have in old Norse quidr, the paunch, the maw ; quida, to fill one's belly ; cud is old English for the stomach ; and Sir David Lindsay of the Mount uses "kyte" exactly as Lukey does in our song.

And, lastly, we have the interesting word "duds," which is still in constant use when rather common clothes are spoken of. Originally a "dud" was a rag, so that to apply the adjective "torn" to duds is surplusage. It comes from the verb to dodder, dudder, or dother, to shake, to tremble. We all know dothering grass. When the corporation were going down the river on barge day, nearly half a century ago, a stalwart Freeman was seated opposite rare old Ralph Dodds, who had a fine shape of jelly near him. He was hailed by the Freeman with, "Mistor Dodds, hinny, rax us sum o' them dothers." And so we pass from dother, or dodder, or dudder, to shake, to tremble, to duds, rags, not things which make us tremble, but in which we tremble, or which tremble in the wind.

It has been pointed out how this connection between rags and shaking or trembling exists in many languages, and thus we come to understand that a rag always bears with it this idea of shaken by the wind. We have the word "tatters," rags and tatters. Now, in Bavarian, tateren is to shiver, and tater-man is a scare-crow, a man made of rags, of tatters, the very object being that they shall shake in the wind. In Switzerland, lodelen is to shake, to be loose, loden, is a rag : hudeln is to waver, to dangle, hudel, a rag. The French driller, to twinkle, gives us drilles, tatters ; and so I might go on with several more instances of a like kind.

But I have got a long way from our song which goes on to describe the varied contents of the "bit shop," and to make many sweet promises which you will learn when you hear it sung :—

> Reed harrin, broon syep, and mint candy,
> Black pepper, dye-sand, and sma' yell ;
> Spice hunters, pick shafts, farden candles,
> Wax dollies wi' reed leather shoes,
> Chawk pussy-cats, fine corley greens,
> Paper skyets, penny pies, and yule doos.

> A'se help thou to tie up thy shuggar,
> At neets when frae wark a' gets lowse !
> An' wor Dick, that leeves ower by High Whickham,
> He'll myek us broom buzzums for nowse,
> Like an image thou's stand owr the coonter,
> Wi' thy fine muslin, cambricker goon :
> An' to let the fowks see thou's a leddy,
> On a cuddy thou's ride to the toon.

> There's be matches, pipe-clay, an' broon dishes,
> Canary seed, raisins, and fegs ;
> And, to please the pit-laddies at Easter,
> A dish-ful o' giltey paste eggs ;
> Wor neibors, that's snuffers an' smokers,
> For wor snuff and backey they'll seek,
> An', to show them we deal wi' Newcassel,
> Twee blackeys sal mense the door-cheek.

Let us hope that in this case, at all events, the realisation of an ideal wedded life, to be begun "next Whit-Sunday," equalled the anticipation.

I should like to have instanced "Jemmy Joneson's Whurry" as a song which must always retain its interest for quite another reason. It perpetuates the remembrance of a common and favourite mode of conveyance before the days of steam-boats and railways. It has thus quite a quasi-historical interest, entirely independent of its own great merits as a song. But I must only make a passing allusion to it now, and that because of a certain quaint touch in one of the verses which is worth remembering, because, if sufficiently pondered over, it will remove many artistic, critical, commercial, and social delusions. The happy Newcasseler, who is making the great voyage from the Newcastle of ninety years ago to Shields, had a different scene to survey to that which greets his successor who does the same passage to-day in the steam ferry instead of the old wherry. And yet, not so very different after all. He says :—

> Tyne-side seem'd clad wiv bonny ha's,
> An' furnaces sae dunny ;
> Wey, this mun be what Bible ca's
> "The land of milk and honey !"

There is real good homely genius in those lines.

I have made no mention of a few fine old songs which we claim here in Northumberland as ours, such as the simple and pathetic "Sair Failed, Hinnie," or "O, cam ye frae Newcastle," because of the lack of time, for it seemed impossible for me to mention our local songs without making special reference to the first of all our Newcastle song writers, Joe Wilson, who was still amongst us only twenty-three years ago. You may ask me why I place him so certainly at the head of our multitude of song-writers. My answer is that he has succeeded, beyond all the others, in reaching the heart of the people ; in writing songs which are actually sung, and which have entered into our local life. This is surely the true test of the great song-writer. There are songs which are instinct with the divinest spirit of poetry : there are songs which stir the blood like the blast of a trumpet : there are songs which ring through the heart like the chime of marriage bells : there are songs which pour forth the wail of the life-weary : there are songs which drop like soothing balm upon the stricken heart : there are songs which seem to reach even beyond the grave. And there are the songs which please the bairns, and the songs of common domestic life ; and to this class do Joe Wilson's belong. I speak of the best of them. Like nearly every writer of verse, he wrote far too much, and he wrote some few things which we could well do without. But these are very few, and Joe Wilson is, when we take his work as a whole, a man of whom we may justly be proud ; a man, too, who had a message for us, which he gave us in his own simple way, and who was, though he little knew it, truly a teacher. Upon his tombstone in the Old Cemetery at Jesmond are engraved the lines in which he himself describes what the object of his life has been :—

> It's been me aim t' hev a place
> I' th' hearts o' th' Newcassel people,
> Wi' writin' bits o' hyemly sangs
> Aw think they'll sing.

This is really the highest aim of the song-writer, and it means much, for that which is mean, or poor, or base will not live. The man must purify his inmost heart, and be gentle, loving, true, lowly of spirit, who would say of his work :—

> All my ambition but to sing a song
> That men should listen to, and say, we would
> We knew the singer, for he speaks from God
> Straight to our souls.

Joe Wilson's life was a short one. He was born in Stowell Street on the 29th November, 1841, his father being a joiner and his mother making straw bonnets. He was brought up to be a printer, published his first book when seventeen years old, wrote his famous song " Aw Wish yor Muthor wad Cum," and the scarcely less famous " Dinnet Clash the Door " in 1863, began to sing his own songs and give recitations in music halls and such places in 1864, married in 1869 ; became landlord of the Adelaide Hotel in New Bridge Street in 1871, but found the life unbearable in a twelvemonth, so gave it up and became a firm and convinced teetotaller. To a friend who asked him how he was getting on with his public house, he replied, " Badly : if aw drink wiv iv'rybody that asks us aw's a drucken beast ; if aw dinnet, aw's a surly beast—aw'll heh to be oot on't."

And out of it he was. From this time he worked hard and earnestly, by temperance songs, readings and recitations, to uphold and advance the cause and doctrines of the Good Templars, whom he had joined. The spirit of his work is admirably shown in the lines :—

Ye may talk aboot clivor men bein' greet drinkers,
  An' reckon yorsel as a one o' that sort,
An' run doon tetotal te chaps that's not thinkers,
  But, hinny, what say ye to Cowen an' Burt?

His writings were still racy of the soil : his inspiration was drawn from the actual life around him : his pictures are those of the real homely life of the people whom he loved and amongst whom he lived.

But lived for too brief a space. Early in 1874 consumption showed signs of its dreaded presence, and, although he struggled bravely on for nearly a year, he passed peacefully to rest on the 12th February, 1875, being but thirty-three years old.

Although they are so well known, let me say a few words about the two songs which I have mentioned, and first as to " Dinnet Clash the Door," which, to the apparently inappropriate tune of " Tramp, tramp," gently inculcates the restful quiet which old folks need and which young folks are apt to think so little of, either for themselves or others.

Oh, dinnet clash the door !
Aw've telled ye that before,
Can ye not let yor muther hev a rest ?
Ye knaw she's turnin' aud,
An' for eers she's been se bad
That she cannet bear such noises i' the least.

Then comes the " korus ":—

Then, oh, lass, dinnet clash the door se,
Yor yung an' yor as thowtless as can be.
But yor muther's turnin' aud,
An' ye knaw she's varry bad,
An' she dissent like to hear ye clash the door.

Just see yor muther there,
Sittin' feeble i' the chair,
It's quiet that she wants to myek her weel ;
She's been yor nurse throo life,
Been yor guide in peace an' strife,
An' her cumfort ye shud study an' shud feel.

And, in two more verses, Joe Wilson tells how she was once young and strong, and urges that now she should have no cause to complain. A good, homely, simple song, full of real life.

And so is the next one I mentioned. Nearly all of Joe Wilson's songs are founded upon fact : they spring from some scene which he

has actually witnessed ; and we have thus bits of genuine, un-
adulterated and wholesome realism, which are refreshing to listen to.
In the famous song I now speak of the wife, who is really not "strang,"
has to get "coals and flooer," but will not be "lang," so she asks
Geordy to "haud the bairn for fairs" during her absence : he'd "often
deun'd for fun !"

Geordy, who is a good-hearted Newcasseler, "held the bairn,"

> But sair agyen his will,
> The poor bit thing wes gud.
> But Geordy had ne skill,
> He haddint its muther's ways,
> He sat both stiff an' num,—
> Before five minutes wes past,
> He wished its muther wad cum.
>
> His wife had scarcely gyen,
> The bairn begun te squall,
> Wi' hikin't up an' doon,
> He'd let the poor thing fall,
> It waddent haud its tung,
> Tho sum aud teun he'd hum,—
> "Jack an' Jill went up a hill,"
> Aw wish yor muther wad cum.

Then Geordy begins to reflect upon the weary toil which women have
to go through, and which men so habitually overlook.

> Men seldum give a thowt
> To what thor wives indure,
> Aw thowt she'd nowt te de
> But clean the hoose, aw's sure,
> Or myek me dinner an' tea.

But the lord of creation is learning a grand lesson. The bairn's
"startin to chow its thum ; " he "sees tuts throo its gum :" but he
is true and patient, and reaps the due reward of kindness.

> At last,—its gyen te sleep,
> Me wife 'll not say aw's num,
> She'll think aw's a real gud norse,—

But, the perplexed mind craves for rest, and so, in spite of victory,

> Aw wish yor muther wad cum.

And so with these simple, useful, truthful, teaching verses I bring
these glimpses into the history, language, literature, and art of our
beloved Northumberland to a close. We have seen what a proud
position Northumbria held in the early history of England, how she

was the home of the earliest English poetry, and may be truly said
to have led Christendom in education and enlightenment. In the
first works which remain to us we find the keynote struck which
has resounded through all the ages since, for we hear the same
simple earnestness, intensity of purpose, and religious devotion in
the voices of Cædmon and Cynewulf as in those of Tennyson and
Browning. We have spent some time with the songs of earlier days
before newspapers and printed books existed, and with those which
lie about our own day, and have heard how, in these things, Northumberland holds her own and honoured place. We have traced
the leading part which a Northumbrian played in the great religious
changes of the sixteenth century; the independent position which
a Northumbrian won amongst our country's didactic poets; and
have learned how, from our county, went forth a sailor of unsur-
passed skill, of unequalled devotion, of perfect courage, and of
stainless life, who shone without a compeer alike in the gentle art
of letter writing, and in the power of planning and carrying out
successfully great naval exploits and vast diplomatic combinations;
and we have glanced at the distinction which our county has won
in various departments of the fine arts.

But far more remains to be done than we have accomplished;
far more than will have been accomplished when this whole course
of Northumbrian lectures shall have come to an end. Surely the
work which we have humbly but faithfully begun will not end here,
but younger and abler hands and minds will continue the labour
of love until every Northumbrian shall have the opportunity of
understanding from the fullest knowledge what a happy thing it is
to belong to so glorious a county.

DIALECT SPEECH IN NORTHUMBERLAND.

BY R. OLIVER HESLOP.

If we take our modern literary English as a standard, we understand by a dialect "one of its subordinate forms or varieties arising from local peculiarities of vocabulary, pronunciation and idiom."

But when we trace back the dialect of Northumberland to its earliest phase we find it in use as a literary medium. And, on the other hand, it is found that the standard English of the present day, represented by the speech of the cultured and the literary form of our writers, is itself the development of a dialect. Traced to its source it forms one of the three main divisions or dialects of Early English; and is found to be that dialect which, by its historical association and its favoured locality, has obtained prominence, been developed as the standard speech, adopted as the literary form, and used in preference, to the more or less exclusion of the rest.

At the outset we are reminded of the simple fact that our language is not the original speech of this island; and that, even at this day, English is not the spoken tongue in every part of it. In the ancient kingdom of the Scots the Gaelic language prevails over a considerable area, and in Wales the language yet remains British.

The date assigned to the arrival of the English in Kent is A.D. 449. The first detachment was followed by successive immigrations, which debarked at separate parts of the coast line. So that whilst Hengist and Horsa are the historical figures associated with the landing in Kent, Octa and Ebussa, their kinsmen, are the traditional leaders of an English descent upon the Northern seaboard.

Their name is Latinised in Tacitus, and in the *Ecclesiastical History* of Bede as Angli; but if one of themselves had been asked he would probably have called himself, like a modern Tynesider, *Ing-a-lish*.

"Those who came over," says Bede, "were of the three most powerful nations of Germany: Saxons, Angles and Jutes." After specifying the locality occupied by the first and last named, Bede adds, " From the Angles, that is the country which is called Anglia, and which is said from that time to remain desert to this day, are descended the East Angles, the Midland Angles, Mercians, and all the race of the Northumbrians, that is of those nations that dwell on the north side of the river Humber, and the other nations of the English." *

As Bede was born in A.D. 672, and probably wrote his history two hundred and fifty years after the first English arrivals, the settlement of his countrymen was described by him from the traditionary narratives of the event. In keeping with these is his genealogy of Hengist and Horsa, which follows, and in which their ancestry is traced to Woden.

The main fact realised by Bede was the kinship of the English race, in which he recognised three leading families, or *gentes Anglorum.*

But the story had been related at a much earlier date, and by a historian who was not, like Bede, of the Angle-cynn. The British writer, Gildas, was probably born A.D. 520, and his *History of the Britons* is ascribed to the year 564, or a little more than a century after the date affixed to the arrival of the English in Kent. Gildas not only shares the humiliation of his countrymen in their defeat by English arms, but deplores the success of the invaders as the triumph of the pagan followers of Woden over the church of Christ. In the bitterness of his soul he realises the judgments that are abroad as the punishments sent in consequence of his people's sins. We do not expect to find much historical enlightenment from either the History or the Epistles, because they are little more than dirges, the burden of which may be summed up in :—" Woe to the conquered ; the heathen are come into the inheritance ; the sin of the people has brought forth death, and the land is a desolation." But there is the interesting fact, that Bede, on more than one occasion, copies the very language of Gildas. Bede either quoted these passages direct, or else both Gildas and Bede quoted from a third source. Whatever, therefore, may be the ultimate verdict as to the *Historia Gildæ*, the inference is that the passages repeated by each writer in this manner possess an antiquity which is beyond dispute.

The statement that the first of the English came by the invitation of Vortigern, and arrived in three ships, is made by Gildas, repeated

* *Eccl. Hist.* i. 15.

by Bede, and copied into the *Anglo-Saxon Chronicle*. If Gildas is not himself the source of this statement, it may belong to yet earlier tradition. It is, in any case, the very earliest mention by a writer of the coming of the English ; and, what is of still greater interest to us, there stands out from the Latin of the sentence one English word. It is expressed in hatred of the people and in scorn of their barbarous tongue ; but there it is, the very earliest English word ever recorded. It is impossible not to feel the strongest veneration for the first word noted of our language, but speaking from this standpoint our veneration is turned to affection for a word which is more to a Tynesider than to any other Englishman. I mean the word *keel*. Elsewhere the term is restricted in its meaning ; but on Tyneside it has maintained its original integrity as the name for the entire vessel.* It has prompted that song of songs "The Keel Row," which, with its stirring tune, is not only our Tyneside anthem, but has gone out into all the world as a marching song of the Englishman in his new and strange lands. Rudyard Kipling, writing of it in India, says †:—"The man who has never heard the Keel Row rising, high and shrill, above the rattle of the regiment going past the saluting-base, has something yet to hear and understand."

The passage in Gildas reads as follows :—"Then a litter of cubs " (that is his name for the English) "issuing forth from the lair of the lioness of Barbaria, in three *cyuls*, as it is expressed in their tongue, in ours long ships."‡

In A.D. 547 Ida had established his sovereignty in what was known as the kingdom of the Beornicas, the district between Forth and Tyne. From Humber northward was the country of the Deras.§ Ethelfrith not only united the two states, but drove his conquest

---

* It was also so used in East Anglia. "*Keel:* a kind of boat employed on the Yare ; now very rare." Walter Rye. *Glossary of Words used in East Anglia.* Eng. Dialect Soc. No. 75. 1895.

† Kipling, *Plain Tales*, Macmillan, 1896, p. 216.

‡ Tum erumpens grex catulorum de cubili leœnæ Barbariæ, tribus ut lingua ejus exprimitur *cyulis*, nostrâ linguâ longis navibus. *Historia Gildæ*, chapter 23. In the Tyneside pronunciation of *keel* at the present day a fractured vowel sound is heard. This can hardly be better rendered than by the phonetic form [kyul] given by Gildas.

§ The terms Bernicia and Deira were not in use, I believe, to the east of the Severn till after the Norman Conquest. Those of "Bernicians" and "Deirans" have absolutely no contemporary authority, and as they merely mean "the inhabitants of the kingdoms of the Beornicas or the Deras," why not say "Beornicas" and "Deras" at once? C. J. Bates, *Archæologia Aeliana*, vol. xix. p. 147.

westward to Chester and the seaboard there ; and to him we owe the first unified kingdom, thenceforth to be known as the nation of the Northanhumbrians.

Turning backward from these noisy years of the nineteenth to the great days of the seventh century we find that they—

> Are yet the fountain light of all our day,
> Are yet a master light of all our seeing.

For the Northanhumbraland became the bright particular centre which attracted the Christian culture, introduced by Aidan from the west and by Paulinus from the south. And the germination and development of this influence gave it an almost indigenous character, associated, as it became, with a succession of remarkable men whose very names make history. In Cuthbert and Cædmon, in Biscop and Wilfrid, in Acca and Bede we have men not for an age but for all time.

The greatness of the Northanhumbraland was no mere provincialism. It was a pre-eminence unexampled in Western Europe. Wilfrid's church at Hexham was on a scale of magnificence beyond anything on this side of the Alps. Gaul then remained a mere disintegrated portion of the wreck left of the Western Empire, wherein the Romanised Celt and his Frankish invaders were alike menaced by the terrible powers of the Saracen. It was in the first stages of its recovery that Alcuin became the chief agent in founding a school of learning at Tours. "The learned Alcuin, that Northumbrian Erasmus," as Mr. Bates styles him,[*] was a disciple of Egbert who, in turn, had been a disciple of Bede.

The vernacular literature of this great period perished in the Danish invasions which ensued ; all save a few fragments. Among these are the verses attributed to Cædmon, the legends in runes on the Bewcastle and Ruthwell crosses, and the biliteral inscription on the Falstone cross.[†] The most extensive example of the earliest Northanhumbrian dialect is found in the glosses to the four *Linaisfarne Gospels*, the same in three of the *Rushworth Gospels*, and in the *Durham Ritual*[‡]; and from these and from another, which I

---

[*] C. J. Bates, *Hist. of Northumberland*, 1895, p. 82. See also Bede, *Hist. Eccl.* ed. Plummer, pp. xxiv. and xviii. n. 2.

[†] For these see Prof. Stephens' *Old Northern Runic Monuments* and *cf.* Sweet's *Earliest English Texts*.

[‡] The *Durham Ritual* is No. 10 ; the *Gospels* form Nos. 28, 39, 43, and 48 in issues of the Surtees Society. But see the *Lindisfarne Gospels*, ed. by Prof. Skeat, Cambridge University Press.

shall presently indicate, we recognise the mother-tongue of Cuthbert
and Ceolfrid and Biscop and Bede. And, despite its inflected
structure and archaic forms, we can plainly read in it the idioms and
vocabulary of the dialect-speech of the Northumberland of to-day.

The other fragment, to which reference was just made, is given
by the biographer of the Venerable Bede, in his narrative of the death
of his master. His words are these :—" And in our own tongue also
(for he was skilled in our native songs), speaking of the dread
departure of the soul from the body, he sang :—

> Before the need-journey
> No one is ever
> More wise in thought
> Than he ought,
> To contemplate
> Ere his going hence
> What to his soul,
> Of good or of evil
> After death-day
> Deemed will be."

Thus reads the translation into Southern English, given by Professor
Earle.* If, however, we turn it into our northern dialect, we shall be
able to come much nearer to the wording of the original :—

> Afore thor need-fare
> Yen is nivver mair
> Wise in thowt
> Than he owt,
> Think what he can
> Or his way-gan
> What tiv his ghaist
> O' good or ill maist
> Efter his deeth day
> Doom then may say.

For the space of three centuries our northern dialect is involved in
the darkness which followed the Danish invasions, when the pagan
hosts spoiled the churches and monasteries and destroyed their
treasures of literature. And, although our native songs and our
recorded literature perished, yet the spoken dialect remained.
It was necessarily influenced greatly by this important ethnic
addition ; but the Danes and Norsemen were a kindred people, pos-

* Prof. Earle, *Anglo-Saxon Literature*, 1884, p. 110. See Sweet's *Earliest
English Texts* for the poem in its original form.

sessing, possibly, no great physical difference from the English of Northanhumbraland and a dialect which, though strange, was not foreign (for there is little doubt that the two peoples could understand each other's speech.)* The fusion, at all events, became complete ; and, however it affected the spoken language, it is likely to have produced effects in accent and enunciation most strongly in those parts where Danes and Norsemen became settled in the greatest numbers. The effect would be less perceptible in districts, which, although nominally under Danish rule, were yet able to maintain a certain degree of independence. Such was the case north of the Tyne.

One of the indications which enables us to judge of the localities colonised by the northmen is found in place-names. On this coast the test words for these are the termination—*by* for settlements (as Whitby, Thornaby), and the substitution of the word *beck* for the Anglian term, *burn*. And, as far as the evidence of place-names can be relied on, the northern part of the county of Durham and the whole of the modern county of Northumberland are practically unaffected by Danish influences.

This also agrees with the actual history, in which, during the period of the Danelagh, we find Northumberland owning the supremacy, and at times submitting to the overlordship of a Danish earl, yet practically independent, and, ultimately, in the hands of its own line of rulers, maintaining the tradition, if not the power, of a sovereign land.

Scandinavian terms which appear in English may have been, and in many cases were, common to both tongues. But we do not find recorded instances until a much later date. Of these the word *to call* is an example, and in the northern dialect the use of the first-person singular of the verb *is* probably dates from this time. What we do find, when our northern dialect comes to light again after its long eclipse, is a strong and apparently hereditary antipathy to the Norse invaders, who are denounced as paynims and worse.

The Norman Conquest, profoundly as it affected the nation politically, appears to have influenced the northern dialect in the smallest degree. The historic earldom of Northumberland continued, now as a fief of Scotland, or again in the hands of a nominee of the English crown ; but in either case the country itself remained in practical isolation from the main current of English life. Domesday

---

* Prof. Skeat, *Principles of Eng. Etymology*, 1st series, 1887, p. 455.

did not include it; nor, until centuries later, did the king's writs run throughout all the districts north of the Tyne. The palatinate on the south extended an ecclesiastical authority beyond the Tyne, but served the more to demark this outlying and frontier land.

When the dialect reappears it exhibits the results of a development which had gone on during the period of its long obscurity. These are shown in the modification of its inflectional suffixes, and its advance in the direction of a modern form. An example of this occurs in a charter extant in the Treasury at Durham which is written in the vulgar tongue. It is addressed to his thanes in Islandshire and Norhamshire by Ralph Flambard, whose episcopate reached from A.D. 1099 to 1128, in which time he built the nave of Durham Cathedral, and realised the plan of his great predecessor William of St. Carilef. The tendency shown in this document is yet more apparent in the structure of the "Cursor Mundi," which was written in Durham about A.D. 1275 to 1300, and in the text of a truce made between Percy and Douglas in 1324.

In the first of these we still find inflected forms of the pronouns surviving in *hine*, accusative of he, and *thisses*, genitive of this, but even these are already lapsing. The gutturals *noght* and *wroght* have not yet, however, given place to nowt and wrout. *Qua* and *quilk*, the hard forms of who and which, are still current. *That ilk*, for that same, and *sal*, the northern form of shall, are both in use. In our dialect to-day we still use *deed* for death, in the common expressions *caad as deed*, cold as death, *deun to deed*, done to death, and in *tew'd to deed* and *tired to deed*—just as the word is used in "Cursor Mundi." Here, too, the participial form a-n-d is observable. When the modern Tynesider speaks of *fleein*, and *seein*, and *deein*, he is sometimes accused of a careless pronunciation of the ending in i-n-g. But the old present participle is not *deeing*; it is *deeand* ["*Deiand* ai and never deed," in "Cursor"] and from this form has been developed our shortened sound as it is now heard in *deein*, and *seein*, and *fleein*.

The condition of Northumberland in the reign of the second Edward was that of a country wasted by the passage and repassage of armies and camp followers and by the demoralisation of defeat. The head made by the Scots under Robert the Bruce culminated in their demand for the cession of all the country up to the gates of York as the condition of peace. But with the accession of Edward III. and the death of the Bruce the aspect brightened, and the century, whose

early years saw Bannockburn, was yet to become illustrious. Cressy
and Poictiers abroad, and Neville's Cross and Chevy Chase at home,
were evidences of a chivalry that redeemed the lapses of the past.

Two writers of the fourteenth century have especial claim upon
our attention. Richard Rolle de Hampole wrote from his cell at
Hampole, about four miles from Doncaster, and is usually known as
Hampole in consequence. His diction is that of the extreme south
of the ancient Northanhumbraland. His writings include some prose
treatises and his poem *The Pricke of Conscience*, finished shortly
before his death in A.D. 1349. Almost contemporaneously Master
John Barbour, archdeacon of Aberdeen, wrote *The Book of the
most excellent and noble prince, Robert de Broyss, King of Scots*,
which was completed in 1375. From these two works we are able to
make a comparison of the language at points as far south as
Doncaster and as far north as Aberdeen ; that is on the southernmost
confine of the ancient Anglian kingdom and at the far northern point
on the east coast to which the northern English had extended.

The *Brus* is a story-book, recounting, as everybody knows, the
stirring adventures and romantic deeds of the king and his adherents.
It tells us, to begin with, that :—

> Stories to rede are delitabill,
> Suppose that thai be nocht bot fabill ;
> Than suld storys that suthfast wer,
> And thai war said on gud maner,
> Have doubill plesance in heryng.

The Pricke of Conscience is in striking contrast with this, for it is
a lengthy homily ; and in the course of its well nigh ten thousand
lines few passages rise above the solemn tone of exhortation in
which the theme is conducted. But in his meditation on the text
" Eye hath not seen nor ear heard," Hampole describes the joys of
heaven in a strain of exaltation which carries our hearts with it.

> All manner of joys are in that stead [steed] ;
> There is aye life withouten dede ;
> There is youth aye withouten eld [eeld],
> There is al-kind wealth aye to wield.
> There is rest aye, withoot travail ;
> There is all goods that niver sal fail
> There is peace aye, withooten strife
> There is all manner of liking of life ;
> There is, withooten mirkness, leet ;
> There is aye day and niver neet.
> There is aye summer full breet to see,
> And niver mair winter in that countree.

The important facts about these two early writers is the practical identity of their language and the evidence which they afford in showing that northern English was one dialect throughout the limits of the ancient Northanhumbraland. Dr. Murray writes :—

I have been repeatedly amused on reading passages from " Cursor Mundi " and Hampole to men of education, both English and Scotch, to hear them all pronounce the dialect, " Old Scotch." Great has been the surprize of the latter, especially on being told that Richard the Hermit wrote in the extreme south of Yorkshire, within a few miles of a locality so thoroughly English as Sherwood Forest, with its memories of Robin Hood. Such is the difficulty which people have in separating the natural and ethnological relations in which national names originate from the accidental values which they acquire through political complications and the fortunes of crowns and dynasties, that oftener than once the protest has been made, " Then he must have been a Scotchman settled there :" reminding us of the dictum of a learned Scottish judge upon *The Pricke of Conscience:* " You call it Early English, but it is neither more nor less than *Broad* Scots !" To which the reply has been given, " You call the language of Barbour's *Brus,* and Blind Harry's *Wallace,* of Wyntown, James I., and Dunbar, *Scotch;* but this is only a modern notion, for those writers themselves, whose patriotism certainly was not less, while their authority was greater than yours, called their language *Inglis.*" The retort has certainly the facts on its side. Down to the end of the fifteenth century, there was no idea of calling the tongue of the Lowlands *Scotch ;* whenever the " *Scottish* language " was spoken of, what was meant was the Gaelic or Erse, the tongue of the original Scots, who gave their name to the country. The tongue of the Lowlanders was " Inglis," not only as being the tongue of the Angles of Lothian and Tweedale, and as having been introduced beyond the Forth by Anglo-Saxon settlers, but English as being the spoken tongue of the northern subjects of the king of England, those with whom the subjects of the king of Scotland came most immediately in contact.*

It is probable that the present audience includes some countrymen of the Bruce, and in so delicate a subject as the question of their mother-tongue, I have sheltered myself under the language of their distinguished compatriot, Dr. Murray. The Lowlander is linguistically a Northanhumbrian Englishman, and it is by a historical irony that he calls himself a Scot. For the Scot was a Celt, in whom Wallace and Bruce found a foe more implacable in the struggle for independence than they found in their English kinsmen. But it was under the name of Scotsmen that the national party ranked, and, although it was really alien, they endowed it with an association and lustre which transferred from the Gael to the northern English the proud boast of " Scotland yet ! "

* James A. H. Murray, *Dialect of the Southern Counties of Scotland,* Philol. Soc. 1873, p. 41.

The severance of Scotland was followed by an independent development of the language north of Esk and Tweed, and its dialect became
the language of its court, its church system, and its legal tribunals ;
whilst its foreign connections and internal components reacted upon
its colloquial forms and its literary expression.   These circumstances,
needless to say, were all wanting when the border line was crossed
southward.   Northumberland and North Cumberland were remote
provinces of the English kingdom divided from each other by the
franchises of Tyndale, Ridsdale, and Hexhamshire.

Towards the end of the fifteenth century, the Midland dialect
asserted itself as the sole medium of literature.   Hitherto English
had been written in three dialects.   These, in the early period, were
Northumbrian, Mercian, and Wessex—or Anglo-Saxon, and were
developed as Northern, Midland, and Southern English.   Each was a
dialect distinct from the rest.   If a writer lived north of Trent and
Humber he wrote his book in Northern English; if immediately
south of them or towards the Thames he wrote Mercian English ; or,
if in Wessex he wrote Anglo-Saxon.   As each of these dialects
altered in the course of its growth, so its written form passed
through the phases of its development from the inflected form of the
early time to the simpler character of the later period.   But the progress of each was made at very different rates.   Thus the language of
Wessex continued to be written in the form which we call Anglo-
Saxon, and retained its declensions to a much later period, when
Northern English had, to a very large extent, outgrown them.   The
charter, to which I referred, belongs to the early years of the twelfth
century, and shows a comparative emancipation from inflections ; and
the subsequent examples show yet further advancement in form and
structure.   So much is this the case that "Cursor Mundi" and the
Brus and Hampole present no difficulties except in vocabulary ; whilst
the "Metrical Life of Saint Cuthbert," written about A.D. 1450,
appears almost modern in its form.

Printing, which was introduced in 1477, confirmed the supremacy
of a single dialect for English reading.   The printing of the Bible
especially set before the entire people a form and structure of
language which we now recognise as English.   It did more.   North
of the Tweed the language had developed on lines of its own, affected
by its Celtic surroundings and by the growth of Scotland as an
independent state ; and its divergence from that of the English
border became greater in course of time.   The union of the crowns

naturally led to the adoption of the English standard of expression in the written form of the language, at all events. But almost a century earlier the English Geneva version of the Bible had permeated Scotland, and its reaction upon language and literature became an important factor in conforming the Scottish expression to English usage.

The adoption of a single dialect for the purposes of English literature resulted in the eclipse of the other forms. The dialect and sub-dialects of the North have been practically set aside for quite four hundred years.* In this period they have developed as all language must develop. But they have grown as the outcast grows, and if they are not always nicely dressed they are invariably picturesque. From the remote corner occupied by Northumberland and its comparative isolation from external influences we retain a dialect possessed of characteristics which are in many respects unique. These have survived to our own day, stamped with a character impressed at a remote period and yet remaining clear and unmistakable. And there is one consideration to be borne in mind when we contrast it with other forms of dialect. They are usually described as "a form of speech among the uneducated." This, however, was by no means the case in Northumberland down to a comparatively recent period. For as late as stage-coach days the dialect-speech was common to gentle and simple, to lared and lewd alike. It was, with us, no mere vulgarised vernacular. With a vocabulary remarkable in its comprehensive character and discriminating nicety, it included in its archaisms terms which as often refer to the minor moralities of life, to the niceties of conduct, and the care of the person, as to behaviour at table and in society. All these indicate a true refinement, which finds a fuller expression in the social virtues included in such terms as *bonny*, and *canny*, and *hinny*.

Another point to be remarked is : that, whilst the three early dialects differed from each other and the Midland and the Northern English were widely different in their spoken and written forms from Southern English, there was much less difference between Midland English and Northumbrian English to begin with. They were, as Bede describes them, two branches of the same family group. For the Northumbrians were those who fared north of the Humber, and the Mercians (that is, Mark, or March-men, the men who fought

* An attempt has been made in the accompanying chart to represent the comparative lengths of time by drawing the centuries and decades of the Christian era to scale.

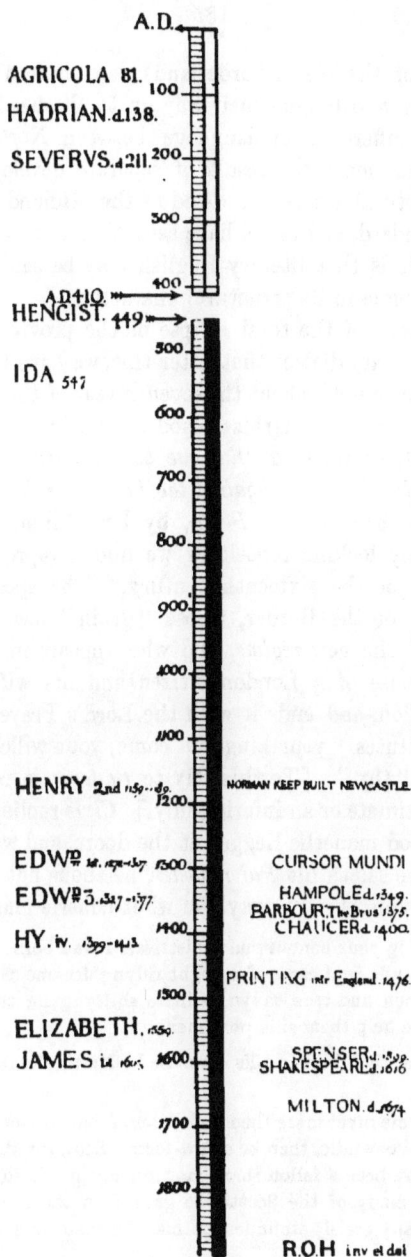

A.D.

AGRICOLA 81.
100
HADRIAN. d.138.
SEVERVS. d 211. 200
300
400
AD 410
HENGIST. 449
500
IDA 547
600
700
800
900
1000
1100
HENRY 2nd 1159...89.
1200   NORMAN KEEP BUILT NEWCASTLE.
EDW.D M. 1272-1307 1300   CURSOR MUNDI
EDW.D 3. 1327-1377   HAMPOLE d. 1349.
                       BARBOUR The Brus 1375.
HY. iv. 1399-1413   CHAUCER d. 1400
1400
                       PRINTING intr England. 1476.
1500
ELIZABETH. 1559.
JAMES 1st 1603. 1600   SPENSER d. 1599.
                       SHAKESPEARE d. 1616.
                       MILTON. d. 1674.
1700
1800

R.O.H inv et del

CENTURIES FROM ANNUS DOMINI
DIVIDED INTO DECADES.

along the line of the Welsh borderland) were those who also entered the Humber but who fought their way up to the head-waters of the river Trent. Difference of language between Northumbrian and Mercian was thus more the result of separate development than of an original structural difference. And as the Midland dialect became the adopted standard, and as we have seen that it was a near relation of our own, so it is that literary English may be said to partake of the Northern tongue in its structural character.

It is significant of the total eclipse of the provincial dialects by the advancing literary dialect that, after this, we have little or nothing to be called our own until about the seventh year of the reign of Queen Elizabeth. Our example of this period occurs in a book printed in London in 1564, entitled, *A Dialogue both Pleasaunt and Pietifull, wherein is a Godlie Regiment against the Fever Pestilence, with a Consolation and Comforte against Death*, by Dr. William Bullein. In this most unlikely looking repository we find a reproduction of the Ridsdale dialect of the sixteenth century. The speaker is one of the broken men of the Border, whose "grain" has been dispersed by the rigour of the new *régime*, and who appears in the guise of a beggar at the house of a London citizen and his wife. He begins with a benediction, and ends it with the Lord's Prayer, in which he reverently substitutes "your kingdom come, your willes be done" for the too familiar "thy." [To this day to *tu toyer* is reserved for an address to an intimate or an inferior only.] *Civis* replies:—"Methinke I doe heare a good manerlie Beggar at the doore, and well brought up, how reverently he saieth his *Pater noster*, he thous not God, but yous Him." *Uxor* enquires : " I pray you what contrie man be you ? "

Mendicus.—Savying your honour gud Maistresse, I was borne in Redesdale, in Northumberlande, and came of a wight ridyng sirname called the Robsons, gud honast men and true, savyng a little shiftyng for their living. God and our leddie help them silie pure men.

Uxor.—What doest thou here in this countrie? Me thinke thou art a Scot by thy tonge.

Mendicus.—Trow me niver mare then gud deam, I had better be hanged in a withie, or in a cowtaile, then be a row-footed Scot, for they are ever fare and fase. I've been a fellon sharp man on my hands in my yong daies, and brought many of the Scottes to ground in the North Marches, and gave them many greisly woundes, ne man for man durst abide me lick, I was so fell.

Then he tells how many of his kinsfolk and acquaintances he had met, among them the very man in charge of the gate, whom he proceeds to commend as : "A Ridesdale man borne, a gud man and a true, whiche for ill will in his youth, did fleem the countrie :—it was laied to his charge, the drivyng of kine hem to his father's byre : But Christe knoweth he was sackles, and live as honestlie in his age, as his sire did when he was yong gud maister." *

Outsiders persist in stating that a Northumberland man is unable to pronounce the letter *r*, and that he elides it in consequence. Attempts to imitate it are generally made with this misconception of its character, and are in native ears ridiculous. The burr is given with a full aspiration, and is really an emphatic and exaggerated *r*. The attempt of the Scotch lassie who rendered it by "swallowing the words and giving them a bit chow as they went down," was, probably, as unsuccessful as others. The ordinary English *r* is, of course, pronounced by the passage of breath between the incurved tongue and the palate. The Scottish *r* is produced by a true trill of the tip of the tongue. The burr, however, is effected by using the base and not the tip of the tongue. Hence it is called the uvular or tonsil *r*.†

This tonsil *r* is by no means peculiar to Northumberland. It exists sporadically as a family peculiarity in places widely separated in this country and in Scotland. It is also common on the Continent, where it has assumed an exclusive character over wide areas. But in no portion of this island does it extend over a wide district except in Northumberland.‡ It has thus attracted special, and, perhaps, undue attention. It is a feature of our speech which carries with it an unmistakable identity and of which we, as Northumbrians, are proud. But, considered philologically, it is a mere casual accretion or accident.

It was a common assumption that we derived the burr from the Danes. It was argued : Because Danes in Denmark use the uvular

* The earliest edition of William Bullein's Dialogue is dated 1564. A reprint is published in the Early English Text Society's Series (1888), from the edition of 1578, collated with the earlier editions. The portion relating to the Ridsdale Beggar will also be found in Stephen Oliver the younger's *Rambles in Northumberland*, 1835, p. 330.

† The "burr," as it is called, consists in allowing the uvula (or little tongue-like pendant to the soft palate at the back of the mouth), in place of the tip of the tongue, as in L, to "flap" quickly by the passage of vocalized or unvocalized breath, thus making the rapid beats or interruptions which give rise to the sensation of "trill." A. J. Ellis, *English Dialects*, 1890. Eng. Dial. Soc. No. 60, p. 125.

‡ The area of this district is shown by a line of dot-and-dash on the accompanying sketch map.

BERWICKSHIRE

"N." *North Northumberland*
S *South* do
W.T. *West Tyne*
T *Tyneside*
Shown by dotted lines thus ......
Limit of the Burr shewn
by outer line

MAIN SUBDIVISIONS OF DIALECT
IN THE COUNTY OF NORTHUMBERLAND.

r at the present day, and because they invaded and colonised parts of the east coasts, therefore they introduced and propagated the uvular *r* in Northumberland. But had this been the case, it would have been expected that in the parts which are especially Danish, in the country of the [Deras south of the Tees, where place-names indicate the clusters]of Danish settlements, we should find this speciality of speech rather than north of the Tyne, which is the part least affected by the Danish settlements. In other words, we ought surely to find the burr in Danish rather than non-Danish Northumbria. But this is just what we do not find..

The question remained until Professor Moritz Trautmann published the result of his exhaustive research into the origin and extension of the uvular *r* on the Continent. He there shows * that the *r* in old Northumbrian as in Anglo-Saxon was a tongue *r* and not a uvular *r*. Neither was the uvular *r* spoken in the old Continental languages and dialects. Its introduction there has been historically recent and he surmises that the Northumberland burr may in like manner be an acquirement dating from a much later period than is commonly supposed.

He is confirmed in this opinion by the fact that the uvular *r* was introduced to France and Germany in recent times.

The sound of *r* spoken in French at Paris in the sixteenth century is established, by particular descriptions, as being then universally the tongue *r* and not the *r grasséyé*. The same evidence exists for Germany. A few decades before 1670 the burr began to be introduced to Paris by the *Précieuses* as an affectation. In little more than a century it had spread extensively as "the fashion," originating in the numerous *ruelles*, or coteries of *Précieuses*, which sprang up in every large French town in imitation of the capital. Not only town people but country folk became infected with the novelty. Its introduction to Germany followed; first to the courts, then to the town society, and thence it has permeated all classes over a very large part of the Continent. Its passage to Denmark is noted by Professor Trautmann, which he says it now dominates absolutely ; and it has already passed to Bergen on the one hand and to Switzerland on the other. A remarkable fact about this phenomenon is its continuous progress; for the spread still continues to increase in area. Just the converse is the case in our own country ; for it has

* Prof. Moritz Trautmann, in *Anglia ;* Halle : Max Niemeyer, 1880, pp. 211, 222.

long been the desire of Northumbrians to emancipate themselves from what was at one time the common speech of all classes in the county.

There can be little doubt that the burr was introduced into our dialect at a date historically recent, and Dr. Murray, in supplementing Prof. Trautmann in *Anglia*, points out the contrast between the Continental and the Northumberland burr, as shown by its spread in one case and its shrinkage in the other. Dr. Murray further mentions the existence of a tradition that the Northumberland burr began as a personal defect of Hotspur, was imitated by his companions and by the earldom as a whole.*

This tradition exists quite independently of Shakespeare's reference. The latter is striking because it refers to the peculiar enunciation of Hotspur as a well-known characteristic. It occurs in the second part of King Henry IV. The third scene of act ii. is "Warkworth, before the castle." The widowed Lady Percy, dissuading the earl of Northumberland from taking the field, recalls the memory of her lost husband, Hotspur; "Her heart's dear Harry," of whom she says :—

> [His honour] stuck upon him as the sun
> In the grey vault of heaven, and by his light
> Did all the chivalry of England move
> To do brave acts : he was indeed the glass
> Wherein the noble youth did dress themselves :
> He had no legs that practised not his gait ;
> And speaking thick, which nature made his blemish,
> Became the accents of the valiant ;
> For those that could speak low and tardily
> Would turn their own perfection to abuse,
> To seem like him : so that in speech, in gait,
> In diet, in affections of delight,
> In military rules, humours of blood,
> He was the mark and glass, copy and book,
> That fashioned others.

That Shakespeare had before him a traditional origin for this delineation is every way likely. The lapse of time from the battle of Shrewsbury to the date of the play was 195 years ; and in Shakespeare's time the hero of the battle of Otterburn had become a household word throughout Southern England by the ballad literature which recounted his exploits. In his defence of poetry Sir Philip Sidney's reference shows how greatly in Elizabeth's time had been the

* *Anglia*, vol. iii. *supra*, p. 376.

spread of the romantic incidents of which Froissart had written minutely. Hotspur, the "Percy out of Northombarlande," is a central figure in ballad literature and tradition, and it may well be that in his own country, and on the minds of his followers and fellow Northumberland men, he wrought a spell. It is with just such fascination that Shakespeare, in another century and far removed from our border-land by distance, dwells again and again upon the character and the name of Harry Percy. The familiarity of this repeated "Harry," and the untiring play upon his nickname "hot-spur," are evidences of this. Yet more remarkable is the circumstance that after Hotspur's death Shakespeare revivifies his hero in his next play, and in the second part of Henry IV. endears him in the personal allusions which I have just read. It is as if the noble Harry Percy were one whom he would not willingly let die.

It is natural to think that the men of Northumberland were actuated by a like fascination when they adopted Hotspur as their ideal. And although he was descended from the proud lineage of a conquering family, yet his life and character made him congenial to the people among whom he lived, just as his

spirit lent a fire
Even to the dullest peasant in his camp ;

and his bravery in the field identified the "Hotspur of the North" with the Northumberland men in whose ranks he fought.

The facts connected with this peculiarity of speech are these :— (1) The uvular r of Northumberland is not an indigenous phenomenon, but an introduction. (2) Although much earlier than the uvular r now spoken on the European continent, its use in Northumberland probably originated no earlier than the fourteenth century. (3) It is still extant, but its area has not extended, and its tendency has been to diminish.

The low-back utterance of the uvular r suits itself to low-back vowel sounds, such, for instance, as the o as pronounced in *thorn*, *for*, *oar*, etc., or to the mid-back a, as heard in *farm*, *armour*, *bar*, etc. But such vocalization as is heard in the modern pronunciation of the palatal sounds in *durst*, *work*, *fur*, *first*, and in *turn*, *burn*, *worm*, *worth* are found to be quite incongruous with the uvular r. With it they are necessarily spoken *dorst*, *work*, *for*, *forst*, and *torn*, *born*, *worm*, *worth*. There can be very little doubt that this remarkable vocalization is a natural development from our original northern vowel sound ; and not, as some may suppose, a mere vulgar lapse. It follows as a consistent practice throughout, and conforms to the laws of language in every instance. The subject is too large to be dealt with except in an extensive series of word lists, but a single instance may illustrate the development of a word sound.

The word *work* (substantive) has a venerable history. It is, of course, the Greek ϵργον. [That Greek word in early examples begins with a digamma ; so that our English *w* preserves, as Professor Skeat has pointed out,* a sound which the Greeks lost *two thousand* years ago. This, however, is by the way.] Work occurs in our earliest English. In Anglo-Saxon it is *weorc* [pronounced *way-ork*]. In Mercian it is *wirc*. From this was developed the Middle English form *werk*, with a levelling of the vowel, and a result in the present obscure sound heard in our modern pronunciation of work (*wəək*). But in the *Lindisfarne Gospels* the form is *woerc;* so that it was spoken in our earliest Northumbrian with a low-back vowel as *wo-ark*, developed with us as work. The effect of the uvular *r* at this stage would be to arrest the further development of the word sound. And this would be quite consistent with the origin of the burr early in the fifteenth century. As soon as we leave the burr country in a southerly direction we find that the pronunciation has probably been affected by the literary language, and we meet with the form *wāk*, as in Yorkshire.

When, therefore, we find thirst, curse, and purse pronounced *thorst, kors, pors*, and words like birth and mirth and skirt pronounced *borth, morth, skort* [and so on throughout a long series of examples], it is that a vocalization of the Middle English period of our northern tongue has been retained because it can be produced with the least effort in enunciating the uvular *r* which follows.

To this cause may be attributed the arrest and consequent perpetuation of the word-forms of an early period. It is this feature which makes the Northumberland burr unique. In order to acquire it the learner must acquaint himself with the dialect form of many words as they may have been spoken in the period of Middle English. The Continental *r grasséyé* but feebly represents what is included in the uvular *r* sound as it is heard in Northumberland. Compare, for instance, the feeble result of such a pronunciation as Otter-burn with the genuine sound which we hear when it is spoken by us as *Ottorborn*. The consideration of this phenomenon adds weight to the

* Skeat, *Principles of English Etymology*, part 1, p. 129.

argument in favour of the traditional account of the date at which the *burr* first became prevalent in Northumberland.

The difficulty of reading our dialect is more apparent than real. When, however, it is either "said or sung" its mere utterance affords us gratification or amusement. Even its more serious forms possess a quaintness which is akin to humour and a charm like the charm of home itself. A conspicuous instance of this is found in the *Pitman's Pay* of Thomas Wilson. This is by far the most considerable modern work in the dialect and its importance can hardly be over-estimated; for it was written between the years 1826 and 1829, when many words were in vogue which have since grown obsolete. It is thus a rich mine to the philologist.

A short example must serve us here. The young pitman just entering upon manhood, *loquitur* :—

> Aw now began te curl ma hair,
>   For curls an' tails were then the go,
> To clean ma een wi' greater care,
>   An' smarten up frae top to toe.
>
> Ma shinin' coat o' glossy blue,
>   Lapelled an' lined wi' breet shaloon ;
> Ma posey jacket, a' bran new—
>   Just figured like ma muthor's goon—
>
> Ma breeks o' bonny velveteen—
>   Ma stockins—clocked a' up the leg—
> Ma nice lang-quartered shoon se clean,
>   An' buckles—real tuyth-an-neg,
>
> Ga' me the shape an' air o' yen
>   O' rather bettermer condition ;
> An' garred the jades a' gorn agyen—
>   A glance frae me was quite sufficien(t).
>
> Like ony chicken efter moot,
>   When its awd coat it fairly casses,
> Aw swaggered then—for ma new suit
>   Played harlekin amang the lasses.
>
> Amang them aw wad a'ways be,
>   Aw cuttered, canny things, aboot them,
> An' varra suin began to see
>   Life wad be varra wairch withoot them.
>
> They help us up its rugged hills—
>   Soothe and support in toil an' trouble—
> Share wiv us a' its thoosand ills,
>   And a' its pleasures fairly double.

With the exception of a few archaisms there is little in the construction of these sentences that differs from our ordinary book English. And we find this yet more apparent in recent works in the dialect. The tendency has been to adopt, with much perversity, a spelling of words which has only resulted in obscuring the text. Taking any one of these works, however, we shall find that it looks in print more uncouth than it is in reality, for in *construction* it presents few variations from literary English.

Sound and breath are so constantly associated in our minds with what is transient that it is not easy to realise that the spoken utterance has been found to be the least perishable feature of our dialect. It is in speech and accent, nevertheless, that we recognise the most archaic word forms, and in the vocalization of the dialect that we fully understand how it differs from standard English. It is English in a comparatively unsophisticated condition. Its inherited speech has been handed down from mother to child without any reference to books, so that in this state of nature it has received a development along lines which are peculiarly its own, and even yet, or until a quite recent period, it has remained a well of Northern English undefiled.

Outside his native speech the Northumberland man is necessarily confronted with uncouth, or, as he would call them, *unket* words. His attempts to enunciate these are not invariably successful. For affidavit he is content to say *accy-davey*. *Polly's-nick-stick* is more comprehensible to him than polytechnic, and *gleedy-scoupy* than kaleidoscope. *Wor Tommy's ropes* is more familiar than the scintillating chromatrope, and do we not hear the latest development of the lantern screen called the *China-matty-graf?* Our Vice-President (Dr. Watson) refrained from recording the circumstance in his delightful *History*, but it lives, nevertheless, in the traditions of this Society that a distinguished local lecturer on this platform turned to his lanternist and requested him to " Wise on the *high-drogan*."

But words less formidable than these are not surmounted without difficulty. What, for instance, is a testimonial? In response to the announcement, "applicants are required to deposit testimonials," a candidate unloosed a gold chain and laid it with an inscribed gold chronometer upon the table, and, like Captain Cuttle upon a memorable occasion, waited with a beaming countenance to see the effect produced. The complacency vanished when the examiner in mining quietly remarked, "You will of course be aware that all testimonials produced become the property of H.M. Home Office."

Every person knows of the gentleman who narrowly escaped a collision on the river, and gasping to the skipper of the offending keel, "Do you know the consequence of running down a small boat?" was told, "Ah, but; di ye knaa the *consecure* o' huz lossin' wor tide?"

Or again, the familiar instance of the keelman who was expostulated with : "You should not have given way to violent language; it would have been far better to have tried *persuasive* measures." "That's just what aa did, mistor ; aa fell'd him wi' the boat-hyuk."

But these instances, valuable as mere stage properties to the local humorist, are no more a criterion of dialect-speech than Mrs. Malaprop's expressions are of literary English.

Such words as *mooth* and *thon*, and *aith*, and *claith*, and *rape* (a rope),.and *sweer* (unwilling), and *mony*, and *foor* (a furrow), and a whole vocabulary besides are the actual forms met with in the earliest English, as are the familiar *poke* (a bag), and *kist*, and *hak* (a pick-axe), and *skrike*, and *thak*, and *birk* (birch).

Some of our dialect words have a literary history of their own. Others are found to be words once current in English literature which have lapsed in course of time, but which continue to live on in our dialect in all the freshness of daily use. It is only possible to glance briefly at instances of each of these classes.

The visitor at a cottage passes the *hailan* and enters the room ; and on being invited to sit by the fireside he may say : "Aa'll just sit doon ahint the *brattish*." Now this word *brattish* is a wooden screen. It is so applied technically in a coal mine to the tubes, or screens, or temporary courses for carrying a current of air. But the word first occurs about the year 1300 on its introduction from Norman French, and its old French form is *bretesche*. At that time it was the military term for the temporary breastwork, or hoarding of wood, erected on the battlements of a fortress to protect the defenders from the missiles of the besiegers. The Early English Alliterative Poems, of about 1325, refer to "Bigge brutage of borde built on the walls." On the Pink Tower in Newcastle there could be seen, as can yet be seen on the towers in Bath Lane, the stone corbels, or cantilevers, which were intended for carrying the *brattish*.

In our dialect we have preserved this word—one example among many—in its almost original form.

In literature it has had a far different history. It became obsolete in the sixteenth century in books, and was thenceforth used only in special forms in the dialects. In a Scottish guise, however, and in an illiterate seventeenth-century spelling, it met the keen eye of Sir Walter Scott, and he forthwith adopted it, formulating it as *bartizan.* Its first appearance in this form was in 1801 in his "Eve of St. John." It is used again in "Marmion" in the description of "Tantallon's dizzy steep" :—

> Whose varying circle did combine
> Bulwark and bartizan and line.

And from a wood screen it has been transformed by the great magician into an angle-turret of stone. Sir Walter Scott, in self-conscious pride of the word which he had evolved, used it again in his novels ; and, such is the effect of a literary example, that architects have adopted *bartizan,* without question, as one of their technical terms.*

If we sit "ahint the brattish" or at the fireside we shall hear that the goodman does not ask a question ; he *axes.* He does not converse ; he *cracks,* or *has his cracks.* Perhaps he has a *crow to pull* with someone. Or he is *mistrustful* that the youngest had *played the wag.* If he had, he would *yark* the *imp* when he *buckled* with him. But he would *liever* not send the *scrat* of a pen to the *maister :* his hand was so stiff and *nummy.* The *yonker* had perhaps been in the *parocke,* or *ferreting* the neighbour's *shotts* out of the barn. But he was a *reesty* lad and would not *kythe.* The words which I have italicised are all in common use in Northumberland, and are examples of words which were in regular literary use up to the latter end of the sixteenth and the early part of the seventeenth centuries. The list of words which have become obsolete in literature but still live on in dialects is extensive, but *one* instance may serve as an illustration.

Nowadays, I believe, boys never absent themselves from school without law or leave. But, in days gone by, irregularities of that kind did occur. At the Royal Free Grammar School of Newcastle-upon-Tyne, the lapse of a boy used to grieve the gentle heart of that brave old soul, Dr. Snape. The malady sometimes overtook the more refractory pupils of the distinguished academy of Dr. Bruce. It was confined, however, to no particular grade and was quite as often heard of at the famous Jubilee school or the then known Corporation school. It was in all cases called *playing the wag.* It is alluded to in one of the lamentations of Ned Corvan :—" Thor's ne pleyce te play the wag

* Dr. J. A. H. Murray, *New English Dictionary, sub voce.*

noo; the grun's a' tuen up wi' High Levels, Central Stations, an' dear knaws what else. Aw used te play the wag doon the Kee thonder. Aw've seen me fish for days tegither." The difficulty of the procedure lay in the return, when the powers that be were faced with an easy going expression, concealing the very far from easy going emotions actually felt. This was to be overcome by *playing the wag* for the nonce. But if this affectation of indifference was not invariably successful it was, nevertheless, the only resource. Florio, who wrote in 1603, translates a phrase thus :—" It is an easie thing to shew stoutness and *play the wag* before one come to the pinch." * How easy it is, must have since been experienced by many a trembling delinquent. Thirty years later in that century, Cotgrave associates the word with the special meaning of playing truant, in his definition of " A wag, or one that loves to be gadding abroad when he should bee at his booke."† When *wag* is applied to a boy it is to one whom he describes elsewhere as a "crack-rope" or "slip-string" (in other words a truant) whom he also calls a " knavish lad."‡ So that the term *playing the wag* has a very venerable history. It was known to Shakespeare's

> Whining school-boy, with his satchel
> And shining morning face, creeping like snail
> Unwillingly to school

—just as it has ever since been known to generations of Tynesiders.

The history of Northumberland forms an important chapter of the history of England itself. All its life is a part of the great flow of the national life current, just as its dialect-speech is a portion, and a most important one, of our great inheritance in the English language. The areas of dialect-speech represent early ethnographical and political differences in the people ; and so permanent are the tendencies—especially in the spoken utterances—that we may trace well-defined divisions and subdivisions which coincide with the historical aspects of each portion of the district. These considerations link our local patriotism to our country's and assure us that in attempting to elucidate even so humble a subject we are in some degree, however small that may be, interpreting one of the phases of our existence as an English people.

---

* *Montaigne's Essays*, translated by John Florio. Booke 2, ch. xii.

† Randle Cotgrave ; *A Dictionarie of the French and English Tongues*, 1632, *s.r. Fripon*.   ‡ *Ibid. s.r. Sagoin*.

NEWCASTLE A HUNDRED YEARS AGO.*

By RICHARD WELFORD, M.A.

Our object this evening is to exhibit and describe the leading features of Newcastle as they existed before steam and gas and electricity had changed the face of nature, and altered the environments and conditions of human life.

Borrowing from some of my own pages, let us take a glance at the position which the town occupied and the life that was lived in it during the early and middle periods of its development.

In the first stages of its history the leading characteristics of Newcastle were solidity, compactness, and strength. Nature had provided its founders with a site which art easily fortified and genius made secure. When the legions of Rome came to Northern Britain, they saw here a place convenient for outlook, excellent for communication, admirable for defence. Towering high above a wide spreading tide was a rocky hill, flanked east and west by deep and narrow gorges covered with thorn and bramble—natural outworks so effective that the addition of ramparts extending from their great mural barrier to the river edge, and the construction of a bridge, gave the Romans a stronghold of the first rank, a practically impregnable fortress. Long afterwards, when the Normans arrived, they found an effective position waiting to be utilised. Upon this broad plateau overlooking the Tyne, they and their Plantagenet successors erected a magnificent castle, extended the mural defences, restored the bridge, and in no long time built up one of the strongest fortified towns in the kingdom.

Standing at the south-west corner of the fortress, where now the High Level Bridge gives easy access to the opposite shore, we see in imagination the castle and its precincts as they appeared in the latter part of the thirteenth century. Before us rises the massive keep,

* This lecture differed from those of the series which preceded it. Instead of a literary discourse it was a running description of a hundred lantern slides, comprising maps, plans, engravings, etc., of old Newcastle. Apart from the pictures, which cannot conveniently be reproduced, the lecture loses most of its interest, for which reason only the introductory portion and such of the descriptive matter as can be read without illustrations has been printed.—R. W.

surrounded by equally massive walls—the outer or supporting wall, with its towers and posterns, the inner wall with its gate and draw-bridge—while on the west side is the grand entrance, the Black Gate, with its barbican in front, and square towers, flanking a second gate, behind. Beyond, partly concealed by the keep, is the Moot Hall, or hall of justice, and round about cluster the store houses and other buildings used by the garrison, the whole covering about three acres of ground.

Strong was the Norman-Plantagenet castle, strong were the Plan-tagenet town walls. A sketch of them, as they appeared to Sir Jacob Astley, sent hither on a mission of defence before the outbreak of the great Civil War, gives us our earliest picture of their actual appear-ance, position, and strength. They were about twelve feet high on the inner side—the outer side being protected by a moat or ditch—and from seven to eight feet thick, with massive gateways covering the principal outlets of the town, and towers at irregular intervals, facing what, it may be presumed, the builders considered the least defensible positions beyond. Between the towers were turrets, or watching places, surmounted, as were also the gates and some of the towers, by effigies of men cut in stone, two on each turret and three on each gate. Had we known this mural barrier in its prime we should have appre-ciated the observation of old Leland, recorded in his *Laboryeuse Journey and Serche for Englandes Antiquities*, that "the strength and magnificens'of the waulling of this towne far passith al the waulles of the cities of England and most of the townes of Europe."

When this system of circumvallation was completed, Newcastle became, as Gray, the first historian of the town, tells us, "a safe bulwark against the Scots," and all other the king's enemies. Within its gates monarchs assembled, and princes and nobles, prelates and warriors took counsel. Here they began great enterprises, planned vast campaigns, held parleys, arranged truces, received homage, and held hostages to ransom. Hither came English armies, with knights and esquires, and all the chivalry of the realm, lightening by joust and tournament, in the fields of Jesmond and Gosforth, the sterner duties awaiting them in the troubled border land and the coveted kingdom beyond.

For more than three centuries the walls of Newcastle remained secure and untaken. Against the ravages of time they were protected by the liberality of successive monarchs and the patriotism of the townspeople; to the power, the art. and the subtlety of man they offered strong and successful resistance. Foemen and freebooters from Scotland, religious insurgents and rebellious earls at home were alike defied and beaten off. Force did not destroy, cajolery win, nor treachery surrender them during all that long and, for the most part, perilous time. And when the hour of conquest did come, their first surrender was their last, the forerunner of disuse, neglect, and gradual decay.

In "the fighting days of old" Newcastle was a centre of industrial energy, distinguished among the trading ports of the kingdom for its commercial and manufacturing activity. When great armies mustered outside the walls, and the king's ships, laden with men and munitions, sailed into the harbour of Tyne, local purveyors, artificers, and navigators, skilled in their respective callings, were ready to provide for every usual requirement, and able to satisfy every reasonable command. As the military spirit declined, and peaceful commerce supervened, the industrial energies of the town expanded, for the townspeople had stronger incentives to action in the competence and fortune which successful trade invariably brings. The earth was burrowed for coal, the hills were carved into grindstones, and, when wind and tide favoured, the river was alive with craft, from the humble keel that plied only in its native channel to the masted ship that carried away the products of the district and brought in corn and wine, and other necessaries and luxuries from fairer fields than even Tyneside knew.

Few towns equalled Newcastle in beauty of situation and picturesqueness of construction. The castle keep rose high above narrow thoroughfares that crept up and down the hill sides, and wandered along the edge of the water. Through the town ran two narrow burns or streamlets seeking, by deep and devious courses, an outlet in the Tyne. Within were patches of verdure, interspersed with blooming gardens, divided by shrubbery and hedgerow. Without were the wooded slopes of Elswick and Fenham in the west, the leafy shades of Jesmond and Heaton in the east, and between them, northward, the green expanse of the Town Moor and Castle Leazes, while to the south ran the clear and sparkling river, hurrying from its sources in the moors of Cumberland and the fells of the Border to the all-absorbing ocean.

The late John Storey, a local artist, has enabled us in a well-known picture, to realise the appearance which the town presented in the reign of Queen Elizabeth, when walls, towers, and gates were stout and strong ; when hills and dales, within and without the town, were as clear to the eye as they were toilsome to the feet ; when the waters of the two principal rivulets—the Lort Burn and the Pandon Burn—came unobstructed from the Leazes and the Moor, the one past St. Nicholas' and the other by All Saints' to their home in the Tyne. The picture shows Newcastle in its beauty and its strength. No one who sees it can wonder at the patriotic fervour of the local worthy who, being asked by one of the judges of Assize if Newcastle was not a very ancient town, replied, "Yis, ma Lord ; and it elwis wes a varry aad, ancient toon, ma Lord !"

Picturesque and beautiful as was Newcastle in the reign of the Tudors, it was not less so in the reign of the Georges. If, on a clear morning a hundred years ago, we had entered the town from the south, we should have beheld, as we came down Sheriff Hill and through Gateshead, as fine a bit of old England as the eye could covet or the heart desire. Spread out before and below us we should have seen a delightful medley of rambling streets and gabled houses, flanked by lawns and gardens, orchards and meadows, interspersed with stately towers and glittering pinnacles ; while the old wall, still standing though decayed, outlined with a rim of mottled grey the checkered scene of brick and verdure within. Around and beyond, our eyes would have roamed over wide prospects of arable and pasture, wood-land and moorland, while deep down in the foreground we should have caught the flash and glimmer of the Tyne, broken up by haugh and islet, shoal and sandbank, and thickly studded with the ever-changing flotilla of the coal trade.

Let us, in imagination, take a tour round the walls of the town a hundred, or say a hundred and five, years ago. For, with the exception of the Quayside wall, which yielded to modern requirements in 1763, all the old fortifications remained till 1795, when Pandon Gate was pulled down, followed by the Close Gate in 1798.

We begin our perambulations at the Close Gate, a dark and dismal looking edifice that spanned the thoroughfare called the Close, near where now stands Davidson's mill. Climbing the steep ascent up which the wall rises, we come to White Friar Tower (removed in 1840), so named because it abutted upon the gardens of the monastery of the White Friars. Thence northward to a point at the back of what is now the Literary and Philosophical Society's Library, and there we see Denton or Neville Tower forming a corner, from whence the wall sheers off to the west. Within a short distance comes West Spital

Tower, which derived its name from the adjoining grounds of the Hospital of St. Mary the Virgin, said hospital being then utilised for the Royal Free Grammar School, and now (*i.e.*, the site) occupied in part by the Stephenson monument. In the closing years of last century West Spital Tower was a dwelling house—the home of Ralph Beilby, Thomas Bewick's apprentice master, and subsequently his partner. In that tower Beilby wrote the descriptive letterpress for the *History of Quadrupeds;* while hard by, in the Forth, with a long garden reaching nearly to the wall, lived Bewick himself, then but newly married and settled down.

Bending our steps north-westerly, to what is at present the foot of Pink Lane, and leaving, as of no interest, Stank Tower, near the east end of the present portico of the Central Railway Station, we recognise an old acquaintance—Gunner Tower, removed so recently as 1885. Then passing a gate in the wall, which gave access to the town's recreation ground, the leafy Forth, we arrive at Pink Tower, late the site of the John Knox Church, and now of the Clarendon Hotel, and thence to the West Gate, which stood facing the Police Station that bears its name According to Leland, the West Gate was "a mighty strong thing." It is said to have been re-edified at the end of the fourteenth century by Roger Thornton, who, coming through the old gate a poor lad from the country, rose to be one of the richest merchants in the North of England. Here it may be proper to digress for a moment for the purpose of adding that Roger Thornton was eight times mayor of Newcastle and a representative of the town in several parliaments, founder of the old Guild Hall on the Sandhill and the Maison Dieu adjoining ; and that, dying in 1411, he was buried under a stately altar-tomb in All Saints' Church, inlaid with a magnificent brass, which is still preserved in the vestry as the mediæval " art treasure " of the town.

From the West Gate (removed in 1811) a walk of a few yards brings into view Durham Tower, portions of which, and of Herber, Morden, and Ever Towers are still in existence, though greatly dilapidated. Behind St. Andrew's Church comes Andrew Tower (pulled down between the years 1827 and 1830), and in front of it the frowning fortress of the New Gate. An etching by the elder Richardson gives us a very effective picture of this New Gate as it is supposed to have existed at the end of the fourteenth century. Massive were its walls—imposing its proportions. Small wonder that resolute rebels and incursive Scots beat their heads in vain against a gate that in the fulness of its strength resembled the keep of a castle. Moat and drawbridge, barbican and portcullis, must have made it practically impregnable. A hundred years ago it was the town prison, and the way to the gallows. Over its northern entrance, facing the road to Scotland, was a statue, which was thought to resemble King James the First. But, whomsoever the time-worn figure may have been intended to represent, there was a curious mixture of uncertainty and delusion about it. So at least, until the destruction of the gate in 1823, felt half-fledged school boys and credulons lads from the country, who were solemnly told that this statue stepped from its perch and back again every time it heard the great clock of St. Nicholas' proclaim the hour of twelve !

Resuming our journey from the New Gate, we follow the wall due east, behind the south side of what is now Blackett Street, and leaving Bertram Monboucher Tower, which stood near the emergence of Clayton Street into that thoroughfare, and Ficket Tower, which occupied the site of the Y.M.C.A. entrance, we arrive at Pilgrim Street Gate, a strong but clumsy edifice (destroyed in 1802), which covered the roadway at the top of Pilgrim Street. Further eastward comes the far-famed Carliol Tower (taken down in 1880 to make way for the Public Library) whence the wall turns suddenly to the south, passing Plummer Tower (still standing in Croft Street), Austin Tower (removed in 1836 for the formation of the North Shields Railway), and then on to Corner Tower, the ruins of which we see to-day beside the railway arch in City Road. Here the wall forms a loop to include the ancient vill of Pandon, and descending the slope across the burn of that name we approach Pandon Gate. This, we observe, is a peculiar structure, unlike any other of the town's gates, with an arched opening at the summit, to which access is obtained by a flight of stairs six feet wide. At one time it was supposed to have been of Roman origin, forming part of the Roman Wall, and its antiquity was preserved in the local phrase—"As old as Pandon Yett."

Now we make our way past the Sallyport, or Wallknoll Tower, with whose present appearance we are all familiar, and down to the Sand Gate, standing near the end of the thoroughfare bearing its name, adjoining the river.

Coming along the Quay we note the narrow streets to the right, of which there were about twenty, called " chares "—a word so purely local that, when a witness at the Assizes deposed to seeing three men come out of the foot of a chare, the judge remarked that he must be insane.

In one of these chares, very near to the Sand Gate, and bearing the poetic name of "Love Lane," was born one of the great men that Newcastle claims for her own. The principal house in that narrow thoroughfare was, for some years, the home of William Scott, a respectable coalfitter. To him and his respective wives, for he was twice married, came sixteen children, and among them a boy named John, who became in after years the Earl of Eldon, Lord High Chancellor of Great Britain, while his elder brother, William (born at Heworth), became Baron Stowell, Judge of the High Court of Admiralty. There is a peculiarity in the birth and career of these two eminent men which is worth noting. They were each twin born with a sister, and although six years divided their ages, they ran their official course abreast of each other. So nearly contemporaneous were their promotions that good old George the Third was tempted to make a mild little joke of it. Being at the death of a stag which had given the field a bad run, while a stag of the same herd had afforded excellent sport the day before, his Majesty said, " Ah ! There are not often two Scotts to be found in the same family."

Having traversed the outside of the town, and viewed its appearance as a decaying stronghold, we proceed to explore the streets and inspect the public buildings. We have arrived at the Sandhill, which in olden times was the commercial heart of Newcastle, the seat of municipal government, the market and the playground of the citizens. Across the Sandhill marched every distinguished visitor ; upon the Sandhill was celebrated every great public event. Time would fail us to tell of the piping and drumming, the torch fires and bonfires, bull-baiting and bear-dancing with which the townspeople commemorated royal birthdays and coronations, mayor-choosings, parliamentary elections, river perambulations and the receipt of good news from our armies, fighting ever, somewhere or other, against Dutchman or Spaniard, Frenchman or Turk. In those bygone days, when great merchants lived in the many-storied houses round about, when noblemen and country squires resided great part of the winter in town, when the incorporated trading companies devoted their surplus funds to dining early or supping late, there were few merrier places than the Sandhill.

Facing the water we see the old Guildhall in all its picturesque beauty. We are but just in time, for in 1796-7 it was modernised, and assumed the dull and formal shape with which we have long been familiar. Till then it was a safe and convenient place for the town's out-door oratory. From its outer staircase, protected by arches and balustrades, John Wesley preached ; from the same spot Blacketts and Ridleys, Liddells and Carrs addressed surging crowds of electors and non-electors, with fair chance of shelter from flying eggs and apples and other savoury missiles which then, and for long after, ranked among the accompaniments of political warfare.

At the west end of the Guildhall, impeding the approach to Tyne Bridge, we view the chapel of St. Thomas à Becket, or St. Thomas the Martyr. It formed a very awkward corner, and when, in 1830, it was pulled down and re-established in the fields of an associated charity—that of St. Mary Magdalen, near another bridge at the north end of the town, the Barras Bridge—a great public improvement was effected.

And here is Tyne Bridge itself, but recently rebuilt, and shining in all the whiteness of a new structure. For five hundred years the great highway across the Tyne, heavy and cumbrous, protected by a gate and a tower, and covered with shops and houses, had stood firm and fast above the ebbing and flowing tide. But in November, 1771, on the morning of Sunday, the 17th of that month, Novocastrians opened their eyes upon a scene of desolation such as had not been witnessed since the siege of the town in October, 1644. The middle arch of the old bridge, and two arches nearer Gateshead had fallen into a raging flood, and six or seven people had been drowned. Next day four other houses and shops gave way, and shortly afterwards the whole range of them to the southward as far as Gateshead, met with the same fate. Local annalists relate, with harrowing detail the fears, the sufferings, the miraculous escapes of citizens in that dire disaster. You may read how the Sandhill was covered with water six feet deep ; how three sloops and a brig were driven upon the Quayside and left there, furrowing up the pavement, and breaking down a great part of the Quay ; how other craft were scattered and stranded all the way to Shields, or borne onward to the sea and lost, while one of the bridge houses was carried bodily down to Jarrow Slake and left there with a cat and a dog in it all alive.

Fortunately there was, even at that time, a Stephenson upon Tyneside who was capable of grappling with a difficulty in locomotion. John Stephenson, father of the architect who designed the new church of All Saints, undertook to complete a temporary bridge from the Sandhill to Gateshead in four months. He fulfilled his contract, and nine years later a new bridge, presenting much the same appearance as it did when we traversed it for the last time, in 1866, was completed. It was by no means so picturesque as its predecessor, but better able to bear traffic and withstand the pressure of the tide.

A few yards to the west of the entrance to Tyne Bridge, in the thoroughfare leading to Close Gate, we pause at the residence of the mayors of Newcastle—the far-famed Mansion House. In the old times Newcastle was celebrated for its municipal hospitality, and it did not lose its character until a wave of reform, sweeping through the country sixty odd years ago stopped the public tap, and left everybody free to indulge—at his own expense. The municipal records of the sixteenth century contain marvellous accounts of the feasting that went on in Newcastle whenever occasion demanded or opportunity offered. Thus, towards the end of that century, a party of notables from the Low Countries passing through the town were received with musketry and music, and regaled at a banquet worthy of the metropolis. For there were veal and mutton, pigs and coneys, geese and capon, wildfowl, quail, and fish, a turkey cock and a swan, a barrel of London beer, twenty-one gallons of sack, twenty-three gallons of claret, and three quarts of muscadine, with sugar and marchpanes, marmalade and liquorice, cherries and quinces, plums and damsons, not to mention comfits, biscuits, "banqueting conceits," and two pounds and a quarter of perfume. So also when two noblemen's sons came "travelling into Scotland from France," the town not only gave them a banquet at night and breakfast next morning, but paid for "washing and starching of their bands, shirts, linen and hose."

The Mansion House of a hundred years ago had replaced, in 1693, an older one which stood upon the same spot. The dining room was fifty feet, the dancing room forty-two feet long, and the drawing room large in proportion. If we had called there, say in 1797, we should have seen his worship Alderman William Cramlington, then mayor for the second time, and if we had enjoyed his hospitality he would, perhaps, have favoured us with a recital of his famous joke upon the undersheriff, Nathaniel Punshon. For it is recorded in local history that once, when the corporation were having a day upon the river, the state barge of the municipality sprang a leak, and Mr. Punshon showed signs of trepidation.

"Don't you be afraid, Nat!" said Alderman Cramlington. "Even if the whole corporation should go to the bottom, you are safe enough."

" How so, Mr. Alderman ? "

" Why," replied Alderman Cramlington, with a twinkle in his eye to indicate that he was hatching a meritorious pun, "everybody knows that an empty puncheon always floats ! "

Returning to the Sandhill, we turn our backs upon the Guildhall, and look up at the stately houses in which the merchants, bankers, and other well-to-do citizens reside. Towards the close of the last century the house with many windows near the north-west corner was the home and the bank of Aubone Surtees, a prosperous and high-minded Novocastrian. It was from one of the casements in the lower tier (marked to-day by a blue pane) that on the night of Wednesday, the 18th of November, 1772, " Bessie " Surtees, the banker's daughter, descended a ladder into the arms of John Scott, son of the coalfitter in Love Lane. " What a silly, wild, mad elopement it was " (so, at least, all the lady's friends declared), " and no good could come of it, never ! " Yet one and twenty years later, bells were clanging in all the steeples of Newcastle because " Sir " John Scott had been appointed His Majesty's Attorney-General, and again, no long time afterwards, because these reckless and improvident fugitives of 1772 were visiting the scene of their youthful escapade as Lord and Lady Eldon.

The Sandhill, we note as we traverse it, is triangular, and at its apex we face one of the two market crosses of the town—the Cale Cross. Behind the cross comes a leading hostelry, known to many generations of thirsty Novocastrians as the Nag's Head Inn. None of us can remember the Cale Cross *in situ*, for, having replaced a much older one in 1783, it was taken down in 1807 and returned to the donor, the first Sir Matthew White Ridley, who rebuilt it in his grounds at Blagdon. But the Nag's Head Inn was a conspicuous place till the late Mr. Andrew Reid, about forty years ago, replaced it by Printing Court Buildings. At the Cale Cross were sold eggs, butter, milk, cheese, etc. ; and even now, upon the very spot which it occupied, one may sometimes see a woman vending milk, as her predecessors did a hundred years ago.

To the right of the Nag's Head, a few doors east, we see the shop in which, on the 9th November, 1721, the poet Akenside was born. His father was one of the tradesmen whose calling gave its name to the street—the Butcher Bank—leading up to All Saints' Church. In honour of the poet, the name has been changed to that of Akenside Hill. Newcastle cherished the memory of its illustrious son, though that illustrious son cherished no good memory of Newcastle. For it is said that in after years, when he had become a famous doctor and poet, he was ashamed of his parentage and of his native town !

Before us, westward, as we stand at the Cale Cross, runs the thoroughfare called the Side, which, at the time of our perambulation, had but lately been connected with the centre of the town by the filling up of the Lort Burn and the construction of Dean Street. Previous to 1787, traffic from Tyne Bridge was obliged to take one of two courses—either ascend the Butcher Bank, behind us, and enter Pilgrim Street, or follow the Side to its termination at St. Nicholas' Churchyard. Up the Side was the more usual, because the more accessible, course ; and it was certainly the more picturesque. Like the Sandhill, the Side, especially its upper portion, was flanked by tall, overhanging houses, with projecting bays and pointed gables, most of them commencing below in well-stocked shops, and continuing above in handsome, many-windowed apartments—the homes of the shopkeepers. Ceaseless traffic, ever-changing groups of well-dressed loungers, a luxurious display of fabrics and comestibles, and, over all, glittering casements, with glimpses of domestic life within, made the Side, in the last century, one of the most attractive thoroughfares in Newcastle.

Let us in imagination fill those windows with youth and beauty, cover the sills with cloth and velvet, hang out flags and banners, and endeavour to realise the appearance of the Side upon great occasions. We may, for example, call up the scene when King James of Scotland, passing through on his way to the English throne, was welcomed with such exuberant demonstrations of joy ·that he exclaimed to his courtiers, " By ma saul, they're eneuch to spoil a gude Keng !" We can picture to ourselves a similar demonstration when his son Charles came hither on the way to his Scottish coronation, before those troubles began which finally led him captive down that same Side and across the Sandhill to his doom at Whitehall. We can see those windows again when Cromwell marched in, receiving "great acknowledgments of love" from every casement. Some, who are still living amongst us, may be able to recall the pageant that down to the middle of this present century accompanied the judges, as with chariots and horsemen, trumpeters and javelin men, and all the pomp and circumstance of semi-regal state they swept up the Side to open his Majesty's commission at the Courts of Assize.

Now we proceed up the "Head of the Side"—a puzzling street name to strangers, and the cause of occasional confusion in correspondence. "Head of the Side?" queried one in the Midlands as he looked at the heading of his correspondent's letter. "What can he mean? It must surely be side of the Head! But what Head? Most likely that old posting house, the Queen's Head." So he addressed his letter to his friend—"side of the Queen's Head, Newcastle," and it promptly came back to him marked "insufficient address."

At the top the road divides. To the left is King Street, which leads to the Black Gate and is continued by Queen Street to the old Castle. Right up to the Black Gate are shops devoted to "making old clothes good as new," the refurbishing of old hats, the translation of old boots, and similar handicrafts which cater to the wants of the poor and needy. Through the Black Gate, into the Castle Garth, the same class of business prevails. Cleaners abound, patchers multiply, menders swarm. A hundred years ago this was the town's emporium for discarded finery—the paradise of the second-hand.

On to the Castle—a dismal ruin, a crumbling wreck of the Norman-Plantagenet stronghold! Little but the keep we see, and that, only a few years earlier (1783) had been advertised in these glowing terms :—

To Be Let,

THE Old Castle in the Castle Garth, upon which with the greatest convenience and advantage, may be erected a Wind Mill for the purpose of grinding Córn and Bolting Flour, or making Oil, &c. There is an exceeding good Spring of Water within the Castle, which renders it a very valuable situation for a Brewery, or any Manufactory that requires a constant supply of water. The proprietor, upon proper terms, will be at a considerable part of the expence. Enquire of Mr. Fryer, in Westgate Street, Newcastle.

Returning to the Head of the Side we observe a tall red brick house near the public pant there. At a time when people lived over their places of business this imposing structure would be considered a genteel and commodious residence for a merchant, with warerooms and store rooms, and every convenience. Now, a hundred years ago, the citizens of Newcastle were watching with interest and expectation not only the career of the Scotts from Love Lane, but that also of Cuthbert Collingwood, who first saw the light in this respectable house at the Head of the Side. Between the ages of John Scott and Cuthbert Collingwood, a difference of three years only existed ; they had been boys together at the Royal Free Grammar School, in the Spital, they had married Newcastle wives, and, although moving in utterly different spheres of action, each of them was steadily working his way to a prominent and a permanent place in English history. John Scott reached the Woolsack in 1801 ; four years later every town in Great Britain was ringing with the praises of Admiral Collingwood, successor of Nelson, hero of Trafalgar.

At the far end of the Head of the Side, abutting upon St. Nicholas' Churchyard and known as Amen Corner, we find a bookseller's shop. From 1756 to 1781, the shop and circulating library of Joseph Barber, of Amen Corner, was a favourite resort of the *literati* of the district. The old bookseller was a man of superior intelligence, and knew something about the inside of his volumes and the merits and demerits of the authors. If he were asked for the first books printed in Newcastle, he would produce two thin little quartos—one a sermon by Bishop Morton of Durham, and the other instructions to the army under the title of *Laws and Ordinances of War*. In all probability the courteous old man would explain that when Charles the First came hither in 1639, finding no printer to publish his proclamations, he sent for Robert Barker, the royal printer, who, from a press brought down to Newcastle from London in a stage waggon, issued these two booklets and a couple of broadsides. Likely, too, he would remark that after Barker left, there was no settled printer upon Tyneside till 1646—seven years later. In his time Joseph Barber, of Amen Corner, was a notable man ; a hundred years after his death his memory was revived by a still more notable person—his great grandson, Joseph Barber Lightfoot, Bishop of Durham.

Round the corner, and at the south-east angle of St. Nicholas' Churchyard, we see the workshop of Thomas Bewick, the famous wood engraver. If the time is suitable we shall probably find the great artist working at the three-light window on the upper floor, or busy directing his apprentices within. In any case this is the scene of his labours, the house from whence issue those marvellous blocks which have revolutionised the art of wood engraving and excited the admiration of the civilised world.

From Bewick's workshop we view the east end of St. Nicholas' Church, note the unrivalled lantern-crown, with its crocketted pinnacles and glittering vane, frown at the utterly incongruous building which Sir Walter Blackett was allowed to build over the old vestry, and admire the mouldings of the three east windows, standing out in mute protest against white glass and white wash. Then, with a wondering glance at the dilapidated wooden railings, the weather-beaten retaining wall upon which they stand, and the time-worn grave stones all awry, proceed to visit the interior.

Here, if we have any sense of fitness in matters ecclesiastical, we wonder still more, for a great scheme of restoration has just been completed and the effect is deplorable. All the monuments on the floor sold by auction for building stone, the choir stalls and the altar screen torn down, the communion table set back under the great east window, only the chancel available for public worship, all the nave empty and bare—such was the idea of church restoration a hundred years ago !

Turning our backs upon the three-decker pulpit, the high pews, and the ugly free seats set up the aisles, we look down the desolate nave. Hatchments on the walls, and inscribed stones upon the floor, remind us that we are in the Necropolis of Newcastle, the burial place of notable men for many generations. And we call up their names—Anderson and Askew, Blackett and Brandling, Carr, Colling-wood and Clavering, Ellison, Forster and Fenwick, and so on down the alphabet to Stote, Surtees, and Widdrington.

In the heart of the city they lie, unknown and unnoticed.
Daily the tides of life go ebbing and flowing beside them ;
Thousands of throbbing hearts, where theirs are at rest and for ever ;
Thousands of aching brains, where theirs no longer are busy ;
Thousands of toiling hands, where theirs have ceased from their labours ;
Thousands of weary feet, where theirs have completed their journey.

In front of St. Nicholas' Church, a hundred years ago, where now the Town Hall obstructs traffic, ran three narrow streets. The central one bore the name of Middle Street, that on the west was called, as now, the Groat Market, that on the east bore, at its lower end, the name of the Flesh Market, while higher up it became Union Street, and all three merged at the top into the Bigg Market. In this cluster of many-gabled houses were the homes of the *Newcastle Chronicle*, of John Cunningham, the pastoral poet, of John Shield, author of "My Lord Size," of Geo. Richardson, an eminent member of the Society of Friends, and other local celebrities of lesser fame, now, alas ! forgotten.

We stroll up Middle Street and reach the Bigg Market. Then down Pudding Chare into Westgate Street, and at the spot upon which the Mining Institute now stands, we see a mansion known as "Westmorland Place." It had been supposed that this house was once the Newcastle home of the powerful family of Nevill, earls of Westmorland. We know now that the supposition was wrong, and that their local residence stood on the adjoining property—the very place which we occupy at this moment. A hundred years ago there was a house upon this spot belonging to Caleb Angas, a member of the wide-spreading family of that name, and an eminent coachbuilder. So it remained till, in 1822, it gave place to the Lit. and Phil. But of this Society and all that it has done, is it not written in that admirable book of the chronicles of the Lit. and Phil. with which Dr. Spence Watson enriched the history of his native town last year ?

Through the lower end of Westgate Street we approach Hanover Square, and find the chapel in which preached the Rev. Wm. Turner, the man who started the Lit. and Phil., and with over six hundred lectures nurtured and sustained its infancy. Within that plain, not to say ugly, tabernacle, the greater part of the " men of light and leading " in Newcastle during the first half of the present century assembled. Thither went James Losh, the Recorder, whose statue adorns the vestibule of this library ; Thomas Wilson, author of the " Pitman's Pay ; " John Buddle, the great mining engineer ; Thomas and James Hodgson, proprietors and editors of the *Newcastle Chronicle;* William Andrew Mitchell of the *Tyne Mercury;* James Clephan of the *Gateshead Observer;* Hugh Lee Pattinson, the famous chemist ; Emerson Charnley, the bookseller ; and many other minor lights in the literary firmament of Tyneside.

Through the Postern Gate adjoining Nevill Tower we enter the wide-spreading recreation ground of the town, the Forth (now covered by the Central Station), and bending westward arrive at the New Infirmary, opened in October, 1752, with its chapel and burying ground adjoining, consecrated a couple of years later. Then back, across the Forth, to the Royal Free Grammar School, formerly the Hospital of St. Mary the Virgin, opposite the south-east corner of St. John's churchyard. Here, under the head mastership of the Rev. Hugh Moises, Lords Eldon and Stowell, Admiral Lord Collingwood, and many other local men of mark received their education, and here, on Michaelmas Monday from 1600 to the passing of the Municipal Reform Act in 1835, the mayors, sheriffs, and corporate officers were annually elected. Michaelmas Monday a hundred years ago was a great day in Newcastle. The mayor, ten aldermen, the sheriff, and twenty-four commoners forming the entire governing body went out of office on that day, and came up for election in the following simple and intelligible manner :—

Twelve of the Incorporated Companies, called Mysteries, separately elected two out of each of their companies, making twenty-four. These twenty-four appointed the retiring mayor and three others who had been mayors and were then aldermen (and for lack of them three ordinary aldermen) to be the first four of a body called Electors. These four Electors chose eight persons, of which seven were to be aldermen, if present, and if not, then such as had been sheriffs, and failing them, other burgesses of the town, and the eighth must be the sheriff, or one who had been sheriff. Next, the twelve Mysteries each elected one, and, out of the twelve so chosen, the four and the eight Electors already appointed elected six. By this process were obtained four, eight, and six—together eighteen Electors. Then the fifteen By-trades each elected one, and the fifteen so chosen elected twelve of the burgesses. Out of this twelve, and the remaining six of the former twelve elected by the Mysteries, the four, the eight, and the six Electors before-mentioned elected other six. Thus the four, the eight, the six, and the other six, made up twenty-four electors, by whom the mayor, aldermen, sheriff, and twenty-four commoners were elected to form the municipal body for one year. And yet, with all this symmetrical precaution there were not wanting cavillers who declared that these fours, eights, and long sixes always managed to return what they disrespectfully called "the same old gang."

Beyond St. John's Church, shut in by a high wall and towering trees, we see the roof of the Vicarage of Newcastle. In front of it is one of the institutions of the town, the Vicar's Pump, yielding a beverage that, at the date of our visit, is delightfully cool and sparkling, as water from wells that abut upon churchyards usually is. Next comes the new Assembly Rooms, and on the other side of the street lofty mansions with gardens stretching down to the Town Wall —the residences of the higher and professional classes.

Along Fenkle Street to Low Friar Street, and there we see the old building known to many generations of townspeople as the Dolphin House. This house figures in most of the pictorial sketches of Newcastle. Yet no man of mark ever lived in it ; no one ever devoted it to any special use ; it is a house without a history.

Hard by we come upon the remains of the great monastery of the Dominican or Black Friars, and enter the church with its beautiful east window, in which, according to tradition, on the 19th of June, 1334, Edward Baliol, King of Scotland, did homage to Edward III. " in the presence of many great lords and commons of both nations."

Emerging from Low Friar Street into Newgate Street we face the second of our market crosses—the White Cross—rebuilt a few years earlier (1787) upon the site of an older one, and now, clean and fresh, glittering in the sun. Along the four sides run the arms of the mayor, sheriff, and aldermen under whose auspices it was restored, and on the top is a graceful spire, containing a clock to warn the market people of the flight of time.

From this neighbourhood eastward and northward we see a wide expanse of meadow and shrubbery, garden and orchard, interspersed with lofty trees, and among them, away in the north-east, rises the great mansion called Anderson Place. In the fields immediately before us stood, formerly, the nunnery of St. Bartholomew; in those beyond, the monastery of the Grey or Franciscan Friars. At the time of our visit both estates had been for many years merged into one. Imagine the roadway of upper Grey Street, between Lambton's Bank and the Central Exchange, covered by a huge mansion facing east; realise the fact that the grounds of this noble pile extended from Newgate Street to Pilgrim Street, and from High Bridge to what is now Blackett Street, and you will agree with Bourne's conjecture, that Anderson Place was the most stately and magnificent house in the whole kingdom within a walled town. That part of it which faced Pilgrim Street—*i.e.*, the front—Bourne tells us, "is thrown into walks and grass plats, beautified with images, and beset with trees," while the west side "is all a garden, exceedingly neat and curious, adorned with many and the most beautiful statues, and several other curiosities." During the Civil War Anderson Place became the head-quarters of the Scottish Army, and the temporary home, or prison, of Charles the First—the house from which he was handed over to the forces of the Parliament.

I scarcely need remind you that upon the grounds of Anderson Place Mr. Grainger erected Grey Street, Grainger Street, the Markets and all their connecting streets and thoroughfares. Elderly people still living can remember the grand entrance in Pilgrim Street and the peacocks strutting upon the lawn.

Time does not permit us to visit all the churches which we have passed in our wanderings—St. Andrew's, St. John's and All Saints'— nor the modest buildings which shelter the growing branches of nonconformity—Friends, Baptists, Presbyterians, Independents, Catholics, and the new sect called Methodists. These, and many other public institutions of the town, must necessarily be left to some more convenient opportunity.

We began our perambulations this evening with Storey's picture of Newcastle in the reign of Queen Elizabeth. For the last hour and a half we have been trying to realise the appearance of the town "when George the Third was king." And now! From the heights of Gateshead let us look at Newcastle in the reign of a greater and better sovereign than either Elizabeth or George. Truly a marvellous change—almost a magic transformation! Miles upon miles of streets where grass grew, and flowers bloomed, and fruit ripened a hundred years ago!

And yet, amid the strife and struggle, the hurry and turmoil of the present day, one feels, with eyes and ears turned back to those days of yore, that, as our friend James Clephan expressed it,

> The air is peopled with the dead,
>   The streets breathe voices of the past;
>   The storied town is but one vast
> Romance of ages that are fled.
>
> And he who makes the tale his own,
>   Where'er he turns—by night, by day—
>   Will have companions by the way,
> And never walk these streets alone.

Newcastle-upon-Tyne: Printed by ANDREW REID & COMPANY, Limited, Akenside Hill.